Mobile Work, Mobile Lives: Cultural Accounts of Lived Experiences

Tracy L. Meerwarth, Julia C. Gluesing,

and Brigitte Jordan, Volume Editors

Satish Kedia and Tim Wallace, General Editors

NATIONAL ASSOCIATION FOR THE PRACTICE OF ANTHROPOLOGY
A SECTION OF THE AMERICAN ANTHROPOLOGICAL ASSOCIATION

napa Bulletin 30

NAPA Bulletin (1556-4789) is published in March and September on behalf of the American Anthropological Association by Blackw Publishing, Inc. with offices at (US) 350 Main Street, Malden, MA 02148-5020, (UK) 9600 Garsington Road, Oxford OX4 2ZG, an (Asia) 155 Cremorne Street, Richmond VIC 3121, Australia.

Mailing: Journal is mailed Standard Rate. Mailing to rest of world by IMEX (International Mail Express). Canadian mail is sent by Canadian publications mail agreement number 40573520. POSTMASTER: Send all address changes to NAPA Bulletin, Blackwell Publishing, Inc., Journals Subscription Department, 350 Main Street, Malden, MA 02148-5020, USA.

Publisher: NAPA Bulletin is published by Blackwell Publishing, Inc., 350 Main Street, Malden, MA 02148-5020, USA. Blackwell Publishing, Inc. is now part of Wiley-Blackwell.

Information for Subscribers: NAPA Bulletin is published in two one-issue volumes per year. Subscription prices for 2008 are: Premium Institutional: £27 (Europe), US$54 (The Americas), £27 (Rest of World); Customers in the UK should add VAT at 7%; customers in the EU should also add VAT at 7%, or provide a VAT registration number or evidence of entitlement to exemption. Customers in Canada should add 5% GST or provide evidence of entitlement to exemption. The Premium institutional price inclu online access to the current and all online back files to January 1st 1997, where available. For other pricing options, including access information and terms and conditions, please visit www.blackwellpublishing.com/napa.

Delivery Terms and Legal Title: Prices include delivery of print journals to the recipient's address. Delivery terms are Delivered Du Unpaid (DDU); the recipient is responsible for paying any import duty or taxes. Legal title passes to the customer on despatch by o distributors.

Back Issues: Single issues from current and recent volumes are available at the current single issue price from Blackwell Publishing Journals. Earlier issues may be obtained from Periodicals Service Company, 11 Main Street, Germantown, NY 12526, USA.
Tel: +1 (518) 537-4700, Fax: +1 (518) 537-5899, Email: psc@periodicals.com.

Journal Customer Services: For ordering information, claims and any enquiry concerning your journal subscription please contact your nearest office:
UK: Email: customerservices@blackwellpublishing.com; Tel: +44 (0) 1865-778315; Fax: +44 (0) 1865-471775
USA: Email: customerservices@blackwellpublishing.com; Tel: +1 (781) 388-8599 or 1 (800) 835-6770 (Toll free in the USA & Canada
Fax: +1 (781) 388-8232 or Fax: +44 (0) 1865-471775
Asia: Email: customerservices@blackwellpublishing.com; Tel: +65 6511-8000; Fax: +44 (0) 1865-471775

Associate Editor: Michelle S. Sathan
Production Editor: Sarah McKay, Email: napa@bos.blackwellpublishing.com
Advertising: journaladsUSA@bos.blackwellpublishing.com

Print Information: Printed in the United States of America by The Sheridan Press.This journal is printed on acid-free paper.

Online Information: This journal is available online at Blackwell Synergy. Visit www.blackwell-synergy.com to search the articles ar register for table of contents e-mail alerts.
Access to this journal is available free online within institutions in the developing world through the AGORA initiative with the FA the HINARI initiative with the WHO and the OARE initiative with UNEP. For information, visit www.aginternetwork.org, www.healthinternetwork.org, and www.oarescience.org.

Aims and Scope: The NAPA Bulletin series is dedicated to the practical problem-solving and policy applications of anthropological knowledge and methods. NAPA Bulletins are peer reviewed, and are distributed free of charge as a benefit of NAPA membership. The NAPA Bulletin seeks to:
facilitate the sharing of information among practitioners, academics, and students.
be a useful document for practitioners.
contribute to the professional development of anthropologists seeking practitioner positions.
support the general interests of practitioners both within and outside the academy.
The Bulletin is a publication of NAPA produced by the American Anthropological Association and Wiley-Blackwell. Through the publication of the NAPA Bulletin, the AAA and Wiley-Blackwell furthers the professional interests of anthropologists while disseminating anthropological knowledge and its applications in addressing human problems.

Submission Instructions: For submission instructions, subscription and all other information visit:
www.blackwellpublishing.com/napa

ISSN 1556-4789 (Print)
ISSN 1556-4797 (Online)

Contents

INTRODUCTION: TRACKING THE CONTEXT OF MOBILE LIVES

Tracy L. Meerwarth
General Motors Corporation and Consolidated Bearings Company
Julia C. Gluesing
Wayne State University and Cultural Connections
Brigitte Jordan
Palo Alto Research Center (PARC)

Many employees recognize that they are doing major amounts of professional work away from what might be considered their official workspace. Some knowledge workers are beginning to see a different world for themselves where work and home are allowed to blur and where periods of paid work alternate throughout the day with periods devoted to family and leisure. Because of rapid improvements in technology and changes in the global economy, worker mobility and distributed work have become a central topic for employees and companies alike. In this volume we begin to remedy a shortcoming in the literature on these topics by center-staging accounts of personal experience. Contributors' narratives revolve around observations they made about their own behavior, illustrations of successes, and descriptions of the tensions inherent in mobile life and work. Thus, the articles reflect the authors' self-conscious awareness of their individual mobile lives and, most importantly, how their lives contribute to and are shaped by larger societal patterns. In this introduction we provide an overview of the individual articles that follow, as well as some background for an informed reading, by discussing some of the driving forces behind the transition from conventional work styles to mobile and distributed patterns of work. We critically review some of the literature on the work and lifestyle transition that constitutes the central theme for this volume, including the effects of globalization, the development of tools for remote collaboration, and the blurring of home and office work. We elaborate our review of the literature on mobility and distributed work to highlight the stylistic, methodological, and topical contributions of this volume, thereby deepening our understanding of how this new mobility fits into the broader cultural and economic landscape. Keywords: mobile, distributed, remote and nomadic work, lifescapes, lifestyles, auto-ethnography.

Several trends have generated transformations in the global economy and major shifts in conventional workscapes and lifescapes.[1] Primary among these trends are globalization, the ever-increasing functionalities of information and communication technologies, and the blurring of home and office work. As a consequence, workplace mobility has become a central topic for workers and employers alike.

NAPA BULLETIN 30, pp. 1–11. ISSN: 1556-4789.
DOI:10.1111/j.1556-4797.2008.00016.x

Globalization now affects virtually every human being, in every country, in every region of the world, regardless of the state of development. As capital moves outward from established centers of economic and political power, work becomes untethered from places of production, is redistributed, outsourced, in-sourced, and off-shored.[2] The rhythm of work that was once delineated by the ringing of the factory bell or the closing of office doors at the end of the day, now responds to a different rhythm. This new rhythm is the rhythm of the marketscapes and econoscapes of the global economy that, like a giant beast, inhales and exhales through integrated supply chains, financial channels, and consumerism in all its forms. These new rhythms have far-reaching effects on workers' lives, lifestyles, and life options, including the construction of their lifescapes. Employees are beginning to feel these shifts in rhythm and are restructuring their lives on both the societal level (regarding such things as Social Security and healthcare), and on the personal level (in terms of career planning, educational opportunities, and life path options).

At the same time, rapid improvements in the capabilities and functionalities of portable communication devices (cell phones, PDAs, laptops, and other devices) and useful applications (such as instant messaging, phone texting, video conferencing, and widespread public Wi-Fi hotspots) have increasingly divorced task from place and have made possible the deterritorialization of work. Connecting to geographically distributed workplaces, often synchronously, is becoming commonplace in employees' lives. Compared to earlier times, when production activities were carried out at localized sites (the fields and forests of preindustrial societies or the factories spawned by the Industrial Revolution), technology has allowed production to expand into multiple, geographically dispersed territories and even into the virtual world. Consequently, work has become mobile, unbounded, and independent of particular localities.[3]

Industrial work patterns that are 200 years old have been changed with the possibilities opened up by the new information and communication technologies, and workers are managing these possibilities in a variety of ways. People recognize that traditional employment is less stable. They witness how real and imagined benefits that were inherent in the image of "the company as family" are being challenged and, in many cases, simply eliminated. As a result, sporadic employment, independent contracting, and temporary consulting work are becoming common, especially among knowledge workers. Clearly, mobile and remote workers are a growing segment in the global economy that deserves the attention of social scientists.

Increasingly, work and home life are blurring. For many, especially knowledge workers, work and home activities may become interspersed, completed in short cycles of activity where periods of paid work alternate with periods devoted to family, community, and leisure activities throughout the day. More traditional work contractors and full-time employees are becoming remote workers who telecommute some days a week from their home to their regular workplace. Others see themselves living a nomadic life—untethered to a worksite while they travel from place to place, producing output in places in between destinations. In many ways, and for a variety of people, there emerges the possibility of returning to a lifestyle that was typical before the Industrial Revolution. This was a time when work and home were intermingling components of a broader life, as people owned and managed the means of production themselves, and home and work life were blended. Beyond that, discussions are now emerging about the possibility of further major changes in work experience and forms of work as the idea of virtual worlds enters public consciousness.

The contributors to this volume are anthropologists who have spent an average of seven years working in remote and mobile settings. Some work in academic institutions, balancing university-based social science research projects with teaching responsibilities. Others work in industry as consultants, managers, or members of R and D (research and development) teams, using ethnographic approaches to solve organizational, communication and design problems for a diverse collection of clients.

The articles in this volume reflect the authors' self-conscious awareness of their individual mobile lives, and feature storytelling broadly as a narrative technique. This was a conscious stylistic and methodological choice made by the editors, as we were aware of an extensive literature on remote and distributed work but had seen little on the actual behaviors that, in accumulation, change established norms. To document these behaviors, we solicited auto-ethnographic first-person accounts from the contributors, including meticulous observations of self and others, detailed accounts of personal experience, as well as illustrations of the successes and descriptions of the tensions inherent in mobile work.

THE INTERFACE OF MOBILITY AND WORK

How mobility fits into the larger societal and cultural landscape has been explored widely in the literature by a variety of social scientists and related disciplines, including organizational development, technology design, market research and economics. What we have found absent, with few exceptions, are ethnographic accounts that focus on understanding the details of the personal experiences of people who are caught up in the process of restructuring their existence as they transition from traditional to flexible work styles. This volume is intended to contribute to remedying that deficiency.

A few anthropologists have placed ethnographic exploration at the forefront of their investigations, framing behavioral changes within a broader social and historical context. For example, a team of anthropologists from San Jose State University carried out an exemplary ten-year study of the adaptations and choices busy two-earner couples and their children make in their lives at home and at work. Although they address mobility only implicitly, they describe the ways in which new communication technologies are integrated (and resisted) in the daily lives of Silicon Valley families, and track the mundane interactions of these families in detail as they use a plethora of techno-gadgets to cope with daily responsibilities and plan activities, both personal and professional.[4] These accounts provide a detailed understanding of how, in an effort to be efficient and productive, working families find themselves overloaded with activities, and often frustrated and even baffled by the lives they are living.[5]

Corporate interests have crept into these investigations, but in so doing they have enriched our understanding of the implications of mobility and remote work. Not surprisingly, there is a concomitant turn toward the concerns of corporations and other large governmental and NGOs by anthropologists and other social scientists—not in the least because these entities are most likely to fund research in this arena. Corporate interests became particularly strong when it appeared clear that, with the decline in the number of onsite office workers, companies could substantially reduce their architectural footprint, thereby saving on real estate and building maintenance costs (Harrison et al. 2004). At the same time, there emerged a concern with how to manage mobile workers, in part conceived of as a control and supervision issue (Staples et al. 1998), but also to some extent as a growing concern with employees' quality of life and work–life balance (Benko and Weisberg 2007; Covey 1989).

As will become evident, the present volume builds on previous studies of the interface of work and technology, yet differs somewhat in style and focus. The eight contributors, themselves engaged in new forms of working and the challenges of having to manage the altered work–life relationships brought about by fast-changing communication and information technologies, turn inward to offer analyses of their own behaviors, using reflection and ethnographic description as a point of departure. Stylistically and methodologically, this results in an auto-ethnographic approach that is shared across the articles. As anthropologists who not only study remote, nomadic, and mobile workers but who are also remote, nomadic and mobile themselves, the contributors offer not only detailed behavioral observations but also a synthesis of the patterns they uncover, as well as insightful interpretations of their meaning. Moreover, the present volume is comparative in nature, in that the authors offer insights into the process of constructing new kinds of lifescapes as they compare life in traditional work roles with the realities of their existence as mobile workers. They thus begin to draw the outlines of what these changes are beginning to mean, both for a large number of the working population and the organizations that employ them.

In addition to the stylistic and methodological difference between this volume and others, there is also a difference in focus. Although other researchers might center their investigations on technology, work, family, or gender, we begin with a definite and persistent focus on mobility and bridge our discussions to other topics from this center.

We have structured the articles around the lived experiences of mobile workers, but we realize that the issues, insights, strategies, feelings, and behaviors that are shared by the authors are not exclusive. Workers from a traditional nine-to-five office may have similar experiences when much of their work is facilitated by information technologies. Examples of issues that both mobile and traditional workers face include "turning on and turning off work," presenting professional value to employers and coworkers, and the need to construct a more fluid identity that can function in a variety of situations. Although the very nature of work is changing, there are nevertheless many common requirements for any workplace. These include adapting to teamwork and team structure, and acknowledging the changing relationships and responsibilities that emerge in new social formations.

Traditional and new-style workers alike feel the effects of keeping people, things, and ideas related to work and leisure connected and integrated as they move through their busy days. It is our intention not to make a strict divide between traditional and mobile workers in this volume. At the same time, however, we do feel that the mobile experience intensifies these issues and gives them more prominence. For example, the physical requirements of mobility and the extensive organizational preparation it requires significantly increase the effort it takes to maintain integration. Thus, by providing some additional insights into this lifestyle based on firsthand narratives, we introduce new concepts related to mobile work and expand existing ideas related to work dominated and facilitated by information technology.

A BROAD DEFINITION OF TERMS

At a time when work patterns are rearranging themselves, it is no surprise to see the emergence of special terminologies for talking about nonworkplace spaces and places in which work is performed. At this time, some of the most common terms are remote work, mobile work, contract and freelance work, or telecommuting. Whatever the label, this work is generally flexible, temporary, nomadic, independent, virtual, or distributed. Because this work–lifestyle is as yet without a consistent definition either in scholarship or in practice, we have left it to the authors to define flexible work from their own perspectives. However, we do want to suggest some terminology in this introduction that might lead to a common understanding of the descriptors that are currently so variably used.

- *Workers* can be "remote." This implies that the location where the work is performed is physically separate from a primary or base office location.
- *Work* can be "distributed." By this we mean that work is no longer accomplished in one central location, but is potentially spread out all over the world. Types of work generally falling into this category include outsourcing, global teaming, virtual work, globally distributed work, and telework.
- *Both workers and work* can be "mobile." That is, we find them in nonconventional locations. For workers, mobility may include frequent location changes, whereas work, when it moves, for example, overseas or is assumed by customers, may be at least temporarily stable, requiring a fairly elaborate technological and infrastructure base. Mobility thus includes both *remoteness* (separation from a resource-rich "home base," and *truly mobile work,* which involves both remoteness and motion, or at least more fleeting periods of stasis (Sherry and Salvador 2002:110).
- Because virtual worlds are foreshadowed (although not specifically discussed) in this volume, we also propose a distinction between the terms "virtual" and "hybrid." Virtual refers to work that is facilitated by, and located on, the Internet. Work that is hybrid is a mixture of virtual work and work done in an office or other physical location.[6]

THE ARTICLES IN THIS VOLUME: AN OVERVIEW

The earlier work related to worker mobility serves as a solid foundation and inspiration for the questions and insights raised by the authors of this volume. Their reflexive, firsthand accounts offer not only a deeper understanding of the daily adjustments in practices, goals, and shared conventions that are required by the transition to remote and mobile work but also provide a strong base for expanding and grounding future social science research in this field. The set of cases explored in the articles that follow is meant to give readers an introduction to the range of issues that arise in the transition from traditional work styles to remote work, with the goal of leading to a deeper understanding of the factors that will increasingly shape life in the global economies of the future.

The personal narratives in this volume illustrate the many challenges and opportunities associated with living a mobile existence. The authors discuss the effects that deterritorialization has had on their daily lives, including how they adapt to, perform, and convey professional value to employers and colleagues as they work at a distance. They also illustrate the processes of renegotiating work behavior, making a place for personal time, and reconceptualize their personal identities as they integrate work and home into a challenging life. Based on their insights and discussions, we recognize that significant challenges emerge when adapting to the changing work context as professional existence evolves from traditional to flexible and mobile work. In highlighting the personal experiences and the perspectives of eight anthropologists who both study and live as remote and mobile workers, this volume deepens our understanding of how the new mobility fits into the broader cultural and economic landscape.

The opening article, *Community, Context, and the Presentation of Self in Distributed Workplace Interaction* by Michael Youngblood, explores many of the challenges remote workers face and offers insights into the strategies they use to manage them. Youngblood raises important questions about collaboration and coengagement with colleagues when they are not proximate to each other in time and space. Drawing on professional observations and personal experiences as a consultant working remotely, he investigates how relationships of collegiality and hierarchy are constructed and how workers manage to communicate their commitment and performance through increasingly narrow channels of social interaction when their actual productive activity is largely invisible to others with whom and for whom they work.

As she looks back on transitioning from the life of a fully employed corporate researcher to the life of a multilocal, often remote consultant, Brigitte Jordan, in *Living a Distributed Life: Multilocality and Working at a Distance,* paints a vivid picture of what it is like to be committed to regular, periodic moves between two home–workspaces, one of which for her is in the Silicon Valley of California, the other in the tropical lowlands of Costa Rica. She contextualizes her personal experiences and insights by drawing on keenly observed patterns of technology development, culture change, and societal transformation as she explores the upsides and downsides of this lifestyle and suggests some strategies for making it a successful endeavor. Her auto-ethnographic account suggests that the micro-patterns she sees in herself and the people she interacts with constitute the negotiated, on-the-ground materials that make up emerging global processes of culture change and societal transformation.

In *Occupational Websites as Locations for Remote and Mobile Worker Culture: An Examination of Temporary Worker Websites,* Loril Gossett illuminates the plight of "temps" and other independent workers who often find themselves on assignments where they are physically separated from the home office and their peers. Drawing on her experience as a temporary worker, Gossett explores some of the websites that are explicitly dedicated to the support of disconnected workers and shows how these sites provide resources that allow them to develop, sustain, and participate in a temporary work-related community of their own.

Julia Gluesing, in *Identity in a Virtual World: The Coevolution of Technology, Work, and Lifecycle,* paints an evocative picture of the parallels and complementarities of her personal and professional life with the recent developments in information and communication technologies, along with the increase in the functionality of the tools knowledge workers use. Aligning the evolution of her professional and personal life, Gluesing draws on personal experiences in work situations that range from a conventional job to her current involvement with a globally distributed system of industry or university-based coworkers and colleagues. These descriptions provide a fascinating and insightful analysis of the ways in which technologies and careers are connected in the progressive construction of an integrated identity.

Perri Strawn, writing about *Remote or Mobile Work as an Occasion for (Re)Structuring Professional and Personal Identities,* speaks about her life as an executive who continuously moves between a home–here and a work–there reality. Because of her comparatively senior position, Strawn is more concerned than most authors in this volume with issues around maintaining a corporate culture, both as an executive and as a remote worker. She insightfully describes the fragmentations that result from constant travel between work, home, and other locations and explores some of the strategies she has found more or less productive in combating this problem.

As an organizational anthropologist who studies employees, spaces, and places where work is conducted, Tracy Meerwarth, in *Disentangling Patterns of a Nomadic Life,* looks at reconceptualizations of physical space (e.g., home and away) and the shifting nature of relationships (e.g., with communities, friends, family), that emerge with increased mobility. Meerwarth introduces the term "nomadic" to describe the experience of traveling to multiple and geographically distributed sites across the landscape where the author is able to accomplish work. She explores the conflicts between media portrayals of seamless and effortless technologies by contrasting them with real-life experiences. Meerwarth reveals the difficulties involved with negotiating role transfers that arise for knowledge workers who actually live the mobile life. She identifies a pattern of increasing adaptability to physical and social relationships as evidence of her personal and professional growth in her role as a nomadic worker.

Developing the concept of *located mobility,* Amy Goldmacher draws on her experience of working in one city while having to manage the logistical and emotional aspects of her home life in another to provide insights into the personal, social, and emotional flexibility that is required for this kind of life. In *Located Mobility: Living and Working in Multiple Places,* she discusses the adaptations that become necessary when living and working away from a primary residence for an extended period of time, and offers insights into managing the challenges associated with that kind of lifestyle.

In *Interruptions and Intertasking in Distributed Knowledge Work,* Patricia Lange uses a self-reflexive investigation of her interactions with family and interviewees to discuss challenges that she faced when doing distributed work from home. Lange challenges theoretical and practical application of the term "multitasking" and instead proposes the term "intertasking" to describe activities that are interleaved in short intervals to satisfy multiple and often conflicting work demands. She reveals these dynamics so that members of distributed projects and teams can design processes, tasks, and tools that accommodate different dispositions with regard to doing several things in a short amount of time.

Taken together, these articles convey a strong sense of questioning entrenched practices and long-held assumptions about what constitutes "work," a "job," and a life worth living. There is an active sense of empowerment in these writings, of possibilities for crafting new lifestyles that fit with both personal circumstances and emerging societal patterns. We hope this collection not only will inspire new thinking about mobile work but also will help mobile workers themselves make sense of their own lives and circumstances and craft their own solutions.

NOTES

1. The idea of "lifescapes" came out of early work at the Institute for Research on Learning and the Workpractice and Technology Group at the Palo Alto Research Center where by the early 1990s workpractice studies had expanded to include the more holistic notion of "workscapes." Jordan, in a project with highly mobile, high-performance executives coined the term *lifescapes* because it became clear that work was no longer confined to work in the workplace but had spread into people's personal lives. The idea of "scapes" as indicating horizontal cultural conceptual domains has been publicized by Appadurai (1996) with "ethnoscapes," Cefkin (2007) with "rhythmscapes," and many others. For an in-depth treatment of the idea of lifescapes, see Jordan (2005).

2. The various forms of outsourcing are comprehensively reviewed by Palm (2006) and Skipper (2006). For World Systems Theory see Braudel (1993), Friedman (2003), Latham and Sassen (2005). Other global references we have found helpful are Appadurai (1996), Bestor (2001), Economist Intelligence Unit (2006), Friebe and Lobo (2006), Lutz (1995), and Sonntag (2005). A contributing factor to changing lifescapes is the demographic trends that underlie increases in life expectancy. For this the inspiring reference is still Laslett (1991).

3. For a review of the growing literature on deterritorialization and mobile work see Halford (2005) and Hislop and Axtell (2007). Other references we have found useful are Bean and Eisenberg (2006), Felstead and Jewson (1999), Felstead et al. (2002), Pittinsky and Shi (2004), Sherry and Salvador (2002), and Trager (2005).

4. They report their findings in two books (Darrah et al. 2007, English-Lueck 2002), several articles, and a number of websites, for example, http://www.sjsu.edu/depts/anthropology/svcp/, accessed September 6, 2008, or http://www.sjsu.edu/depts/anthropology/svcp/SVCPjugg.html, accessed September 6, 2008.

5. Other anthropologically based accounts are reported in the annual Proceedings of EPIC, the Ethnographic Praxis in Industry Conferences (the first of which occurred in 2005), as well as in articles in an increasing number of edited works. Because the topic of mobile work is of multidisciplinary interest, edited

books and proceedings of conferences are particularly likely to include ethnographic research. See, for example, articles in Brown et al. (2002), Ling and Pederson (2005), and LeVine and Scallon (2004). Other articles based on an anthropological approach are Baba et al. (2004), Gluesing et al. (2003), Luff and Heath (1998), and Miller and Slater (2000). We do not have the space here for a comprehensive review of the contributions by other disciplines but have found particularly helpful Bailey and Kurland (2002), Hinds and Kiesler (2002), and Gephart (2002).

6. Virtual worlds are explored from an anthropological point of view by Boellstorff (2008), Hine (2000, 2005), Jordan (in press), and Moore et al. (in press).

REFERENCES CITED

Appadurai, Arjun
1996 Modernity at Large: Cultural Dimensions of Globalization. Minneapolis: University of Minnesota Press.

Baba, Marietta L., Julia Gluesing, Hilary Ratner, and Kimberly Wagner
2004 The Contexts of Knowing: Natural History of a Globally Distributed Team. Journal of Organizational Behavior 25(5):547–587.

Bailey, Diane E., and Nancy B. Kurland
2002 A Review of Telework Research: Findings, New Directions and Lessons for the Study of Modern Work. Journal of Organizational Behavior 23(4):383–400.

Bean, Cynthia J., and Eric M. Eisenberg
2006 Employee Sensemaking in the Transition to Nomadic Work. Journal of Organizational Change Management 19(2):210–222.

Benko, Cathleen, and Anne Weisberg
2007 Mass Career Customization: Aligning the Workplace with Today's Nontraditional Workforce. Boston: Harvard Business School Press.

Bestor, Theodore C.
2001 Supply-Side Sushi: Commodity, Market, and the Global City. American Anthropologist 103(1):76–95.

Boellstorff, Tom
2008 Coming of Age in Second Life. An Anthropologist Explores the Virtually Human. Princeton: Princeton University Press.

Braudel, Fernand
1993 [1963] A History of Civilizations. Richard Mayne, trans. New York: Penguin.

Brown, Barry, Nicola Green, and Richard Harper, eds.
2002 Wireless World: Social and Interactional Aspects of the Mobile Age. London: Springer-Verlag.

Cefkin, Melissa
2007 Numbers May Speak Louder than Words, but is Anyone Listening? The Rhythmscape and Sales Pipeline Management. Proceedings of EPIC 2007:188–199.

Covey, Steven
1989 The Seven Habits of Highly Effective People. New York: Simon and Schuster.

Darrah, Charles N., James M. Freeman, and Jan A. English-Lueck
2007 Busier than Ever!: Why American Families Can't Slow Down. Stanford: Stanford University Press.

Economist Intelligence Unit
2006 Foresight 2020. Economic, Industry and Corporate Trends. London: EIU.

English-Lueck, Jan A.
2002 Cultures@Silicon Valley. Stanford: Stanford University Press.

Felstead, Alan, and Nick Jewson
1999 In Work, at Home: Towards an Understanding of Homeworking. London: Routledge.

Felstead, Alan, Nick Jewson, Annie Phizacklea, and S. Walters
2002 The Option to Work at Home: Another Privilege for the Favored Few? New Technology, Work and Employment 17(3):204–223.

Friebe, Holm, and Sascha Lobo
2006 Wir nennen es Arbeit: Die digitale Boheme oder Intelligentes Leben jenseits der Festanstellung. 3rd edition. Munich: Wilhelm Heyne.
Friedman, Jonathan
2003 Globalizing Languages: Ideologies and Realities of the Contemporary Global System. American Anthropologist 105(4):744–752.
Gephart, Robert P.
2002 Introduction to the Brave New Workplace: Organizational Behavior in the Electronic Age. Journal of Organizational Behavior 23(4):327–344.
Gluesing, Julia, Tara Alcordo, Marietta Baba, David Britt, Willie McKether, Leslie Monplaisir, Hilary Ratner, Kenneth Riopelle, and Kimberly Wagner
2003 The Development of Global Virtual Teams. *In* Virtual Teams That Work: Creating Conditions for Effective Virtual Teams. Cristina Gibson and Susan Cohen, eds. Pp. 353–380. San Francisco: Jossey-Bass.
Halford, Susan
2005 Hybrid Workspace: Re-Spatialisations of Work Organization and Management. New Technology, Work and Employment 20(1):19–33.
Harrison, Andrew, Paul Wheeler, and Carolyn Whitehead
2004 The Distributed Workplace: Sustainable Work Environments. London: Taylor and Francis.
Hine, Christine
2000 Virtual Ethnography. London: Sage.
Hine, Christine, ed.
2005 Virtual Methods: Issues in Social Research on the Internet. Oxford: Berg.
Hinds, Pamela J., and Sara Kiesler
2002 Distributed Work. Cambridge, MA: MIT Press.
Hislop, Donald, and Carolyn Axtell
2007 The Neglect of Spatial Mobility in Contemporary Studies of Work: The Case of Telework. New Technology, Work and Employment 22(1):34–51.
Jordan, Brigitte
2005 [2000] Lifescapes of the Future: Living and Working in the Third Millennium. Electronic document, http://www.lifescapes.org/Papers/lifescapes_of_the_future.htm, accessed August 27, 2008.
In press Blurring Boundaries: The "Real" and the "Virtual" in Hybrid Spaces. Special section, "Knowledge Flow in 'Real' and 'Virtual' Spaces," Brigitte Jordan, ed., Human Organization 68(2).
Laslett, Peter
1991 A Fresh Map of Life: The Emergence of the Third Age. Cambridge, MA: Harvard University Press.
Latham, Robert, and Saskia Sassen, eds.
2005 Digital Formations: IT and New Architectures in the Global Realm. Princeton: Princeton University Press.
LeVine, Philip, and Ron Scollon, eds.
2004 Discourse and Technology: Multimodal Discourse Analysis. Washington, DC: Georgetown University Press.
Ling, Rich, and Per E. Pederson, eds.
2005 Mobile Communications: Re-Negotiation of the Social Sphere. London: Springer-Verlag.
Luff, Paul, and Christian Heath
1998 Mobility in Collaboration. Proceedings of CSCW 98 (Seattle). Pp. 305–314. Seattle: Association for Computing Machinery.
Lutz, Christian
1995 Leben und Arbeiten in der Zukunft. München: Wirtschaftsverlag Langen Müller–Herbig.
Miller, Daniel, and Don Slater
2000 The Internet: An Ethnographic Approach. Oxford: Berg.

Moore, Robert, Caboll Gathman, and Nicolas Ducheneaut
In press From 3D Space to Third Place: The Social Life of Small Virtual Spaces. Brigitte Jordan, ed. Theme issue, "Knowledge Flow in 'Real' and 'Virtual' Spaces," Human Organization.
Palm, Michael
2006 Outsourcing, Self-Service and the Telemobility of Work. Anthropology of Work Review 27(2):1–9.
Pittinsky, Todd L., and Margaret J. Shi
2004 Organizational Commitment and Worker Mobility in Positive Perspective. American Behavioral Scientist 47(6):791–807.
Sherry, John, and Tony Salvador
2002 Running and Grimacing: The Struggle for Balance in Mobile Work. *In* Wireless World: Social and Interactional Aspects of the Mobile Age. Barry Brown, Nicola Green, and Richard Harper, eds. Pp. 108–120. London: Springer-Verlag.
Skipper, William
2006 Services Offshoring: An Overview. Anthropology of Work Review 27(2):9–17.
Sonntag, Selma K.
2005 Appropriating Identity or Cultivating Capital? Global English in Offshoring Service Industries. Anthropology of Work Review 26(1):13–20.
Staples, D. S., John S. Hulland, and Christopher A. Higgins
1998 A Self-Efficacy Theory Explanation for the Management of Remote Workers in Virtual Organizations. Journal of Computer-Mediated Communication 3(4). Electronic document, http://jcmc.indiana.edu/vol3/issue4/staples.html, accessed September 9, 2008.
Trager, Lillian, ed.
2005 Migration and Economy: Global and Local Dynamics. Lanham, MD: AltaMira.

COMMUNITY, CONTEXT, AND THE PRESENTATION OF SELF IN DISTRIBUTED WORKPLACE INTERACTION

MICHAEL YOUNGBLOOD
Cultural Anthropologist and Independent Consultant, New York, New York

Instantaneous communications technology has made it possible for distant coworkers to be interconnected to an unprecedented degree. Despite this, distributed workers often feel deeply disconnected from the production and performance of conventional workplace relationships and workplace culture. As the knowledge economy workforce trends toward ever-greater distribution and globalization, this raises important questions about the practice and experience of creative coengagement by colleagues who are not proximate to each other in time and space. How are shared understandings of workers' behavioral norms disseminated and practiced when workers are physically isolated from the collective workspace? How are relationships of collegiality and hierarchy constructed and performed through increasingly narrow channels of social interaction? How do workers signal their energy and commitment to a collective creative enterprise when their actual productive activity is largely invisible to others with whom and for whom they work? This article draws on my research with distributed knowledge workers, informal observations of colleagues, and personal experiences working as an independent consultant in distributed settings. It focuses on the challenges these workers face in defining their workplace community and effectively representing their professional selfhood when working at a distance. In this article I suggest that one key to alleviating these challenges is to extend the attributes of "placehood" to distant work spaces. Keywords: distributed work, workplace culture, community, performance, placehood

Over the past few decades many of us who are professional workers in the United States and other highly developed economies have become free to engage in our work virtually anywhere we choose. Although we typically see this freedom as a valued job perk and part of an enviable lifestyle, working away from the formal office and away from our coworkers also raises significant new professional challenges. In this article I focus on a few of these challenges, including the difficulties we face in attempting to define our workplace community, communicate our presentness to distant colleagues across space and time, and make visible our contribution to a collective productive process. Although working away from the conventional collocated office often has discernable practical and emotional benefits, my research and my own work experience indicate that, for many workers who enjoy this freedom, our individual efforts to overcome these challenges are often inefficient and sometimes cause us to operate against our own best interests.

NAPA BULLETIN 30, pp. 12–27. ISSN: 1556-4789.
DOI:10.1111/j.1556-4797.2008.00017.x

Popular and scholarly attention to the nature and impact of distributed work is growing and timely. With the rise of multinational corporations and offshore outsourcing over the past several decades, work and workers around the world have become increasingly distributed. In some industries and regions of the world the pace of these changes has been stunning. As a result, work at a distance is often conceptualized as a new phenomenon. In many respects, however, distributed work is not that new at all. Workplace consultant Jim Ware (2003), for example, describes work as distributed when it meets any of three conditions: if individual workers are isolated from each other in space, if normal communications and interactions are predominantly asynchronous, or if individual workers coengaged in the same enterprise are employed by different organizations. Considered in this way, it's not difficult to recognize many examples from the distant past. We might, for instance, point to the dispersed colonial workforce of the British East India Company, beginning in the 17th century; or perhaps the globally distributed organization of the Catholic Church as far back as the fourth century (cf. King and Frost 2002).

One thing that is new in today's distributed work is the way we communicate. Rome used to exchange messages with the far outposts of the church by ship or caravan; communication could take months. Today, we have the tools to interact with almost anyone on the planet as quickly as we can with the person at the next desk. Cell phones, e-mail, and other digital technologies have enabled distribution to expand exponentially—not only across huge distances but also across relatively small ones that are often no greater than the distances people like me used to walk, cycle, subway, or drive every day to go to work. These technologies have liberated many types of conventionally collocated office work from the expectation of collocation. Where workers used to be distributed because the nature of the enterprise actually required geographic distribution (e.g., colonialism or long distance trade), workers today are often distributed simply because the tools enable it.[1]

Pinning down the precise number of people who have the freedom to work away from the office is not easy.[2] This much is certain: our numbers have been growing over the past several years. We see people doing "office work" all around us, not just in offices. As the portability and connectivity of our laptops, PDAs, and other tools improve, the range of locations that we are able to turn into viable personal workspaces continues to expand. The result is that an increasingly large section of the workforce is now conducting a substantial amount of its work in what I've been calling "voluntary spaces"—the home, the café, the neighborhood pub, the verandah of a vacation getaway spot, any location that allows these workers to successfully meet their professional goals and obligations while concurrently maximizing fulfillment of their own broader life interests related to family, society, or personal freedom. As one who is both participant and professional observer of this behavior, I find this new voluntary geography of work deeply intriguing.

Locating our work activity in dislocation from the formal office can be professionally fruitful in many ways. It is often more efficient, enabling us to "go to work" wherever we are, with no obligatory commute. It is often more effective, buffering us from the routine distractions of the office. And it can be conducive to inspiration and innovative thinking, as changes of surroundings stimulate new perspective and fresh ideas. But there's also a real professional downside: dislocation from the collocated office does not simply distance us from a physical space, it distances us from a sociocultural place where relationships are formed and reinforced, collective standards and norms are defined, group knowledge is accrued, and shared meanings are created and invoked. It is a place where collocated workers create and practice their work community through a tremendous range of signs, signals, interactive modes, and sensory channels. The more routinely a worker is absent from the office, and the more narrowly he is connected to this community through decontextualized electronic channels, the more disconnected he becomes from this place.

A PERSONAL DISTRIBUTION ODYSSEY

As owner and sole employee of an ethnographic consulting practice, I spend the majority of my time conducting research and analysis for my clients. In this, I am very often on my own. When I do field research, I am sometimes partnered with a client or colleague, but am just as often venturing out solo (it all depends on client budgets and the nature of the work). When research is completed, the analytical process is often a heads-down affair that doesn't require me to be anywhere near my clients or colleagues. I am, in other words, a very mobile and frequently isolated worker. However, my experience of distributed work is not just personal, it is also ethnographic and observational. Over the past eight years, I've been involved in numerous projects for my clients that have focused on the experiences of other professionals who do their work in situations similar to my own. This has often put me in the decidedly meta position of contemplating the challenges of their distributed work while I myself am typing up my findings in a neighborhood coffee shop either across town or hundreds or thousands of miles away from where my own colleagues or clients sit.

My personal experience with distributed work began conventionally, structured in response to organizational needs rather than worker discretion. I was directing an off-campus study program for a college in the United States. The job required that I live and work in a small town in northern India, where the program was based. This was before the explosion of the Internet, e-mail, and cellular phones, and preceded even the ready availability of landline phones in the Indian outback. During the semesters, I stayed in contact with my department heads and support staff in the United States primarily via the regular postal service and the lone fax machine at a public telecommunications booth down the lane from my apartment. This college, which maintained several dozen concurrent study abroad programs around the world, had a substantially distributed workforce. Aware of the disconnect created by extreme geographic distribution, the college required intensive face time at its U.S. campus and arranged twice-annual collocated workshops for its dispersed employees. These gatherings were designed to help the globally located directors and the North American staff to renew acquaintances, form new relationships, share knowledge, and embrace a sense of mutual engagement in a common endeavor.

This policy of regularly recurring, collocated meetings changed with the rising ubiquity of the Internet and increasing access to telephones in most parts of the world where the programs were based. The college cut back on expensive face-to-face campus meetings, relying on the speed and apparent effectiveness of e-mail and voice communication as a partial and mostly acceptable replacement for direct interaction. True, technological advances made it possible for individuals in many distributed roles to now be more routinely connected with differently located supervisors, colleagues, and staff, but their work lives became, in some ways, much more isolated. Despite overall greater communication through the course of each semester, the reduction of periodic face-time somehow made our communication less conducive to cultural inclusion and relationship building than it had been before. My experience was that, for most directors abroad, their own felt and practiced community of coworkers continued to be defined by the relationships that they had made at the earlier campus workshops, even as new employees joined the organization and assumed roles that should have become valuable nodes within the collective collegial network.

Shortly after up leaving my position with the college, I returned to the United States to begin work with a consulting firm in New York. There, the opposite was the case. Like many companies that specialize in group-based creative work, this organization was designed on a model of "radical collocation" (Olson et al. 2002), meaning that workers were aggregated into teams inhabiting a single common room for the duration of a project. In this context of extreme and sustained proximity, typically lasting several months, relationships and mutual understanding between workers gelled within days of joining a new project team and continued to evolve every day of the engagement. Inside the team rooms, distinct work cultures would form within the first week; up-to-the-minute bits of insight were shared orally and expressively across the common table throughout each working day. The daily collegial bonding was so intense that those of us whose roles required us to be away from the team to conduct field research or attend meetings for more than a few days would inevitably feel disconnected from the group on return, having missed out on the stories, the activities, the newly formed "insider" understandings, and the camaraderie shared in our absence. The team was the key to our professional world. Good, cohesive teams did better work. Teammates who had talent, worked hard, and contributed to team spirit and effectiveness were preferred picks for future project teams. If you weren't a good teammate, you didn't have a bright future at the company.

My current pattern of work began in 2002, when I started working on my own as an independent consultant. Today, my collocated time with colleagues falls somewhere in between the two extremes of my preceding work situations. Equally distinct from both, however, is the extent to which much of my work has become liberated from the requirement that it be done in a particular location—whether a specific office or a specific part of the world. In New York City, where I now live, I have four different spaces that I consider to be my "office." One of them is a desk in my home, and the others are coffee shops that I enjoy in different parts of the city. When I'm on the road to conduct research or other project work, the office is often wherever I happen to find a comfortable and inviting place to settle in and open up my laptop. My clients and colleagues and work locations are continuously changing. With no consistent place of collocation in which to do my work, and usually no consistent or geographically proximate team members with whom to collocate, I frequently find myself engaged for long periods of time with clients and coworkers who I rarely and sometimes never meet face to face. But in contrast to my own isolation, these clients and coworkers with whom I am engaged are most often themselves fully or frequently collocated. Their own collocation enables them to practice and produce a culture of project-specific and community-specific shared knowledge and behavior from which I am always at risk of being cut off.

Today, when I'm working on the patio of a café on a sunny summer day in T-shirt and shorts, I am the envy of some of my more conventionally employed friends and colleagues who wish for a "dream job" like mine. Indeed, it can be an enjoyable way to work. At the same time, however, I'm acutely aware of the many subtle and significant ways that my interactions with my communities of coworkers have become far less rich than they have been before.

DISTRIBUTED WORK AND CONVENTIONAL WORKPLACE RELATIONSHIPS

But does any of this matter? Aside from having less social time with our workmates, do distributed workers suffer any professional loss from being away from the office? Unfortunately, research on the professional impact of distribution for individual workers has been scant. As we might expect, much of the popular and scholarly literature on collocation and distribution has been oriented toward what it means for efficient workflow, effective collaboration, or corporate innovation—that is, what it means for organizations rather than for individual workers (cf., Castilla et al. 2000; Cramton 2001; Fleming and Juda 2004; Lechler 2001; Lowry et al. 2006; Olson et al. 2002). Some of this work focuses on the challenges of building collective work culture or collective ways of thinking across distance (cf., Baba 2005; Baba et al. 2004; Gluesing et al. 2003) but there has been little attention to the trials of individual workers who are isolated from these collective outcomes.

Another stream of literature, taking a broader sociological perspective, has examined the larger societal impact of distribution. Political scientist Robert D. Putnam, in his classic *Bowling Alone* (2000), argues that working away from common and local spaces such as the conventional office is one of several factors that have contributed to the decline of social fabric in the United States. Putnam argues that participation in community builds what he calls social capital, which he defines as individual access to the collective resources of a group, including knowledge, skills, behavioral norms, values, and reciprocity. Although Putnam sees an individual's social capital as a by-product of participation in many different types of communities (not just workplace communities), his writing often strikes a sympathetic chord among those of us who are distributed and have reduced access to these group resources enjoyed by many of our collocated professional peers. More recently, Putnam and Lewis M. Feldstein have highlighted examples of communities and organizations that have been resisting or even reversing this trend (2003), but have found that one important requirement for doing so is regular face-to-face contact. For similar reasons, sociologist Ray Oldenburg (1997) praises "third places"—corner cafes, neighborhood pubs, and other very local gathering grounds—as key loci for revitalizing interpersonal familiarity and concern for the common welfare in our neighborhoods, towns, and cities. The significance of such local socialization spots for community development is inarguable. (My own case in point: I personally have come to know many more people in my neighborhood since I began working independently.) But for workers who occupy these spaces as work sites there is an ironic twist: nestling in with our laptops and cell phones at the local coffee joint may help us to bond with our neighbors and neighborhoods, but this comes at the expense of our bonds with the people who actually have a stake in the work we're doing while we're there.

The work of Putnam and Oldenburg connects in many ways to another set of concerns focused on the balance between work and life. There is a substantial literature on this topic, and it has been an important consideration in many public health debates as well as corporate human resource initiatives. The work–life perspective points to an interesting paradox: although many workers view information technology as a liberator that has helped them to more seamlessly accommodate work alongside other dimensions of their lives, many observers argue that these same technologies have blurred the distinction between work and life, enabling work to penetrate deeper into our homes, our family lives, and other locations and activities that were once havens from the stresses and demands of the workplace. Thus, journalist Madeleine Bunting (2004) finds many distributed or mobile workers to be delusional about their personal quality of life and describes them as "willing slaves."

Although there has been a valuable (and much less prominent) literature touching on the costs and benefits of distance interaction for individual workers' productivity and job satisfaction (cf., Bos et al. 2004; Hinds and Mortensen 2005; Kruger et al. 2005; Lesser and Stork 2001; Peña et al. 2007; Staples and Webster 2007), we still know relatively little about the impact of distance on workers' professional relationships and careers. How do these workers understand and practice a workplace community with a group of other individuals with whom they may rarely or never meet in a common place? How do these workers define and live up to their own roles or signal their energy, contribution, and dedication to a collective enterprise when they are physically isolated from the collective workplace, interacting with others through increasingly narrow channels of communication? These are questions of great significance to distributed workers—especially freelance and contract workers who are heavily reliant on work relationships and client referrals to build their practices. For independent professionals like myself, they have bearing not only on how we do our work and represent our work in the present but also on how, how often, with whom, and at what level of compensation and collegial regard we will work in the future. They are career issues.

To illustrate the point, I'll elaborate on two related sets of professional challenges faced by workers who are dislocated from their workplace communities. The first is the challenge of identifying the actual members of one's workplace community and determining the most appropriate ways to interact with them. Second, and closely related, is the challenge of self-representation within that community.

IDENTIFYING AND PRACTICING COMMUNITY IN DISTRIBUTED WORK

Distributed work can actually be highly conducive to some types of work-related relationships that conventional collocation does not as readily support. Consider for example an independent copywriter who spends afternoons doing work for her client from the voluntary space of a coffee shop. Although separated from her colleagues, she may become friendly with other distributed workers using the same space. As these relationships grow, they may lead to a network of reciprocal knowledge sharing and other mutual support that is beneficial to her professional development and future opportunities even though the members of this network are not engaged in the same work project or the same organization.[3] These offsite relationships and information exchanges may be valuable, but working away from the office tends to substantially reduce the distributed worker's opportunities to develop important relationships with the community of individuals most immediately engaged in the activity of a shared work effort. Distant workers, in other words, can often become invested in a different primary work community than the community of their collocated coworkers. And in this latter community, distributed workers can find themselves to be considerably "out of the loop."

In today's advanced communication age we may not see this as a big problem. Most organizations have by now become adept at providing distant workers with the resources to stay in contact with the formal office and to stay abreast of formal communications. But that's only part of the challenge. Informal and unscheduled conversation among coworkers—the classic chitchat around the office water cooler or coffee station—is sometimes equally important, and distributed employees and contractors are largely excluded from this. (Compounding the problem, many distributed workers are not even conscious of the significance of these channels of information. They don't know how much they're missing.) What makes face-to-face interaction so valuable, in part, is that it occurs within a shared, multisensory context that normally adds a great deal of additional insight in the exchange of information. Face-to-face interaction is not only more nuanced but also it is usually more memorable and influential than our interaction with people at a distance (Latané et al. 1995). And, as some of my informants have pointed out, face-to-face interaction enhances our sense of mutual personal engagement toward people with whom we interact—that is to say, dealing with people personally and directly usually makes us care more about them.

All of these attributes of collocated coworker interaction are important in formal meetings, but they may be equally or more important in casual workplace interaction. In their review of literature on workplace proximity, human–computer interactionist Sara Kiesler and management theorist Jonathon Cummings suggest that spontaneous, casual communication among colleagues is crucial to the development of workplace communities; it enables coworkers to "learn how one another's work is going, anticipate each other's strengths and failings, monitor group progress, coordinate their actions, do favors for one another, and come to the rescue at the last minute when things go wrong" (2002:66). The interpersonal nuance, gravity, and emotional engagement that make these interactions important and possible are difficult to foster when workers are at a distance.

Face-to-face, content-rich interaction is not only important to developing relationships with coworkers but also for understanding the roles and personalities of our coworkers who populate those relationships. Without the nuance of face-to-face interaction, workers often have a tough time recognizing differences in those relationships based on defined or semidefined roles, hierarchies, and mutual responsibilities. Workers who are routinely removed from the collocated work community often have trouble even identifying who its key members are or should be. One reason for this is that these types of information may not be effectively conveyed to distant workers, if deliberately conveyed at all, because subtle variations in roles, expected behaviors, and expected contributions on a collaborative team are often evolutionary, created and revealed throughout the actual process of work. Moreover, some important details that coworkers need to understand about each other are not always documented or even documentable—that is, they may be most effectively noted through informal communication and behavioral observation. As a result, relative roles (incl. the worker's own) end up being a matter of interpretation and guesswork for the distributed worker who lacks much or all of the rich contextual insight derivable from such clues as who sits where, who interacts comfortably or respectfully or timidly with whom, or who seems to be the resident fount of knowledge in those casual but all-important impromptu conversations. The less time distributed workers spend in the workplace context, the more challenging it can be for workers to not only define the contours of their workplace community but also to understand the individuals within it and to be, in turn, understood.

CONVEYING PRESENTNESS AND VALUE AS AN ABSENTEE COLLEAGUE

This brings us to the problem of how the community views the distant worker—or, in other words, the challenges we distributed workers face communicating to the community who we are and how we are contributing to the common productive effort. This seems to be particularly challenging when the nature of our work is highly creative (Cramton 2001; Davenport et al. 2002). In creative work, compared to other types of work that are more applied, linear or repetitive,[4] a worker's inputs of effort and outputs of work product are usually far more difficult to quantify. This is especially problematic if a worker's work peers, overseers, or other stakeholders have had no personal experience doing the same or similar types of work. How long does it take to create the perfect graphic design? Or a compelling brand concept? Or to analyze a unique set of research data? How much time must be devoted to the critical processes of rumination and experimentation to get it right, and what are the specific tasks involved? This vagueness of required time and activities to reach a given objective in these types of work creates a situation in which distributed workers feel a need to perform their input of effort for their distant colleagues in an attempt to reify and quantify the value of their labor that is inhered in their final output.

There are a number of different ways that I've seen noncollocated creative workers attempt to demonstrate their value and effort to a larger workplace community. One important and extremely common solution is an exaggerated frequency of contact with the people they perceive to be the key members of their workplace community. Many workers I've interviewed have described feeling compelled, when working outside of the office, to respond more quickly and more often to coworkers' phone calls and e-mails throughout the day to demonstrate that, despite being somewhere else, they are on the job. As social psychologist Justin Kruger and coauthors have shown, distributed workers commonly lose substantial productive time responding to more types of communications, from more coworkers, than they would if they were actually collocated with their colleagues and visibly engaged in other more pressing work (Kruger et al. 2005). When this occurs, communications can be self-propagating; calls and e-mails and instant messages (IMs) beget more calls and e-mails and IMs.

Initiating and maintaining a fusillade of electronic communications is just one response workers employ to signal that they are on the job. Sometimes these interactions are carefully timed to enhance their impact or significance. One typical example of this is when a remote worker sends an e-mail first thing in the morning, often on a topic of fabricated importance, with the backstage agenda of letting coworkers know that he or she has begun his or her day and is officially "at work." Workers often bookend these communications with another late in the afternoon or the evening, intended to signify that they are still on the job—or, as one freelancing friend of mine put it, to show that "my day is just as long, if not a lot longer, than yours." This solution is not always effective in meeting its objectives—especially, for example, when the worker's colleagues are in different time zones and may pay little attention to the time of day or night that messages were actually sent. But even in situations where time zones are shared, the strategic timing of remote communications can be complicated other by variables that may or may not be visible to distant colleagues. One woman I know who works from home to care for her child reports that she feels the greatest need to send e-mails and instant messages during the times that she's feeding her baby. It's irrational, she admits, but she feels convinced that her colleagues will suspect her of "slacking off" if she openly defers some of her work effort until evening when her child has gone to bed.

Frequency and timing of communications are not the only considerations, there is also volume. Many distant workers attempt to demonstrate their value through the sheer largeness of their output and interaction. This entails creating longer, more detailed than necessary documents, and longer e-mails, phone calls, or voice mails, to demonstrate an impressive quantity of thought, and a depth or breadth of engagement. I have seen distributed workers adopt this practice often, especially when working with collaborators with whom they have had the fewest face-to-face opportunities to communicate their selfhood or the significance of their contribution. It is a solution that commonly backfires, often planting suggestions in the minds of the worker's colleagues that their absentee teammate is seeking constant feedback, has difficulty working independently, and requires more attention and management than other workers. Despite the intended result of establishing presentness and value, this results in inefficiencies for distant workers, taking effort away from actual productivity to enact performances of productivity. And of course, this creates inefficiencies for their coworkers as well.

The problem of how the community sees the worker is also a problem of how the worker communicates her personal identity back to the community. In this way, it's just the inverse of the challenges distributed workers have in trying to figure out the other members of their community. It's a two-way street, one that can be particularly difficult when the interacting individuals have never met, or have met only in the most formal of circumstances. Many distance workers have expressed to me not only their concern about how little they know their colleagues but also how little their colleagues really know about them. This is not an experience unique to distance work. Having trouble "figuring out" a coworker or worrying about how a coworker perceives or judges us is common even in collocated work. In distance work, however, there are fewer channels for interpersonal understanding, fewer extralinguistic cues (facial expressions, body language, tone of voice, etc.) about the spirit in which communications are sent and received. And there are fewer opportunities for a "do over" if the impression given turns out to be not what we intended. As a result, distance workers often feel trapped within the narrow frames of formal role-play and a Goffmanesque on-stage representation of self from which they are afraid to stray for fear of being misunderstood. These carefully scripted "strictly business" communications may seem to be efficient and to reduce the possibility of misrepresentation, but they leave little room for forming actual bonds of familiarity and positive emotional ties.

Distance work, at least as it is normally practiced today, introduces perceptual and communication challenges between remote workers and their workplace communities and vice versa. The strategies that distributed workers adopt in response do address real needs and concerns, but they are also double-edged solutions that can lead to unintended self-representations and new work challenges in the process of alleviating others.

CASE STUDIES OF COLLEAGUES AND INFORMANTS

All of these difficulties of distributed work are things that I have consciously grappled with in my own career. Their significance, however, became much more clear to me when I began observing other distributed workers. A few examples from the experiences of friends and research informants will highlight the impact of these issues more objectively and candidly than any stories that I could relay from my own personal history. Each of these examples focuses on micro-level strategies that, though they may seem insignificant, have substantial impact on the workers' communities and reputations.

Take for example a professional acquaintance who I'll call "Dave," a contract web designer for a large bank. Dave works at home most days of the month and visits his client's office only occasionally. When I met Dave, he expressed concern that he was unclear about who the specific people were that needed to know what he was doing on a day-to-day basis. He was even less sure about who he most needed to impress to win his next freelance opportunity with the bank. Unsure for whom he should be performing, and in which situations, his strategy was to send frequent e-mails, voice mails, and interim work products to a broad assortment of individuals, including people who had never formally expressed interest in receiving or observing his work. Dave wasn't sure about the social contours or composition of his workplace community. He was attempting to make his value visible and signal his presentness to an appropriate and advantageous community of stakeholders by casting a broad net. But this backfired. I also interviewed "Anika," a technology director at the bank. Anika was someone who may have been in a position to hire Dave on a future project but who had little stake in his current work. When she received unsolicited e-mails from Dave, most of the time she simply deleted them without reading a word, assuming they would contain nothing that she needed to know. Dave's attempts to make his value evident and to draw Anika into his community resulted in the opposite of his intentions, creating an impression that he was wasting Anika's time and had little to contribute.

"Cheryl," an informant in a research project that I conducted on highly mobile workers, exemplifies an alternative approach. Cheryl is a freelance customer relationship consultant who had been working for one of her most steady clients for two years. She lived several states away from the client's formal office and had little face-to-face contact with any of her client stakeholders. Like Dave, Cheryl was uncertain how to identify her workplace community, but her strategy was to focus her performances of value and presentness on a few key people that she perceived to be most important to recognizing her contribution. In my interviews with other people involved in the project, however, I learned that some of them perceived Cheryl to be conspicuously unengaged. They weren't on her e-mail list. Moreover, having little insight into the depth of her actual work activities, some of these distant colleagues were quietly suspicious that she was absorbed in personal business when she was supposed to be on the job. This was doubly disconcerting to these individuals because Cheryl had been contracted to serve, in part, as a manager of several other independent consultants. Her failure to make her value, and that of her subcontractors, appropriately visible to the right people greatly diminished perceptions not only of her own contribution but also of the contributions of the other distributed people on her team.

The cultures and subcultures of workplaces and workplace communities are always distinct, but the distinctions can be subtle. Cultural conflicts between workers and their communities can be much more visible when a distant worker has been enculturated in a workplace context very different than that of his or her colleagues. Take for example the case of an informant named "Rajiv." Rajiv, a graphic designer and an Indian national, explained that he was trained in an Indian organizational culture in which deference to authority was important to signaling not only his understanding of workplace roles but also his future value and compatibility with the company. After arriving in the US and becoming a predominantly home-based (and café-based) distributed contractor to a web design firm, Rajiv frequently sent e-mails to his perceived overseers seeking input on his work product. His intent was to acknowledge his subordinate role and express his readiness to follow advice and direction. Concerned that his work was invisible, and that "being out of sight means being out of mind," Rajiv sent voice mails and e-mails to his client colleagues with a frequency that he himself felt to be "excessive." Rajiv's managing client—an American, enculturated in a relatively flat and self-directed organizational setting—interpreted these frequent communications as evidence that Rajiv was floundering and possibly not up to the job. The client shared these concerns with other office-based colleagues, leading to a broad misperception of Rajiv's personality and capabilities. As Rajiv experienced, information about how to "read" other people and understand a workplace's cultural expectations for interaction builds up slowly at a distance. Without the assistance of nonverbal cues and more candid, collegial, face-to-face communication, it took Rajiv several months to correct course, readjusting his strategy and ultimately redirecting his reputation within the workplace community.

As these experiences illustrate, effective practice of workplace community depends on being able to identify not only the appropriate members of one's community but also the most appropriate channels, character, and frequency for interactions with each individual member. These are not skills that can be taught or learned generically; social boundaries and patterned expectations for interaction are often unique to specific workplaces and specific groups of people within those places. Workplace communities are subcultures that are best understood through richly contextualized immersion. Each of these examples demonstrates this, and underscores ways that isolation can compound the cultural and interpersonal disconnects.

CONCLUSION

Effective interaction and self-representation within a workplace community always entail challenges. Even in a collocated setting, workers' efforts to express their selfhood and to participate in a community can have unintended consequences and undermine their interests. But distance work heightens these challenges. Distance isolates workers from exposure to the rich pool of community behavioral norms, informal feedback, boundary-defining cues, shared knowledge, values, mutual support, and other types of social capital that the collocated office more typically enables. Viewed in these terms, it appears that the root of the problem is not distance but rather the interpersonal and contextual isolation that distance—even very minor distance—tends to enforce. And in this respect, our current tools and practices for managing distributed workforces still have a long way to go toward meeting these challenges that distance continues to pose.

When people work together in a common space, their presence and interaction generates a unique and complex cultural system. This cultural system is what makes the difference between an inert space of work and a contextually rich place. In other words, workplaces are work locations that are characterized not just by people "doing their jobs," but also by aggregated layers of collective experiences that inform the emergence of a community identity, shape and nuance understandings of workers' relative roles and relationships, qualify each member's contribution and value to the community, and set the terms for ongoing interpersonal engagement and mutual assessment. Individuals who conduct their work outside of the collocated work site have substantially reduced opportunities to participate in these community experiences and to immerse themselves in the sensory channels through which the culture and context of the workplace community are transmitted and shared.

Of course, any durable solution to the challenges discussed above cannot simply reside in sending workers back to the collocated office. Workforces are becoming too complex and too global to reverse the distribution trend. Moreover, as we know, many workers enjoy working in locations of their own choosing; it is a benefit that they would be hesitant to give up. Is there a way to overcome the isolation of distant workers without removing the distance? Is there a way to foster vibrant workplace communities without losing sight of the unique needs of workers who aren't collocated with the rest of the team? These are questions of increasing importance for workers as well as for the companies they represent; highly functional workplace communities are not only more satisfying for individual workers but are also more efficient and effective in their collective work.

One way to address isolation could be through management techniques that better anticipate the challenges of remote workers. These techniques could be quite simple, with team leaders identifying and encouraging the adoption of best practices for communicating across collocated and distributed colleagues. Team leaders could, for instance, make a point of engaging all members of the community in both formal and casual discussions about mutual roles and expectations. They could also facilitate ongoing dialogue and feedback that would help distant workers bond with their colleagues and better understand the relationships, implicit behavioral rules, and expectations within the team. Another solution may be for collocated team leaders to make better use of the information technology toolbox at their disposal. Collective interaction via voice and video, both now readily accessible over the Internet, can easily and effectively add a great deal of context and interpersonal nuance to the interactions of dispersed colleagues. Most workers who have discovered services such as Skype would likely agree that the addition of vocal inflections and personal imagery to even short discussions between distant colleagues can do more to cultivate a sense of mutual understanding and connectedness than dozens of individual e-mails. As anthropologist Julia Gluesing and colleagues argue, solutions similar to these can be demonstrably effective in helping globally dispersed workgroups to come together as coherent and effective teams (Gluesing et al. 2003). However, in situations where most workers are collocated in a single place and only a few workers are distributed, there are barriers to the routine use of such techniques. In these situations, worker isolation is more often viewed by managers and collocated colleagues as primarily a problem for the remote worker rather than for the entire team. For the rest of the community, conference calls, video calls, and policies mandating occasions of unnatural, contrived, "informal" dialogue can seem like a poor use of precious time.

If we are to really address the issue at its core, it seems to me that we will need to imagine and design new processes and technologies that seamlessly and efficiently extend the qualities of "placehood" into the workspace experiences of nonproximate workers. This means envisioning communications technologies that are configured by default to facilitate more contextually rich and nuanced communicative experiences. It means envisioning technologies that enhance group awareness of each user's personality and his or her commitment to the shared effort, but without becoming big brotherly, compromising privacy, or facilitating the uninvited penetration of work ever deeper into workers' lives. And it means envisioning technologies that expand each user's opportunities to effectively participate in the routine practice of the workplace community, perhaps concurrently helping users identify actual and potential members of their own work community and lending some insight into the most appropriate methods and occasions for interacting with each. Any solution that accomplishes these things will need to be as fast, efficient, and intuitive as e-mail as well as create clearly discernable value for all users, both collocated and distributed. Falling short of this, it will not get used.

This may be a tall order but it is a goal that we should take seriously. Inevitably, work will become even more portable than it is today; the numbers of distributed workers both at home and abroad will continue to expand. As the spaces in which we conduct our work become more dispersed, more voluntary, and more unpredictable, the extension of placehood beyond the confines of the office space could be the key to ensuring that distributed workers have access to the same social capital of the workplace as their collocated colleagues—and that their collocated colleagues, in turn, get maximum benefit from working with their distributed counterparts. Working remotely will always be different from working in a collocated setting, but it need not be as isolating as it is today. As applied anthropologists and observers of culture and behavior, we are in many ways uniquely equipped to help inform the design of work processes and work tools that reduce this isolation. This is even more the case for those of us accustomed to distributed work—not only because we know its challenges first hand but also because we have self-interest in improving the conditions for our own professional lives.

NOTES

1. I've noticed this most overwhelmingly among peers and informants who are creative workers—consultants, graphic designers, information architects, copywriters, and others engaged in generative knowledge work (Drucker 1959). Technology has dramatically altered assumptions of how and where these types of workers work. Within the past decade, their means of production have become dramatically more compact and portable, their media has become relatively intangible, and their actual work product (documents, images, audio and video files) have become speedily, easily, and cheaply transportable across any distance.

2. The U.S. Department of Labor (2005) reports that, in 2004, there were 20.7 million people in the U.S. workforce who conducted their work from home or from a location of their choice at least one day per week and that 70 percent of these workers depended on the Internet or e-mail to do their job. Urbanist Richard Florida (2002) suggests that the segment of the U.S. economy that he calls the "creative class" constitutes more than 38 million people.

3. I've found that distributed workers in coffee shops, and even bars, often share information about, for example, the use of complicated software applications or leads about potential jobs and clients. These are types of discussions that a freelance contractor may not be comfortable having with members of the actual collaborative team with whom she is currently contracted.

4. Not all knowledge work is creative by requirement. Some knowledge work entails relatively structured, standardized inputs and outputs, including jobs or job activities such as order fulfillment, benefits administration, invoicing, and accounts management (Davenport et al. 2002).

REFERENCES CITED

Baba, Marietta L.

2005 Virtual Community: An Oxymoron at Work? Creating Community in Globally Distributed Work Groups. *In* The Ties that Bind: Building Community in the 21st Century. Stan Hyland, ed. Pp. 133–165. Santa Fe: School of American Research Press.

Baba, Marietta, Julia Gluesing, Hilary Ratner, and Kimberly H. Wagner

2004 The Contexts of Knowing: Natural History of a Globally Distributed Team. Journal of Organizational Behavior 25(5):547–587.

Bos, Nathan, N. Sadat Shami, Judith S. Olson, Arik Cheshin, and Ning Nan

2004 In-Group/Out-Group Effects in Distributed Teams: An Experimental Simulation. *In* Proceedings of the 2004 ACM Conference on Computer Supported Cooperative Work. New York: ACM Press.

Bunting, Madeleine

2004 Willing Slaves: How the Overwork Culture is Ruling Our Lives. London: HarperCollins.

Castilla, Emilio J., Hokyu Hwang, Ellen Granovetter, and Mark Granovetter

2000 Social Networks in Silicon Valley. *In* The Silicon Valley Edge: a Habitat for Innovation and Entrepreneurship. Chong-Moon Lee, William F. Miller, Marguerite Gong Hancock, and Henry S. Rowen, eds. Pp. 218–247. Stanford: Stanford University Press.

Cramton, Catherine Durnell

2001 The Mutual Knowledge Problem and Its Consequences for Dispersed Collaboration. Organization Science 12(3):346–371.

Davenport, Thomas H., Robert J. Thomas, and Susan Cantrell

2002 The Mysterious Art and Science of Knowledge-Worker Performance. MIT Sloan Management Review 44(1):23–30.

Drucker, Peter F.

1959 Landmarks of Tomorrow. New York: Harper and Row.

Fleming, Lee, and Adam Juda

2004 A Network of Invention: Creativity in a Community of Inventors Hinges on a Few Well-Placed Players. Harvard Business Review 82(4):22.

Florida, Richard

2002 The Rise of the Creative Class: And How It's Transforming Work, Leisure, Community and Everyday Life. New York: Basic Books.

Gluesing, Julia, Tara Alcordo, Marietta Baba, David Britt, Willie McKether, Leslie Monplaisir, Hilary Ratner, Kenneth Riopelle, and Kimberly Harris Wagner

2003 The Development of Global Virtual Teams. *In* Virtual Teams that Work: Creating Conditions for Virtual Team Effectiveness. C. Gibson and S. G. Cohen, eds. Pp. 353–380. San Francisco, CA: Jossey-Bass.

Hinds, Pamela J., and Mark Mortensen

2005 Understanding Conflict in Geographically Distributed Teams: The Moderating Effects of Shared Identity, Shared Context, and Spontaneous Communication. Organization Science 16(3):290–307.

Kiesler, Sara, and Jonathon N. Cummings

2002 What Do We Know About Proximity and Distance in Work Groups? A Legacy of Research. *In* Distributed Work. Pamela Hinds and Sara Kiesler, eds. Pp. 57–80. Cambridge, MA: MIT Press.

King, John Leslie, and Robert L. Frost

2002 Managing Distance over Time: The Evolution of Technologies of Dis/Ambiguation. *In* Distributed Work. Pamela Hinds and Sara Kiesler, eds. Pp. 3–26. Cambridge, MA: MIT Press.

Kruger, Justin, Nicholas Epley, Jason Parker, and Zhi-Wen Ng

2005 Egocentrism Over E-Mail: Can We Communicate as Well as We Think? Journal of Personality and Social Psychology 89(6):925–936.

Latané, Bibb, James H. Liu, Andrzej Nowak, Michael Bonevento, and Long Zheng
1995 Distance Matters: Physical Space and Social Impact. Personality and Social Psychology Bulletin 21(8):795–805.
Lechler, Thomas
2001 Social Interaction: A Determinant of Entrepreneurial Team Venture Success. Small Business Economics 16(4):263–278.
Lesser, Eric, and John Stork
2001 Communities of Practice and Organizational Performance. IBM Systems Journal 40(4):839–842.
Lowry, Paul Benjamin, Tom L. Roberts, Nicholas C. Romano, Jr., Paul D. Cheney, and Ross T. Hightower
2006 The Impact of Group Size and Social Presence on Small-Group Communication. Small Group Research 37(6):631–661.
Oldenburg, Ray
1997 The Great Good Place: Cafes, Coffee Shops, Bookstores, Bars, Hair Salons, and Other Hangouts at the Heart of a Community. New York: Marlow.
Olson, Judith S., Stephanie Teasley, Lisa Covi, and Gary Olson
2002 The (Currently) Unique Advantages of Collocated Work. *In* Distributed Work. Pamela Hinds and Sara Kiesler, eds. Pp. 113–135. Cambridge, MA: MIT Press.
Peña Jorge, Joseph B. Walther, and Jeffrey T. Hancock
2007 Effects of Geographic Distribution on Dominance Perceptions in Computer-Mediated Groups. Communication Research 34(3):313–331.
Putnam, Robert D.
2000 Bowling Alone: The Collapse and Revival of American Community. New York: Simon and Schuster.
Putnam, Robert D., and Lewis M. Feldstein
2003 Better Together: Restoring the American Community. New York: Simon and Schuster.
Staples, Sandy D., and Jane Webster
2007 Exploring Traditional and Virtual Team Members' "Best Practices." Small Group Research 38(1):60–97.
U.S. Department of Labor
2005 Work at Home in 2004. Bureau of Labor Statistics News, September 22. Electronic document, http://www.bls.gov/news.release/homey.nro.htm, accessed September 22, 2005
Ware, Jim
2003 Understanding Distributed Work. The Design Work Collaborative. Electronic document, http://www.thefutureofwork.net/assets/Understanding_Distributed_Work.pdf, accessed October 7, 2005.

LIVING A DISTRIBUTED LIFE: MULTILOCALITY AND WORKING AT A DISTANCE

Brigitte Jordan
Consulting Corporate Anthropologist, Palo Alto Research Center

In the last few years, new collaboration and communication technologies have led to a deterritorialization of work, allowing for the rise of new work- and lifestyles. In this article, I use my own transition from the life of a corporate researcher to that of a multilocal mobile consultant for tracking some of the patterns I see in a changing cultural and economic environment where work and workers are no longer tied to a specific place of work. My main interest lies in identifying some of the behavioral shifts that are happening as people are caught up in and attempt to deal with this changing cultural landscape. Writing as a knowledge worker who now moves regularly from a work–home place in the Silicon Valley of California to another in the tropical lowlands of Costa Rica, I use my personal transition as a lens through which to trace new, emergent patterns of behavior, of values, and of social conventions. I assess the stresses and joys, the upsides and downsides, the challenges and rewards of this work- and lifestyle and identify strategies for making such a life successful and rewarding. Throughout, there emerges an awareness of the ways in which the personal patterns described reflect wider trends and cumulatively illustrate global transformation of workscapes and lifescapes. These types of local patterns in fact constitute the on-the-ground material reality of global processes that initiate and sustain widespread culture change and emergent societal transformations.
Keywords: multilocality, lifestyle, culture change, work and technology, lifescapes

As the world is globalizing, many of us are leading lives that are to a greater or lesser degree mobile and distributed. As the papers in this volume show, many people are now doing professional work away from what might be considered their official workspace. Some of them do this sporadically, some semipermanently, whereas others have gone to live in a foreign country on assignment for lengthy periods of time. Although maintaining professional ties to their original or official workspace, some of these mobile knowledge workers retain varying degrees of emotional attachment to their "workplace of origin." They may work in far-flung places but they regularly and expectedly come back to their home base where most of their personal and family life is located. For others, the mobile life means a permanent condition of existing in two or more places at once. Some of them experience this as chronic homelessness, others as the integrated life, raising questions about how much integration between work and home is freeing because it provides options and alternatives, and how much becomes an intolerable invasion.

NAPA BULLETIN 30, pp. 28–55. ISSN: 1556-4789.
DOI:10.1111/j.1556-4797.2008.00018.x

For a growing number of people the very idea of a home in the traditional sense has become nebulous. I am one of those. In the pages that follow I track my transition from a more or less conventional job as a corporate researcher into a complex, multilocal, distributed life that now has me moving regularly between two integrated home–work spaces that are separated by thousands of miles. In the lifescapes I have constructed, what is local and what is remote flips regularly. Every three months to be exact.

And so I find myself exemplifying both sides of the "new mobility:" one side being the global mobility of work, the fact that tasks and work processes that were tied to specific locations have moved to wherever they can be done the cheapest and most efficient way (Palm 2006; Skipper 2006; Sonntag 2005); the second being the mobility of those doing the work (Hislop and Axtell 2007). Actually, mobility has been common and widespread prehistorically, historically and cross-culturally, much in contrast to popular opinion that sees it as a recent phenomenon (Cobb 2005; O'Leary et al. 2002; Trager 2005). There have always been nomads, people who have been leading distributed lives, although maybe not in quite the way we do now. I am thinking of the homeless in our inner cities, the thousands of migratory workers that cross our borders every year from Central America, the "shuttle traders" that Ken Anderson studies as they ply the border region between China and Russia (Fiske 2007), or herders like the Maasai whose seasonal migration paths anthropologists have studied for a long time. What has changed is that with the rise of modern communication media the patterning of mobility has been altered.[1]

In this article, I will be exploring some of the major trends within which the experiences of my own mobile life have played themselves out. I begin by highlighting what may be the most significant factor of the many that have led to making this kind of life possible for me and other knowledge workers: the blurring of the boundaries between work and home life that has occurred with the introduction of new collaboration and communication technologies, especially the Internet and mobile telephony. I continue with a somewhat personal account of my transition to a multilocal existence and distributed work, exploring the ways in which new architectures and technologies make this kind of lifestyle possible. I discuss the patterns of adaptation I see emerging as global economies, organizations, and individuals adjust. Throughout I focus on emerging patterns, tracing the connecting lines between global trends, my own life, the lives of my mobile colleagues, and the participants in the consulting projects in which I am involved. I look at some of the ways in which the emergent technologies of today affect the way we work, live, and relate to each other and, in the course of doing so, again change our ideas of what is possible.

WORK AND HOME: BLURRING BOUNDARIES

The boundaries between homelife and worklife, whose blurring we observe at the current time, were created by the Industrial Revolution. Removing production, for example, from a shoemaker's hut and the shop that was part of his family's living quarters to a factory, the Industrial Revolution erected barriers that are only now beginning to be breached.

By cutting up the day into (then) 12-hour shifts, it established regular working hours and with whistle and factory bell managed to split home from work and work from home, as temporally and locationally separate spheres.

It has been an unquestioned fact of life ever since the Industrial Revolution that work is at work and home is where the family is. Now much of what knowledge workers used to do at work has spilled over into their private lives. And this is not only true for routine activities such as reading professional journals, keeping up with disciplinary trends, and answering e-mail and voice mail but also increasingly includes strategic, heads-down activities such as planning and writing. As a matter of fact, many knowledge workers say that they can't get any "real" work done at the office. Work that formerly was tethered to a defined workplace is now routinely done at home, in the car or in the kinds of public third spaces described by Churchill and Nelson (in press). As a matter of fact, for many people work activities and related obligations have proliferated into almost all aspects of daily life.

Work has invaded the home in many ways, some of which are not obvious. For example, Darrah et al. (2007), in their ten-year study of family life in Silicon Valley, document that many families have begun to conduct their home life with the management techniques they learned at work (see also English-Lueck 2002; Ruhleder et al. 1996).[3]

As is the case at work, time has become the critical resource for these families. There is a premium on noncommitted time that they can spend as "quality time" with each other and especially with their children (Darrah et al. 2007). They feel the need for devices that help with efficient time management and eagerly adopt any technology that might help them monitor the activities of family and friends.

But what may be more surprising is that a parallel change is proceeding at the same time, as a visit to any Google campus will confirm. Digital technologies have allowed home and leisure-related activities to make inroads in the workplace, so that for many people work life has become very much like home life (Hochschild 1997, 2007). Our "other life" in all of its myriad realizations has crept into the times and spaces that used to be reserved for work (Hochschild 1997). The home has domesticated the workplace almost as much as work has settled itself in the home.[2] Knowledge workers' private lives are increasingly colonized by a work mentality that has moved in on the back of the technologies that have worked well for coordinating connections with the workplace. Cell phones and PDAs were quickly seen to provide similar services for organizing one's family (Darrah et al. 2007; Hochschild 2007). This constitutes a structural shift in family life and a major, cultural transformation that is widely visible at least in the Euro-American sphere.

These two worlds, the world of work and our personal, private world of children and friends, of community life and hobbies, of sports and quiet meditation places in the garden, used to be cleanly separated from each other. They were protected by generally accepted rhythms and schedules and by institutions like "the end of the workday," which dumped untold numbers of commuters onto the freeways at 5 p.m. For many knowledge workers like me, the two worlds are now interdigitating or even fusing. The barriers have become more transparent and "stuff" is leaking through. Invited or not, stealthily or welcomed, work has snuck into our home lives and has staked claims to a variety of other places and spaces as well. We grapple with the consequences, as the papers in this volume show.

BOUNDARY MANAGEMENT: MENDING THE FENCES

There is no doubt that well-established boundaries are being breached. But there are as yet few societally sanctioned rules for handling this new situation. As a consequence, individuals, families, and work communities are beginning to develop strategies for managing it, including resisting the constant monitoring that digital devices permit. With ever-increasing availability and visibility, many people feel the need to fence off certain areas of their lives so that they are not open for inspection and colonization by just anyone, at any time.

Families work out explicit rules about technology use and the conditions under which technology-generated interruptions may intrude into family life by manipulating their techno-gadgets and inventing new rituals and boundary markers (English-Lueck 2002; Darrah et al. 2007; Lange this volume). Some make new rules that renegotiate the interface between family and work—balancing the demands of children and homelife on the one side with those of work on the other side. Mealtime may be off limits for answering phone calls, both for adults and teenagers. Uninterruptable work times may be agreed on within the family, though, as Lange (this volume) suggests, the verdict is still out about if and under what conditions that works. When is it all right to interrupt a parent working at home, and what does a child do when Mommy is at home but not available for homework? These parents often find it very difficult to make clear to their children what their status is. As they connect to their virtual office from their kitchen, living room or home office, symbols of transition from work to parental status are gone. The working men and women who used to leave home in business clothes with briefcase in hand, now, in T-shirts and running shorts, appear totally available and interruptible to their children as well as to household help.

Boundary work is particularly urgent for two-earner families with children where crisis times seem to be pickup and delivery for school or childcare, bedtime routines, and meal preparation. Often we see elaborate divisions of labor developing around these critical junctures where the requirements of home tend to conflict with those of work. For me, given that my children are grown, these issues don't apply anymore. My home–work life is no longer quite as complicated, although I am constantly mindful (and often being reminded) of the restrictions under which many of my collaborators who telework from home have to manage. While we are on IM (Instant Messaging) or a pc (phone call), there is always the possibility that on the other side a child walks in with a bloody knee or the gardener sticks in his head asking for instructions.

Domestically, my partner and I have worked out a mutual agreement to minimize interruptions and thereby avoid the associated penalties (primarily the cost of recovering).

Because I do much work at home, often in a recliner in the garden or in a hammock chair by the fire, my partner has developed the habit of approaching without saying anything until I give an indication that I can talk. This allows me to do the multitasking that is part of my lifestyle and to give proper attention to these other parts of my life without incurring the negative consequences of multitasking to a large degree. I do the same for him. We also use IM extensively for communicating between our physically separated home offices (one upstairs, the other downstairs), which eliminates many of the interruptions generated by the "maintenance requirements" of a shared operational household ("You hungry yet?"), as well as the myriad "urgent" items that would otherwise generate an interruption ("Did you see the message from the airline?").

In this new work ecology, fresh behavioral clusters, values, and conventions appear. For example, distributed workers tend to differentiate between "work time" and "my time," although these are no longer linearly arranged but rather intermingled in variably sized chunks. Others organize their activities spatially, by explicitly distributing tasks and time allocations between work space and domestic space in their homes (Halford 2005; Woodruff et al. 2007).

For many, the blurring of the boundaries between work and home is a double-edged sword: on the one hand, it gives (some) people the freedom to arrange their lives in ways that are more satisfying to them and fit their needs better; but on the other hand, people fight again and again to maintain some semblance of order and predictability as the pressures in the office combine with those of a hectic family life. Individually and collectively they create new boundaries by manipulating the techno-gadgets and inventing new rituals and props, creating new institutions like meeting-free days at the office, and agreeing on new physical and behavioral no-trespassing signs for family members working at home (Lange this volume).

Although many chafe under these arrangements, we might consider that this interpenetration of work and home is neither good nor bad in itself. We might want to remember that traditional jobs are a fairly recent invention, kicked off by the rise of factories in the 1800s. During earlier times, when human beings simply followed the rhythms of nature, they worked hard during periods when wild or domesticated crops could be harvested, but during slack times devoted lots of time to social, ritual, and artistic activities. Before the Industrial Revolution people didn't have jobs in the modern sense at all, but did whatever was required to bring in the harvest, make goods for home consumption, and trade or sell their wares (Bridges 1994a, 1994b). Might the new technologies provide the possibility to return to a more "natural" rhythm? Some of us think so. As worklife and private endeavors again become intermingled (at least for knowledge workers), many of us believe that this offers an opportunity for a better integration that intersperses paid "work-work" with other kinds of worthwhile activities.

Yet, for many, it is not freedom and options they are acquiring but coercion and outside control. As Halford (2005) points out, there exists a major dividing line, a "significant fault line," between low-paid, semiskilled or unskilled workers who are given no choice but to work from home and managerial or professional workers for whom the opportunity may appear to offer greater autonomy and flexibility. As a society, we have not yet worked out our priorities and what makes sense for whom.

Technology adoption is one of the forces that make all kinds of borders increasingly permeable (Jordan in press). Techno-gadgets are colonizing our homes and workplaces, our entertainment spaces and learning environments. Observing ourselves and the world around us, we might ask, "What other borders are being breached?" Or the other way around, "What kinds of boundary lines are still intact? How much of our world still remains off-limits to techno-gadget intrusion?" Or again looking at it from the other side, "What activity domains are barred from technological 'enrichment?' What are the spaces that we, as a society, will agree to keep protected from invasion by techno-gadgets?" I used to think that fear of surveillance would motivate people to guard certain physical places, private activities, and conceptual domains against technology intrusion. In particular, I thought that the intimate and spiritual parts of our lives would remain technology-free sanctuaries for a long time. But as I visit my mother's grave in a cemetery in a small town in Germany, there is, on a grave nearby, an "eternal light" powered by a solar cell.[4] This took me by surprise, but the use of communication technologies in spiritual life, ritual and religious practice is extremely common and widespread (Bell 2006; Miller and Slater 2000) and has been incorporated even in indigenous communities without a hitch (Jordan 2007). Now that people are using cell phones and laptops in bed it appears that neither the spiritual nor the intimate is safe. Should it be?

HOW I GOT HERE: A CONFESSIONAL

Earlier in my career, I and everybody else I knew used to "go to work," and that was a particular physical place. For me it was at first a faculty office at a university and then a corporate research lab, where I had all the resources I needed, from libraries to administrative support. Most significantly, I could meet up with my colleagues face-to-face, real live people with whom I had developed significant and satisfying working relationships.

My life changed in 1998 when I switched from being an employee to becoming an independent consultant. A period of downsizing at work coincided with a periodic desire to try something new. So I took a "golden handshake" and "retired."

I wish there were a better word for "retirement." To some people it still implies shutting down. Retreating to the knitting and the fishing, depending on your gender. But for me it was to a large extent life as before. Outwardly, not much changed. I was still doing R and D (research and development) projects, although now with accountability to my own partners rather than to clients contracted by my employer. I still traveled a lot, lived in hotels a lot, came "home" to *Springhill*, my house in the Santa Cruz Mountains above Palo Alto, to catch up, take a look at my garden, and take off again. I still had an office at the Palo Alto Research Center, and continued to interact with my colleagues there pretty much the same as before. As a matter of fact, many of them didn't realize for a long time that my status had changed.

FIGURE 1. My Home Office at *Springhill.*

FIGURE 2. My PARC Office.

I had a minor "identity crisis" at the transition. I wasn't sure at first about how I should refer to myself now, but my past boss suggested I simply put "consultant" in front of my former title. I printed up new business cards that made me a "Consulting Principal Scientist." For a while I contemplated the possibility of starting my own company. It would be called "OnSite Insight," but looking at the difficulties my formerly employed friends encountered (the office rent, the assistants they had to hire, the communication systems they had to install, etc.), I decided to stay lean and simple.

* * *

A few years earlier my partner and I had taken a vacation in Costa Rica. We immediately felt an affinity for the land and the people. Both Bob and I had lived in the tropics before (he in Africa, I in Mexico) and had found that lifestyle appealing. We bought a piece of property high up on the side of a mountain, looking down on miles and miles of beach. There were some old trees on our land but much of the property was cattle pasture, recently abandoned, and now overgrown with weeds and the first generation of forest

FIGURE 3. Miles and Miles of Beach.

regrowth. Amongst fantasies of regrowing the original jungle, we dreamed of building a house there where we would live whenever we could manage some time off, a place that we could use as a base for exploring other areas in Central and South America. This seemed increasingly a possibility as our consulting engagements settled into a predictable pattern of high-intensity work interspersed with occasional slow times.

Whenever we could squeeze in a few days, maybe because a project required time for analysis, for preparing a workshop, or for writing a client report, we began to work on building *Besos del Viento* (Kisses of the Wind), our house on the mountain. Bob designed it and built it little by little with the help of a motley group of local workers. I had only two requirements: this house had to be round (I hate square boxes) and without walls (I also hate to be caged in). We both wanted it to be open to the wind, the butterflies, the birds, the snakes, and whatever other animals might want to share our lives there. It took

FIGURE 4. *Besos del Viento.*

FIGURE 5. First Step in a Long Commute.

years before *Besos* became livable. We finally inaugurated it on the last day of the 20th century with a smashing New Year's Party.

By now, eight years later, we have settled into a fairly regular pattern of three month chunks of time in California twice a year, with the rest of the time in Costa Rica. My work patterns in California and Costa Rica are quite similar, the main difference being the lack of face-to-face interaction with my partners outside of Costa Rica. At the same time, it is remarkable how similar my life is in both places. The majority of the consulting work I do now is done remotely, by e-mail and telephone, with only occasional face-to-face meetings. And those are as easy or difficult to accomplish from Costa Rica as they are from California. As a matter of fact, it takes me less time to get to the U.S. East Coast from San Jose, Costa Rica, than from San Jose, California.

Before *Besos del Viento* became a part of our lives I had always traveled a lot. But I had always had a "home." Now I am living with the necessities, the routines, the pleasures and the excitement of constantly negotiating my two lives—the one that is physically located in Costa Rica, and the other that plays itself out in Silicon Valley. Why do I run my business half of the year from a mountainside in that little country, looking down on 30 miles of surf and watching a family of *coati mundis* steal my bananas while I do my e-mail?[5] Why am I not sitting in California's Silicon Valley for twelve months of the year when that is where most of my business connections are? Good questions.

One of the most obvious changes that the shift to remote work and a mobile lifestyle has generated is visible in the changing architectures of our physical environment, in private, domestic domains as much as in the public sphere. Both of them are interesting spaces in which to track emergent cultural shifts.[6]

As information technologies have decoupled work from physical spaces and face-to-face interaction (Gluesing this volume), the shift to distributed work and a mobile lifestyle has blurred the relationship between home and office. The layout of both *Besos* and *Springhill* accommodates the colocation of domestic, personal, and work activities, and that has modified our expectations of what behaviors can occur in our home–work spaces. Archeologists keep coming up with fascinating insights about the influence of subsistence technologies on home, hut, or cave shelter design. I am old enough to remember the disappearance if not of the "parlor," then definitely of the "rumpus room," the "den," and then the "family room," all of which vanished as people reordered the priorities in their lives. The recent changes in the reconfiguration of our physical spaces are similarly indicative of the ongoing negotiations over redefining when and where work happens and when home life rules.

I do have a home office at *Springhill* (in California) but that may be mostly for historical reasons, mainly because it's always been there and serves as the place that collects the papers, books and tapes I need for my work. At *Besos del Viento* (in Costa Rica) I don't really have an "office," and in both places I appropriate different locations as the place where I do work for a while. It is worth noting that for most of the people who have "real" home offices, that home office is stationary, a specific place to which they may even be able to shut the door. For others, the home office has become mobile and multilocational. For me it happens to be wherever my laptop makes an appearance. Sometimes it shows up on a nine-foot slab of wood (our dining table at *Besos*) or in the *palapa,* my retreat on the hill above the house. This is particularly important for me because at *Besos,* due to the open construction, it becomes difficult to generate something approaching a space (not to speak of a room) of one's own. My partner, too, has his favorite spaces and one might easily find him, laptop on lap, in a shady spot on the steps going up to the pool. Our laptops allow us to colonize a space of our own, when we need it and where we need it, by appropriating different parts of both houses and their environment.

Reflecting on the ways in which we have constructed, reconstructed, modified, and adapted the structures and functionalities of our two abodes, I see myself participating in the wholesale global repurposing and multipurposing of dwellings. When I think about it, I see me doing a version of what everybody else is doing and has been doing for eons—that is, redesigning our environments so that they become esthetically beautiful and functionally efficient, according to whatever current conditions and cultural preferences require. When I look at the Great Rooms in contemporary upscale home construction, so insightfully described by Allison Woodruff and colleagues (2007),[7] I wonder now if it was only my desire to be close to nature that got me to ask Bob for open construction. At a

FIGURE 6. Three Workspaces at *Besos.*

FIGURE 7. Working on the Go.

different time and in a different environment, would I have yearned for the protectiveness of cozy little rooms that made one feel safe and cherished? It is in these subtle ways that "culture has us by the throat," as Harvey Sacks used to say, and that is precisely why examining one's own actions can generate a deeper understanding of these "invisible-in-plain-sight" cultural shifts that we experience, even as we contribute to them.[8]

But it is not only in our own private environments that we can observe the evolution of new spatial architectures. The same is true in the public sphere. Work has scattered beyond our bedrooms and living rooms into a variety of spaces that are becoming hospitable to working remotely by providing resources and a place of refuge for the mobile worker. In the competitive public sphere, this has created considerable pressure to offer services for workers on the go, a pressure that is visible in the changing layout of a variety of structures, from banks to retail stores. For me, because I travel so much, two of my favorite observation points have been airport lounges and hotel lobbies.

Global transportation economies are adjusting to the pressure exerted by the demands of frequent travelers. These pressures affect changes in architecture to changes in services. Now there are spas and massage stations as well as novel and innovative shopping opportunities in practically every large airport, train station or megahotel that caters to a crowd of "transumers" (consumers in transition), global travelers who increasingly live a transient lifestyle. In most airport cafes and bistros your latte now comes with internet access and a convenient outlet for your laptop, for travelers as well as pilots.

I am also fascinated to watch the ways in which airport lounges are beginning to adapt to the needs of working travelers. Old-style lounges, on the one hand, are almost institutional in the layout of their uncomfortable parlorlike seating arrangements, old-fashioned phone cubby holes, and scarce outlets for your laptop. Newly constructed or remodeled lounges, on the other hand, have tables with ergonomic chairs where one

FIGURE 8. Old-Fashioned Airline Club—Bad Design for the Working Traveler.

can prop a laptop, free wireless broadband access, plentiful connections, and may even let you do your e-mail in a luxurious massage lounger. Patently visible here is the slow diffusion of these kinds of innovation. Travelers who don't have access to airport lounges are still crowding around hard-to-find outlets in the gate areas, sprawling around floor level outlets with their laptops and backpacks (and sometimes babies). One might expect that the next remodeling of those facilities will catch up with mobile workers' needs and provide convenient access of the kind that is already common in the airports of Hong Kong and Singapore.

I also continue to track what is happening in hotels, where lobbies are changing from drab, somber walk-through places to brightly lit, cheerful seating areas where you can easily have a private business conversation or hole up with your laptop, never far from an outlet. And many public restaurants and hotels are now providing free Wi-Fi and internet access, a terrific boon to the traveler.

A LONGITUDINAL VIEW: CRITICAL ENABLERS

We have come a long way since we started to experiment with locating half of our work–life in Costa Rica, and I do not underestimate the role of regional economic development and technological development that made this possible. The dozen years since we began building *Besos* saw wrenching changes in the regional economy, including a comparatively rapid progress in upgrading infrastructures such as phone and broadband connectivity, visible in most of the Central and South American countries. Doing distributed work, of course, wouldn't be possible without the increasing functionalities of the technologies that connect us remote workers with our clients and partners.

What we see clearly outlined here is the coevolution of technology with work and lifestyle, with the technology playing a critical role as an enabler, as Julia Gluesing (this volume) has so cogently demonstrated. Today's emergent technologies are affecting the way we work, live, and relate to each other and, in the course of doing so, make different kinds of lifescapes possible.

When I am not in face-to-face contact with clients or colleagues, my main work activities (and I believe this is true for most knowledge workers) are computer work (much of it e-mail), writing (most of which involves editing computer printouts),[9] and telephone calls (Brown et al. 2002; Julsrud 2005). With the laptop, all of these have become divorced from a fixed location.

But in the early days in Costa Rica, phone calls used to be a major headache. When we happened into Matapalo on that first trip in 1993, it was a sleepy little beach community. There was one public phone at a local "soda" (roadside eating place) where villagers stood in line to call family and friends for news, or a potential employer for upcoming jobs—not exactly a place where you could conduct business. In those days the only way we could get e-mail was to stand in line with the rest of the villagers, connect our laptop to the phone line, and hope that nobody was sending us longwinded messages or attachments.

When we acquired a cell phone, it had reception originally only in very restricted locations. One of those was in the pit of Manuelito, the village mechanic. (Remember the days before hydraulic lifts?) The other one was available at low tide. If one waded far enough out into the ocean, one could sometimes get a phone call through, but it was a hazardous enterprise. Now this little community has land phone lines and villagers can call anywhere in the world, send faxes and e-mail, and, incidentally, so can I when I need to communicate back to my partners from this still remote place. What we are beginning to see is a communication network that spans the globe, linking individuals, institutions, and communities.

We still don't have a landline at *Besos* up on the mountain. But Bob, always the inventor–tinkerer, somehow cobbled together a two-kilometer Wi-Fi connection down to the village to the house of a *tico* family who were kind enough to share the use of their landline with us.[10] So now we check e-mail several times a day—a luxury we appreciate immensely because, together with the cell phone, e-mail is our most important link to professional counterparts and family.

Technological development may be most visible around cars. In the early days, there was one car in Matapalo, then (and still) owned by Micki, who might be pressed into taxi services at times. Now you see almost as many cars in the village as there are television antennas on the roofs. In the beginning, we used the rickety buses that ply the dirt road between Matapalo and the communities to the North and South, like everybody else. We also hitchhiked a lot, a practice we continued when we bought *Mulita,* a rather decrepit Toyota Land Cruiser (by now 35 years old) that for a long time had the endearing habit of breaking down rather regularly. But as time went on, Bob, who had driven such a thing across Africa earlier in his life, repaired her bit by bit, and now it is we who give locals and stranded tourists a ride. During the dry season we take the top off and she becomes our safari vehicle.

UPSIDES, DOWNSIDES, REWARDS, AND PENALTIES OF THE DISTRIBUTED LIFE

I believe that the upsides of leading this kind of life are obvious, at least for the privileged professionals who lead a life similar to mine, and indeed, people often envy this lifestyle. But there are also considerable difficulties one encounters and penalties one pays. I fully appreciate that where there is still a single fixed home to which the nomad returns, especially one where family members await her or him, there is likely to be a lot more conflict and negotiation than is the case for me because my partner is with me, no matter where we are for the moment. The consulting trips I take, whether from California or Costa Rica, have the same flavor of absence and return as they used to when I had a single work–home location. My work is still sprinkled through my "other" day in kaleidoscopic fashion, alternating cycles of serious head-down work with breaks of "other." So in many ways, my home life and my work life have not changed.

The Upsides

Probably the biggest upside for me in living a distributed, seminomadic life is the excitement of constant change, mixed with the security of the familiar. I love the tropical life at *Besos* where I continually discover new sources of delight, of joy, and of adventure. I love the early morning hours before the sun rises, doing my exercises on a tile floor downstairs that is still warm from the sun of the previous day; a pale moon floats in a star-filled firmament; a kinkajou makes its way across the branches of a tree, silhouetted against the moonlit sky. At *Besos*, I experience an expansion of my senses, an increased peripheral awareness that notes a gecko on the wall munching on a grasshopper, a toucan in our bananas, a beautiful parrot snake that turns and takes off in a green flash as soon as she sees me raise my head from my laptop.

FIGURE 9. Green Parrot Snake.

FIGURE 10. Visit from a Butterfly.

I find a new kind of joy in watching a jeweled beetle make its way across my laptop, or a butterfly landing on it while I take a sip of my coffee. On a mountain where traffic is rare, I've learned to tell who is coming up the steep gravel road (and may stop for a chat) by the sounds of their engine. I know that a car or truck horn sounding three times repeatedly somewhere on the mountains means "I'm in trouble, need help." It is those recognitions of familiarity, of insider knowledge, of awareness of local routines and events that give me the feeling that I actually live here, that I am not "just" a tourist.

I continue to take breaks between my work cycles, but they now may consist of a walk down to the star fruit tree to check what is ripe, or a chat with Ricardo, our worker, who wants to know if he should cut the coconut trees that are beginning to obliterate the skyline. My tropical garden is a new delight now and I spend lots of my breaks there. Our reforestation efforts have brought monkeys and other animals that need forested travel paths back into our area. And then there is always the beach. I know California quite well, but in Costa Rica, whenever we drive into the jungle or cross a river with our "safari vehicle," there is still a sense of newness, of discovery, of adventure that keeps me from falling into all too rigid routines in the rest of my life, too.

FIGURE 11. Adventures with Mulita and Granddaughter.

But after living three months in the rainforest I find myself ready to return to *Springhill* and to the familiar haunts and faces that continue to define, to a large extent, my work persona. I reconnect with colleagues and friends, reinforce professional bonds, and enjoy having an extensive research library once again at my fingertips. I even enjoy trading the incessant call of toucans for the raucous screeches of blue jays, and looking up once again at redwoods rather than teak and palm trees.

The Downsides

Although the upsides of this kind of life are obvious, the downsides are maybe less so, but it is the downsides that require conscious effort and extra energy because they have to be actively managed. (The upsides are only to be enjoyed or possibly to be prioritized.) Compared to a stable workplace where much information gets exchanged in the hallway, at lunch, the gym or other in-between places, most of the troubles that descend on the nomadic worker have to do with the disruption of social relations and the loss of context. This is the bane of the consultant anyway, and one that I certainly experienced when I did external projects while still tied to a fixed workplace. Not having access to the corridor conversations, those of us working remotely often have no clue about what is happening until a decision has been made "back at the office." But even after return, having missed a major chunk of informal knowledge transfer, having missed subtle changes in company and client goals, not having met new employees or even the new boss when one returns, it is crucial to manage surprises by quick assessment and soliciting updates. For this, ongoing relationships are crucial. One of the hidden costs in working remotely is the tremendous amount of energy that successful distance workers invest in maintaining these kinds of relationships. Potentially serious problems flow from neglecting their maintenance, including unanticipated decisions that may significantly affect the remote worker's or consultant's project.

All knowledge workers who lead distributed lives face changes in their social relationships. Most painful is the unavoidable shrinkage of prior collegial and personal relationships, but there is also a significant increase in new relationships. In my case, although I definitely experience a certain impoverishment in the connection to my colleagues at PARC and to the lab culture, I now have a second set of permanent relationships, namely those I am developing in Costa Rica with colleagues, expats, and ticos from the village and surrounding areas. To overgeneralize, I would say that the number and variety of relationships is up, but the intensity is down. The reality is that I am away for six months out of the year as seen from either side. As Meerwarth (this volume) points out, having face-to-face connections in one place automatically means remote relationship maintenance for the other. And that is a serious issue if one doesn't want to run the risk of letting those relationships shrink into oblivion.

I do have some consulting projects where there is no face time whatsoever. I've never seen these people and they've never seen me. We do wonder how much of a problem that is and have tried to patch it up by sending photos like the one below. In the course of time I have learned interesting bits about them (like that one of them is six feet two inches

FIGURE 12. Remote Work with Canadian Team.

tall and has trouble in airplane seats, or that the sister of another team member just had a baby), but these are isolated bits that don't hang together. Nevertheless, at least in this case, the relationship works perfectly. And I don't know why. Maybe it is because it is the kind of project that I have done a lot, where I can predict what the tasks are that have to be done in sequence, where I can be a watchdog helping them avoid making the most common mistakes and missing those obvious but invisible opportunities. Nevertheless, for me and many of my mobile colleagues the questions remain: When is face time really necessary? How much is enough? And enough for what?

What is definitely certain, however, is that I pay special attention to maintaining these relationships of familiarity, availability, and mutual commitment to the best of my ability. I know that requires special work. I keep lists that tell me both who I need to meet with when I get back and who "at the other end" I want to continue a conversation with while I am gone. In some ways my life has become richer but also more complicated.

There are many, rather mundane reasons why, in our lives, the problems could easily have outweighed the advantages. I do not underestimate the fortuitous idiosyncratic circumstances that enable our particular version of a mobile life. Without my partner's ability to build a dream house from scratch, his technological expertise that keeps our communication networks intact, and his constant attention to the myriad maintenance requirements of our multilocal lifestyle, little of this would be possible. Nevertheless, I believe that there are enough parallels to what other mobile workers experience to make it worthwhile to look at the kinds of strategies we have developed to make this a challenging but deeply satisfying and often exhilarating existence.

STRATEGIES FOR LIVING AND WORKING IN TWO PLACES

As other contributors to this volume have shown, knowledge workers have adopted a variety of different strategies for adjusting to a life where boundaries are blurred and relationships are tenuous and in constant need of maintenance. These adjustments range from choosing socially acceptable patterns of activity management to an assemblage of heuristics, "tricks of the trade," and experiential wisdom that accumulates based on individual and collective experience.

Boundary Keepers and Integrators

As I observe people trying to figure out what strategies to adopt for living this new distributed life where the barriers between work and non-work are disappearing, I see them struggling to adjust. There seem to be two kinds of strategic solutions for dealing with the pervasive interdigitation of work and off-work spheres. Some people fight the disappearance of time-honored boundaries. They struggle to establish new borders and rules so that both family-related and work-related tasks get done. These "Boundary Keepers" fit well into a regulated workplace. They like a clear division between work and non-work. They thrive on set hours for each and do best with a formal, structured workday. They are the ones who maintain separate e-mail accounts for personal and work e-mail. As a matter of fact, they may actually open their "work mail" only during the work part of their day and they definitely are not going to take their laptop on vacation.

Those of us who interleave activities of different kinds, such as intensive head-down work while writing a report with a spell of pulling weeds in the garden, we might call the "Integrators." I confess that I am an unabashed, unmitigated, dyed-in-the-wool Integrator. For me, there is no strict division between work time and "other" time. I prefer to look at the list of what I need to do and what I want to do at the beginning of my day and then spread my energy around to give cycles of maybe 30 minutes to tasks according to their priority. What this means is that many things are in progress. Many things do not get done. Yet items move up in the ranking as they become more urgent. I might end up with spending several cycles on a project proposal with a close deadline. Still, even if that happens, I prefer to get up between cycles, check the laundry, look up a reference, pick some flowers, and come back to the task.[11] The advantage of balancing non-work activities with work-related tasks is that I can juggle many different projects and interests at the same time, including allocating time to myself. With this system, nothing gets consistently ignored: clients, family, friends, and colleagues all remain in my peripheral awareness. It is rare that something actually falls between the cracks. However, it's a wonderful way of supporting procrastination, an ever-present temptation for the solitary knowledge worker. If there is something I really don't feel like doing, I can always push it down on the list.

Integrators don't object to interruptions (although they do manage their negative consequences). The door to their office (if they have one) is always open. They are the ones who keep their e-mail program on all of their nonsleeping hours, and they rarely resist the temptation to look at a mail if it pops up on their screen. If you send them a message, you can expect an answer within minutes. (However, if you are working with a Boundary Keeper, don't expect an answer before the next working day.) The Integrators are avid users of Instant Messaging (IM). They mix personal and business items in the same e-mail and on their to-do lists. They think nothing of doing a grocery run in the middle of a workday and their workplace shows it. I knew I was talking to an Integrator when I met with a manager recently whose cubicle was a lively collection of the pictures of her customers' kids and of colleagues, several magnet photo frames of her cats, a candy dish for drop-ins and even a copy of the New Testament Psalms and Proverbs lying there on her desk. This was an Integrator whose home had happily colonized her workspace. She actually said: "My cube is home for me," and I would bet that she runs errands during the day, talks to friends and family during work times, and stays late in her cube-home whenever required.[12]

Clearly, both Boundary Keepers and Integrators are struggling to establish and maintain some semblance of order and predictability, the Boundary Keepers by establishing new barriers and rules that allow them to preserve some form of separation between their work life and their private life, the Integrators by obliterating them. Both are in the business of making new rules that renegotiate the interface between family and work.

Managing the Transitions: Lists and Routines

Actually, the most hazardous aspect of being continuously on the move is the transition stage, the period of time when you are neither here nor there, when here and away flip. Meerwarth (this volume) calls this a liminal time, the experience of moving through space and time without solid grounding. For me, especially in the early days, there always loomed the fear (and often the experience) of impending double disaster: the chaos of leaving one place and the chaos of arriving at the other. At the same time, these transitional days are full of energy, tinged with the excitement of change, of new adventures, of making plans, of hoping for the repetition of what attracted us to *Springhill* and *Besos del Viento* in the first place. There is a sense of pulling loose, of leaving behind, of uncertainty but also of anticipation of the changes that are in store. This is the time when memories have to be refurbished for the new place.[13]

A major way to conquer chaos for me has always been making lists. I live by lists. They allow me to get some idea of what's out there, and thereby an idea of what I can handle and what will remain a problem. So lists are not really a way to get things done (the tasks and problems are still there after I've written the list) but they provide a feeling of control. At least I know now what the feeling of doom is about, what the chaos consists of and I can make a worst-case scenario in the knowledge—based on experience—that the outcome is never as bad as I think.

Active workload management by making lists is a joint enterprise. Both Bob and I draw up various lists and post them in public places (like the kitchen table). And we make lots of lists. Many of them are tri-partite: of here (wherever that may be at the time), of there, and of in-between. Of things to do before leaving (disconnect the car battery), things to do on the way (last phone calls from the airport lounge), and things to do when there (check which bridges are down). Of items to purchase here, in between, and there. Of things to remember when we are here, in between, and there. These lists bind the here with the there, they smooth the disjuncture, and make the nonordinary again familiar, ordinary, and tractable.

A specialized list that I have on my desktop no matter where I am is our exit list. It, too, has a flip-flop nature, depending on where we are exiting from. It is a boundary object for that wholesale reconfiguration that needs to happen whenever we move from "CR" to "CA" or "CA" to "CR." "Things to take back" in the exit list means things to take back to CA when we are in CR, but take back to CR when we are in CA. The "talk to when we get back" list will have the names of clients, colleagues, and family in California while I am in Costa Rica, and the other way around when I am in California.

Double the Effort, Double the Fun: Duplicating the Necessities

So what does it take to make a structure of massive beams, tile floors, and cement columns home? A functioning work–home? For us, the operant questions were: How much do you really have to duplicate? And how much stuff can you carry on a plane? It turns out a lot. Especially in the early days, little could be acquired locally. For ten years we brought down tools, building supplies, computers, phones, books, office supplies, car parts, dehumidifiers, exercise equipment and more, not to speak of the favorite foods we couldn't get in Costa Rica. If you are addicted to Reese's candy bars or brie cheese, you will have a hard time finding those in our tiny village grocery store. We still travel with our full baggage allowance but now much of that is taken up with clothes, tools, and household goods for our Costa Rican friends, and coffee and Costa Rican rum for our U.S. friends. (I am, however, still dreaming of walking off the plane with only a handbag, and a book under my arm—my idealized version of what a mobile life should look like.)

Finding Way Stations

What has become very important to us in our journeys back and forth are our way stations, places of refuge in the transition that are, in many ways, akin to the "third places" described by Oldenburg (1991) and the "in-between" and "transition spaces" discussed by other authors in this volume. These are familiar islands of comfort and convenience that make a stressful, daylong journey tolerable. All mobile workers who travel particular routes routinely find them sooner or later. For us, the way stations that have become particularly important are airport lounges and our arrival and departure hotel in Costa Rica.

Airport lounges are prime candidates for "third places." They facilitate all kinds of business, recreational and personal maintenance activities (like showers) for the out-of-home, out-of-office nomads that frequent them. At this point in time, they show some measure of stress to adapt to the changing routines of travelers. In the past the design trended toward a pseudo living-room atmosphere where one could watch a movie, read a book, and meet friends and colleagues. Business-related pursuits were relegated to a windowless conference room and a corridor of narrow cubicles where travelers could make a phone call or hook up their laptop. Although less innovative than home office design, which has become very much attuned to work-at-home activities, one can see small steps toward making lounges more responsive to the emergent needs of working travelers. My own observations suggest that cubicle occupancy is declining, while laptop work in the open areas of lounges seems to be more common, leading again and again to the spectacle of travelers searching for scarce outlets.

Our favorite arrival and departure hotel in Costa Rica has also taken on special significance. Arriving there, no matter what time of the day or night, I breathe a sigh of relief. Things here are familiar. We are greeted like family. I ask the maid how it is going with her long-dying father and the gardener inquires after "Mateo," our grandson, who at the age of seven stole his heart. Routine interaction and the expectation of continuing visits generate a kind of pseudo family atmosphere. In the course of the years there has been a progressive exploration of what kinds of favors and special treatment we can ask of each other that may be quite typical for these kinds of ongoing relationships. We bring tools and consumer items that are difficult to get or of inferior quality in Costa Rica for friends among the hotel staff. We keep our car in the hotel parking lot while we are gone. The kitchen staff keeps the cheeses we bring in a cold pack from the United States in the hotel refrigerator for us while we are there. What contributes a lot to this sense of "almost home" is that we know things that nonregular travelers don't know, like to ask for a favorite room such as the Orchid Suite (which is adjacent to the pool) or the fact that we can get coffee at 6 a.m. although breakfast isn't served officially until eight. What is important in this kind of relationship are the personal connections, the small favors exchanged, and the help offered and given whenever the need arises, even if inherently modulated by the basically commercial nature of our stay.

Managing Social Relationships

As Meerwarth (this volume) notes, as a remote worker, no matter where you are physically, you are always managing two sets of relationships simultaneously, those at a distance and those that exist locally. This adds substantially to the workload of the remote worker, taking not only time and effort but also requiring a fair amount of emotional energy. Not paying sufficient attention to this issue crops up as a significant cause of dissatisfaction on both sides, the worker's and the employer's, and may even lead to the abandonment of what often is begun as an experiment.

Youngblood (this volume) explicitly names two strategies for building and maintaining effective collaboration over distance. One revolves around self-presentation and identity; the other around making the work (the "value add," in corporate language) visible to a distant partner or client. There is a set of rarely vocalized questions that always lurk in the background, needing to be answered unexpectedly in interaction with clients and colleagues, such as Who am I to them? How do they see me? How can I make myself and my value visible? What do they need to know about my past, my competencies, my limitations? My work style and my lifestyle? Obviously, I would want to communicate what they need to know to carry out the work over which we are building a relationship, but that itself, in my type of consulting, is often ill-defined to start with.

Again, as in the Boundary Keeper–Integrator question, personal preferences and well-established habits loom large. I know of people who keep any indication of their personal life out of such exchanges, and others who, like me, believe that work is more productive and more satisfying when our outsider status is in some ways mitigated. Research shows that judgment about the performance and competence of remote team members is often negatively affected by the absence of personal contextual information, resulting in what is known as the "fundamental attribution error" (Cramton 2002). If a project fails or a task is not carried out properly, the cause may be attributed to the actor's lack of leadership, motivation, or skill, or, alternatively, it could be seen as owing to situational factors such as lack of support, not enough time, too difficult. Negative behavior by an inside member of a group is likely to be attributed to situational factors ("child sick at home") but similar behavior by an outsider is often judged as owing to personal deficiencies ("incompetent," "unreliable"). This affects how credit and blame are allocated, performance is evaluated, and, as a consequence, how resources are distributed. It would appear then that even apart from personal preference, there are good reasons for not withholding all personal information. In any case, maintaining a strict division between what is private and what is business related is not likely to come naturally to Integrators who tend to mimic the progressive disclosure of personal information in face-to-face encounters in their remote relationships.

This speaks to the larger issue of self-presentation in the absence of colocation. Without the immediate feedback available in face-to-face relationships, I often experience a nagging uncertainty about how my work is being evaluated and how I am seen. There are band-aid solutions to this problem, such as quick phone calls for "checking in," prompt responses to e-mail and voicemail, frequent updates on progress, though, as Youngblood (this volume) has pointed out, that has its own dangers as well. The underlying issue remains. In the last analysis, for social creatures like us, the pervasive ill feeling that comes from lack of frequent responsive feedback is something that, at least at the current state of technology, remote workers will have to live with. It is one of the many stresses they have to manage.

I am fortunate in that my enduring home base at PARC provides a solid anchor for continuing relationships with my professional colleagues there that allows me to retain many of the benefits of colocation. PARC continues as my primary intellectual community but I have also found it important to compensate for the unavoidable shrinking of established relationships by strengthening my participation in other professional communities. Here the anthrodesign community, the SfAA (Society for Applied Anthropology), NAPA (the National Association of Practicing Anthropologists), and most recently the EPIC (Ethnographic Praxis in Industry) community have become major resources for building, maintaining, refreshing, and adapting my professional self-image to the changed conditions in my life. Their websites and support groups make up for the lack of face-to-face communication to some extent, apparently a common way for remote workers to build virtual communities, as Gossett (this volume) describes as well.

My lifestyle is often seen as enviable and I know that I am likely to overemphasize its positive aspects. For example, I often find myself launching into an enthusiastic, overly positive account of life in Costa Rica. But this, after all, is also a country where theft and robbery are endemic, where torrential downpours can sweep you off your mountain, where it takes forever to get something done, and where unbridled development is rampant. I know that living in a tropical country in the midst of natural beauty is intrinsically subject to suspicion of vacationing, retiring, or other kinds of unavailability. So I have learned, as has Strawn (this volume), that actively managing one's remote status rather than being defensive or overly advocatory about it is part of managing remote social relationships.

CONCLUSIONS

The rise of new information storage and communication technologies has despatialized many kinds of work and has made possible for many people a different set of options for rebuilding their workscapes and lifescapes (Latham and Sassen 2005). In times of cultural shifts and societal change new rules and standards have to be built: on the individual side, in the corporate sphere, or by society at large.[14] But at this time there are no fixed rules yet for how to deal with these emergent possibilities, either in the sphere of work or at home. We are living in a time of experiments being conducted and new social contracts and agreements being worked out and what will finally emerge is by no means self-evident.

Let me end this article by returning to blurring boundaries, the phenomenon with which I began. For many of us who have adopted a mobile lifestyle the blurrings are most compellingly, most powerfully experienced in two aspects of our existence: the first revolves around the vanishing distinction between work and non-work; the second around the parallel fact that home and away flip; that here slips into there and there becomes another here, over and over again.

For me, "home" and "work" have become nebulous concepts. If home is where family is, then both *Besos* and *Springhill* are my home. I see my children and grandchildren about as often in Costa Rica as in California. And as far as work is concerned, am I working when I read the American Anthropologist? Wired Magazine? Coastal Living? I used to have a pretty good understanding, shared with colleagues at the office, of what was work and what wasn't. The American Anthropologist, yes; Wired, maybe; Coastal Living, definitely not. But now the question arises: Am I working when I have dinner with my daughter who works in a high-tech company? We discuss the logistics of an impending family get-together, but she also explains to me the nuances of how Indian technologists relate to their superiors.

I do a lot of mentoring in my current life. Is this work? It is not very different from the "cothinking" I do with senior managers in my corporate practice. The main difference is that I get paid for one and not for the other. I do it because it gives me pleasure to be helpful to others. I build personal relationships. I learn a lot. So should I think of those activities as non-work activities? Especially for an anthropologist, the differentiation has never made much sense anyway because we tend to operate in a participant-observer mode no matter where we are or what we are doing. But in the past, the distinctly separate physical location of what I call "work-work" encouraged and actually enforced this separation even in the minds of ethnographers for whom the social–physical world is always the field in which they operate.

The all-important questions of what effects the new technologies will have, how much distance or colocation we shall have, if we shall enjoy solitude or battle loneliness, enjoy connectedness or suffer from overcrowding, what shall be normal and expected and what will be seen as strange, what shall be privilege and what shall be considered substandard, these kinds of issues have not yet been negotiated at the beginning of the 21st century, although the boundaries are blurring. We have the new technologies, but the societal rules that allow them to be domesticated and adapted to human life have not yet appeared (Arthur 2003).

As a society, we are in a period of intense experimentation about how we might conduct ourselves with the new communication and information devices, in families as well as in workplaces. We look for ways of using these new gadgets and the functionalities they represent to help us lead richer lives, be more connected to our fellow human beings, maybe even generate a rhythm in our lives that abandons the nine-to-five regime generated by the Industrial Revolution—in favor of a lifestyle that is more suited to what our bodies and souls need to function optimally.

NOTES

Acknowledgments. I gratefully acknowledge Robbie Davis-Floyd, Anja Eichler, Julia Gluesing, Robert Irwin, Tracy Meerwarth, and Barbara Pillsbury for comments that shaped this article. My thanks to the community of researchers and staff at PARC who continue to provide an intellectual home and support for me whether I am "here" or "there." Their constructive comments and critical suggestions shaped this chapter in innumerable ways.

1. Less familiar than undocumented Mexican labor migration are any number of emerging mobility patterns that have arisen as a direct result of globalization. For example, in the families of professional Taiwanese immigrants, it is not infrequent that the husband returns to Taiwan where he can get a better paying job because of a booming economy, while the wife and children stay in Southern California because there are better educational opportunities there for the family's children. The commuting husbands in these transnational, upper middle class "split households" are often referred to as "parachute husbands" because of their periodic dropping in on the family (Avenarius 2002).

2. In the sections that follow I draw extensively on the Silicon Valley Cultures Project of my colleagues at San Jose State University who have carried out inspiring ethnographic research on high-tech, two-earner families in Silicon Valley for more than a decade. Many of their papers and presentations can be found at http://www.sjsu.edu/depts/anthropology/svcp/, accessed July 29, 2008. See also Darrah et al. 2007; English-Lueck 1997.

3. This trend is reinforced and often initiated by a new type of corporate retreat seminar in which employees are encouraged to reevaluate their "work/life balance" (Covey 1989). These seminars specifically target family life as amenable to effective management techniques. Having participated in several of these in the course of my consulting work, I now think it is quite likely that the exhortations to identify and prioritize tasks and responsibilities in one's professional and personal life lead for many employees to a heightened sensitivity about the rift. As a consequence, many of them reprioritize their time allocations in favor of family and personal growth activities. In my observation these "life changes" quickly wash out under the pressures of

unchanged corporate demands and schedules. If I look at the way I have organized my own life, I realize that I too have been influenced by these trends (a point that will become abundantly clear later in these pages).

4. What does that mean? Does it change the cycle of maintenance visits to this grave? Does it mean fewer visits to the cemetery? A change in the family's Sunday walk route? Or is it a sign of besting the Joneses?

5. A coati mundi or pizote is a small mammal, similar to a raccoon.

6. For an interesting example of how kitchen architecture reflects such shifts, see Bell and Kaye (2002).

7. Of generous dimensions, Great Rooms are prototypically centered on a large multifunctional family room, often with a high ceiling, combining the functions of kitchen, family room, living room, and space for public reception and display. Not a home for permanent laptop installation, these rooms, however, are valued as a site of working in the presence of others, a kind of multitasking in "being alone together" (Mainwaring and Woodruff 2005; Woodruff et al. 2007).

8. The reader may notice that earlier I gave a personal, psychological reason for this preference for openness: "I hate to be cooped in."

9. Yes, I am of the generation whose brain doesn't engage and whose body doesn't comply with a computer screen for writing. Much as I love (and hate) my laptop, it has a long way to go before it can even approach the functionalities of plain paper. At the same time, I ask: Is this really a generational issue?

10. Costa Ricans refer to themselves as *ticos*. The term, unlike *gringo* for North Americans and Europeans, has no negative implications.

11. The rapid succession of bouts of activity looks like a form of multitasking, but is more akin to what Lange (this volume) calls "intertasking." I used to think that my predilection for this kind of piecework came from my early experiences raising three children as a single mother, when I juggled at first the demands of graduate school and then the demands of academic employment with being present at home and there for my children. I became rather good at making lists (I live with lists!) and prioritizing, looking ahead to what needed to be done today, this month, during the year, squeezing the last bit of usable time out of my day.

12. This raises the question of whether the work styles of Boundary Keepers and Integrators can mix. I think not easily. I know that it is important for me, a hard-core Integrator, to figure out what style my remote partners prefer. Boundary Keepers can easily become annoyed if I bombard them with short updates, questions or requests, while a fellow Integrator would welcome that. It may well be that there is a fairly hard-wired (or early-wired) preference for one style or another, nevertheless observation also suggests that hierarchical (boundary-favoring) environments seem to favor (or attract?) Boundary Keepers, whereas flat, distributed work environments tend to favor Integrators.

13. I am thoroughly convinced that memory is location-specific, at least for me. It has happened to me more than once that I can't remember my own phone number or the names of people in the place where I have just arrived, even though recalling them is no problem otherwise. Why do I find myself turning into the bathroom at *Springhill* looking for chicken bouillon? Because at *Besos* I would find it also to the right, in the bodega (store room). And why am I looking for my car in the wrong parking space at PARC? After a frustrating search, I realize that's where I parked it the last time. But that was three months earlier!

14. For an unusual attempt to design corporate policies that are responsive to changing career realities see Benko and Weisberg 2007.

REFERENCES CITED

Arthur, Brian
2003 Why Tech Is Still the Future. Fortune, Nov. 24:119–125.

Avenarius, Christine B.
2002 Work and Social Network Composition among Immigrants from Taiwan to Southern California. Anthropology of Work Review 23(3–4):3–15.

Bell, Genevieve
2006 No More SMS from Jesus: Ubicomp, Religion and Techno-Spiritual Practices. *In* Ubicomp 2006. P. Dourish and A. Friday, eds. Pp. 141–158. Berlin: Springer Verlag.

Bell, Genevieve, and Joseph "Jofish" Kaye
2002 Designing Technology for Domestic Spaces: A Kitchen Manifesto. Gastronomica—The Journal of Food and Culture 2(2):46–62.
Benko, Cathleen, and Anne Weisberg
2007 Mass Career Customization: Aligning the Workplace with Today's Nontraditional Workforce. Boston: Harvard Business School Press.
Brown, Barry, Nicola, Green, and Richard Harper, eds.
2002 Wireless World: Social and Interactional Aspects of the Mobile Age. London: Springer-Verlag.
Bridges, William
1994a The End of the Job. Fortune, September 19:62–74.
1994b Job Shift: How to Prosper in a Workplace without Jobs. Reading, MA: Addison-Wesley Publishing Company.
Churchill, Elizabeth, and Les Nelson
In press Information Flows in a Gallery-Work-Entertainment Space: The Effect of a Digital Bulletin Board on Social Encounters. Special section, "Knowledge Flow in 'Real' and 'Virtual Spaces,'" Human Organization 68(2).
Cobb, Charles R.
2005 Archaeology and the "Savage Slot": Displacement and Emplacement in the Modern World. American Anthropologist 107(4):563–574.
Covey, Steven
1989 The Seven Habits of Highly Effective People. New York: Simon and Schuster.
Cramton, Catherine Durnell
2002 Attribution in Distributed Work Groups. *In* Distributed Work. Pamela Hinds and Sara Kiesler, eds. Pp. 191–212. Cambridge, MA: MIT Press.
Darrah, Charles N., James M. Freeman, and Jan A. English-Lueck
2007 Busier than Ever!: Why American Families Can't Slow Down. Stanford, CA: Stanford University Press.
English-Lueck, Jan A.
1997 Juggling Digital Devices at Work and Home in Silicon Valley. Paper presented at The Fourteenth Annual Contact Conference, Santa Clara, March 8. Electronic document, http://www.sjsu.edu/depts/anthropology/svcp/SVCPjugg.html, accessed July 28, 2008.
2002 Cultures@Silicon Valley. Stanford, CA: Stanford University Press.
Fiske, Shirley
2007 Coming of Age in Corporations. Anthropology News, November:30–31.
Halford, Susan
2005 Hybrid Workspace: Re-Spatialisations of Work, Organization and Management. New Technology, Work and Employment 20(1):19–33.
Hislop, Donald, and Carolyn Axtell
2007 The Neglect of Spatial Mobility in Contemporary Studies of Work: The Case of Telework. New Technology, Work and Employment 22(1):34–51.
Hochschild, Arlie Russell
1997 The Time Bind: When Work Becomes Home and Home Becomes Work. New York: Metropolitan Books.
2007 Through the Crack of the Time Bind: From Market Management to Family Management. Anthropology of Work Review 28(1):1–8.
Jordan, Brigitte
2007 Technology in Sacred Spaces. Anthropology News, April:29.
In press Blurring Boundaries: The "Real" and the "Virtual" in Hybrid Spaces. Special Section, "Knowledge Flow in 'Real' and 'Virtual Spaces,'" Brigitte Jordan, ed., Human Organization 68(2).

Julsrud, Tom Erik
2005 Behavioral Changes at the Mobile Workplace: A Symbolic Interactionistic Approach. *In* Mobile Communications: Re-Negotiation of the Social Sphere. Rich Ling and Per E. Pederson, eds. Pp. 93–111. London: Springer Verlag.
Latham, Robert, and Saskia Sassen, eds.
2005 Digital Formations: IT and New Architectures in the Global Realm. Princeton: Princeton University Press.
Mainwaring, Scott D., and Allison Woodruff
2005 Investigating Mobility, Technology, and Spaces in Homes, Starting with "Great Rooms." EPIC 2005. Pp. 188–195. Arlington: American Anthropological Association.
Miller, Daniel, and Don Slater
2000 The Internet: An Ethnographic Approach. Oxford: Berg.
O'Leary, Michael, Wanda Orlikowski, and JoAnne Yates
2002 Distributed Work over the Centuries: Trust and Control in the Hudson's Bay Company, 1670–1826. *In* Distributed Work. Pamela Hinds and Sara Kiesler, eds. Pp. 27–54. Cambridge, MA: MIT Press.
Oldenburg, Ray
1991 The Great Good Place: Cafes, Coffee Shops, Community Centers, Beauty Parlors, General Stores, Bars, Hangouts, and How They Get You through the Day. New York: Paragon House.
Palm, Michael
2006 Outsourcing, Self-Service and the Telemobility of Work. Anthropology of Work Review 27(2):1–9.
Ruhleder, Karen, Brigitte Jordan, and Michael B. Elmes
1996 Wiring the "New Organization": Integrating Collaborative Technologies and Team-Based Work. Paper presented at the Annual Meeting of the Academy of Management, Cincinnati, OH, August 13. Electronic document, http://www.lifescapes.org/Papers/96.academy.html, accessed July 29, 2008
Skipper, William
2006 Services Offshoring: An Overview. Anthropology of Work Review 27(2):9–17.
Sonntag, Selma K.
2005 Appropriating Identity or Cultivating Capital? Global English in Offshoring Service Industries. Anthropology News 46(3):22.
Trager, Lillian, ed.
2005 Migration and Economy: Global and Local Dynamics. Lanham, MD: AltaMira Press.
Woodruff, Allison, Ken Anderson, Scott Mainwaring, and Ryan Aipperspach
2007 Portable, But Not Mobile: A Study of Wireless Laptops in the Home. *In* Proceedings of Pervasive 2007. Pp. 216–233. Berlin: Springer-Verlag.

OCCUPATIONAL WEBSITES AS LOCATIONS FOR REMOTE AND MOBILE WORKER CULTURE: AN EXAMINATION OF TEMPORARY WORKER WEBSITES

LORIL M. GOSSETT
Associate Professor at the University of North Carolina at Charlotte, Department of Communication Studies and Organizational Science

This article examines the instrumental role that websites play in developing and sustaining a work-related culture for remote and mobile employees that often find themselves working alone or without coworkers from their parent company. More specifically, this article focuses on temporary worker websites, such as www.notmydesk.com and www.Temp24-7.com, to illustrate how these on-line communities foster a distinctive occupational community for temporary workers. Specific stories, postings, and other information contained on these sites reveals the lived experiences of temporary workers. The author's personal experiences in the industry, combined with examples taken from specific temporary worker websites, illustrate how the remote and mobile nature of this occupation impacts workers both on and off the job.
Keywords: nonstandard work, occupational websites, organizational culture, temporary workers, resistance

Individuals employed in remote or mobile work arrangements (such as independent contractors, temporary workers, telecommuters) often find themselves working alone, without people from their home companies to interact with on a regular basis. Although these workers may be physically separated from their peers, their participation on occupational websites can provide these individuals with an opportunity to locate and share information with other people in similar work situations. There are a number of different occupationally focused websites that enable geographically dispersed workers to connect with each other. For example, www.notmydesk.com is a website dedicated to office temporary workers (temps), www.telecommutingmoms.com, is an on-line community for mothers working from home, and www.gamewatch.org highlights issues relevant to independent contractors working in the video game industry. This article explores the instrumental role that these websites can play in developing and sustaining a distinct occupational culture for remote and mobile workers.

I became interested in remote and mobile labor arrangements while completing my Ph.D. in organizational communication at the University of Colorado at Boulder. For my dissertation, I decided to examine communication issues within the temporary help industry. I wanted to get a firsthand perspective on this industry and so I decided to become a temp. Over the period of two years I worked with a number of different clerical

NAPA BULLETIN 30, pp. 56–69. ISSN: 1556-4789.
DOI:10.1111/j.1556-4797.2008.00019.x

and light-industrial temporary agencies. While I was temping, I unexpectedly stumbled on a rich on-line culture created and sustained by the members of this industry.

There are a number of different websites that help to foster a distinctive occupational community for temporary workers. Participation on these sites enables workers to compare their wages, share information about particular agencies and job assignments, and communicate directly with their fellow temps. These on-line communities can also help temps cope with the stress of working in an industry that often has a negative social stigma attached to it. In this article I will discuss stories, postings, and other information contained on these sites to demonstrate how these on-line communities help temporary workers make sense of and function within the temporary work environment. Through this analysis, I will illustrate how temps and other remote and mobile workers are able to create and sustain distinct occupational cultures on the Internet.

THE REMOTE AND MOBILE NATURE OF THE TEMPORARY HELP INDUSTRY

The temporary help industry represents a particularly interesting type of remote and mobile employment. Temps are physically isolated from their agency supervisors and coworkers while on an assignment and often socially isolated from the permanent staff of the companies that contract for their services (Gossett 2002; Gottfried 1991; Henson 1996; Parker 1994). In addition to the inherently remote nature of this occupation, temps are constantly on the move and are expected to quickly adapt to each new client's surroundings, task assignments, and work norms. Temps are organizational nomads who occupy the middle ground between organizational outsider and insider, never fully belonging in the environments in which they work, but not having another location where they are more at home.

Since the early 1990s, there has been a rapid expansion in the staffing industry, both in the United States and abroad. Following the wave of corporate downsizing and reorganizations in the late 1980s, companies embraced just-in-time staffing strategies that resulted in an increased reliance on various forms of contingent labor (e.g., temps, contractors, consultants) so that firms could quickly increase or decrease their staff as conditions demanded (Aaronson et al. 2004; Rifkin 1995). In recent years, the staffing industry has expanded into almost every industrialized nation and has become the fifth fastest growing industry in the United States (Berchem 2005; Houseman and Osawa 2003; Storrie 2002). Recent labor statistics indicate that 47 percent of the people employed by temporary agencies in the United States are male, more than half have attended college, and 80 percent work on a full-time basis. Although most temps would still prefer a more traditional employment arrangement, 32 percent now claim to favor temporary work as their primary occupation (Bureau of Labor Statistics 2005).

As the number of people working in the temporary help industry has grown, so has the number of websites devoted to helping them succeed in this highly ambiguous work environment. There are several reasons why temporary workers might gravitate to the Internet to connect with other temps. Some professions provide opportunities for workers to develop relationships with their peers at occupational conferences and training programs. Employees may also forge communal bonds with each other through more informal communication channels; examples of these are compiled in anecdotal works about work-related graffiti (Dundes and Pagter 1992), comics, newsletters, magazines, and autobiographies (as reported in Daisey 2002; Levine 1998). Although these are all methods by which workers can interact outside traditional organizational frameworks, all have important limitations, particularly with respect to remote and mobile labor arrangements. Remote workers may not be able to attend meetings or other events with people who share their occupational experiences. Newsletters and other physical, printed material typically have restricted distribution networks, because of the fact that they are often centrally produced, only periodically available, and may be difficult to send out to all interested parties. Labor unions and professional associations offer another resource for workers to share information with each other. However, temporary workers in the United States do not currently have a union or formal association to provide them with this sense of community and common purpose. The lack of such organizations should not suggest that temps do not wish to share resources or connect with one another. Rather, temps and members of other remote or mobile occupations might be better served by alternative communication resources that have lower barriers to entry and limited involvement requirements—such as occupational websites that can be accessed at any time and in any location.

Cyberspace is a logical place for disenfranchised or otherwise marginalized organizational members to find each other (Mitra 2001). Previous research has documented ways that members of particular firms have used websites to share information with their peers and organize collective acts of resistance (Gossett and Kilker 2006; Real and Putnam 2005; Taras and Gesser 2003). By searching the Internet for websites dedicated to specific occupational concerns, workers can reach out to people they may not have the opportunity to interact with in their traditional work environment. Individuals involved with remote or mobile work may use occupational websites to learn about various opportunities and issues related to their specific industries. These workers can also use websites to connect with others who hold similar remote or mobile positions. As indicated in previous research (Bishop and Levine 1999; Gossett and Kilker 2006), on-line communities can substitute for the intimacy of the office break room or coffee cart. They are spaces where industry rumors can be shared, job-related problems are debated, occupation-specific humor is appreciated, and a distinct professional identity can be created.

The on-line environment is particularly well suited to the communication needs of temporary workers. The basic nature of the temporary work makes it particularly challenging for these individuals to locate and spend time with one another. Temps are employed by almost every industry and work at all hours of the day. Additionally, temps may not even know the other people employed by their own agency. Given these physical and temporal constraints, occupational websites provide temporary workers with one of the best opportunities to connect with one another and form a distinct occupational culture.

MY INTRODUCTION TO THE ON-LINE CULTURE OF TEMPORARY WORKERS

In 1999, I began my temping career at a national agency that specialized in clerical and light-industrial staffing. I was in graduate school at the time and trying to support myself as a temp during the summer months. When I first arrived at the agency, I was not sure that I wanted to commit to one firm for the entire summer. However, after spending nearly three hours completing a battery of skill tests, filling out legal documents, and retyping my résumé into the agency's computer system, I felt compelled to give this company a try before repeating the process at another firm. After the agency manager reviewed my paperwork and determined that I might be a good candidate, I was shown into a small room where I sat alone to watch the company's orientation video. This 20-minute film focused on a variety of administrative processes (e.g., how to get your paycheck) and legal issues (e.g., how to file a worker's compensation claim). At the end of screening and orientation process, all of my relevant skills had been tested, my contact information had been entered into the agency's system, and I left the office with a job assignment in hand. My first job was a weeklong assignment as a receptionist for an engineering firm. I had no prior experience as a receptionist and no idea how or why I had been assigned to this particular job. However, I was happy to have something to show for my afternoon at the agency and so decided not to ask too many questions.

Although my first temporary agency's screening process was extensive and time consuming, I found it interesting that there was no mention of what it might mean to be a particularly "good temp" for this agency or for the company where I had been assigned to work. In fact, the notion that temping might be a unique occupation worthy of discussion, special training, or guidance was not brought up at any point during the screening or orientation process. The agency focused exclusively on testing and cataloguing my various skill sets, and did not offer any information that might help me prepare for working as a short-term member of an unfamiliar company. Perhaps it was naïve of me to think my agency would train me how to be a temp. However, if the agency does not provide this information, how does a new temporary worker figure out the tricks of this trade? How does a temp learn how to become good at this job rather than simply proficient?

Because the agency failed to provide occupation-specific training, I decided to seek out this information on my own. I searched the Internet to look for books or other information that might help me to prepare for my first temporary assignment. Through this process I found several websites that appeared to be geared directly to temporary workers rather than to staffing agencies or client firms. These websites caught my attention primarily because of the unique nature of their URLs (e.g., www.Temp24-7.com, www.Disgruntled.com). As I reviewed these sites, I discovered they were on-line communities of temporary workers who came together to discuss agency practices, challenging clients, and industry rumors. I had never realized that such websites existed. The agency certainly had not mentioned them during my interview, nor had I seen them referenced in any of the academic literature I had been reading on the temporary help industry in graduate school. At first I dismissed these on-line communities as interesting but unimportant diversions. However, once I started temping, I found myself repeatedly returning to these websites for both my own amusement and for the valuable, job-related advice they also contained. In the next section I will illustrate how these websites collectively establish and sustain a distinct occupational culture for temporary workers.

EXPLORING THE ON-LINE CULTURE OF TEMPORARY WORKERS

There is no single dominant website that defines the occupational culture of temporary workers in the United States. Rather, it is a constellation of different, collaborative on-line communities that help workers define what it means to be a temp. When I was temping, I found that I visited these websites whenever I wanted to kill time on a boring assignment, relieve job-related stress, or find solutions to problems that I felt I could not easily resolve through more conventional organizational channels. When things were going well (e.g., I had enough work, I liked my coworkers) I did not have a need to visit these websites. However, these on-line communities became vital occupational lifelines whenever I felt isolated or frustrated on an assignment. These websites connected me to my occupational peers; people who understood what it was like to work in a place where no one knows your name and you can never find the bathroom or coffee machine.

Communication on temporary worker websites is seldom done in "real time." Instant messaging, chat rooms, and other simultaneous communication systems are not common features of these on-line communities. This may be because of the fact that a temp's schedule (and computer access) is seldom under his or her control. As a result, most information exchanges take place on threaded forums, message boards, or through the posting of documents (e.g., news articles, stories, agency reviews) prepared specifically for the website. As I have continued to explore this industry as both a temp and as an organizational researcher, I have identified three distinct types of temporary worker websites: collective sensemaking sites, career advice sites, and entertainment sites. When considered together, these different websites help to define a distinct culture that allows temps to make sense of their work experiences and articulate the unique nature of this occupation.

Collective Sensemaking Websites

As I mentioned earlier, temps, in their individual work environments, are often physically separated from each other. This makes it difficult for them to share information or compare their experiences with particular agencies or client firms. Additionally, most agencies restrict the type of information temps are allowed to discuss with their coworkers. For example, every agency I have worked with has prohibited employees from sharing salary or job assignment information with their fellow temps. The temporary agency negotiates with each temp separately to determine the wage for a particular assignment. This salary negotiation process is complicated by the fact that temps seldom know what the client is actually being charged for the service or what other temps at the agency are being paid for similar work. The inability to share wage or job information within the temp agency environment puts these workers at a distinct disadvantage when it comes to determining the value of their labor. This process can result in temps from the same agency earning different wages for the same job. These discrepancies typically work to the advantage of the agency because the client pays the same amount for each employee regardless of what the agency actually pays the workers. The inability to discuss their experiences with each other or debate issues of common concern effectively disempowers temps within this industry. Previous research has noted that this communicative isolation prevents temps from determining if they are being paid a reasonable wage (Gottfried 1991). It also makes it difficult for temps to voice concerns about agency or client practices (Gossett 2006; Rogers and Henson 1997) or determine if they are being discriminated against by their agencies with respect to job placements (Parker 1994).

One way that temps have attempted to overcome these various communicative restrictions is through the development of collective sensemaking websites. Participants visit these sites to share industry-related information with their peers and gain insight about particular labor practices. Temps also use collective sensemaking sites to research answers to specific questions or seek out advice from more experienced members of the community. These websites provide a place for remote and mobile workers to have the types of conversations they might otherwise have at the watercooler or in a quiet office hallway. These are focused exchanges about particular topics of common concern. Wage issues, policy questions, and industry rumors can be debated on these websites by people who have something to add to the conversation, and can be overheard by others who are simply interested in the topic being discussed.

I turned to a collective sensemaking website when I was asked by my temp agency to set a pay rate for my services. As noted above, agency rules prevented me from openly discussing salary issues with the other temps. Because of my lack of knowledge on this issue, I initially set a rather large range for myself, assuming that this would show the agency I was flexible and eager to work. However, I soon discovered that I rarely got offered any jobs that paid more than the lowest wage I had requested. Out of curiosity, I went on-line and pulled up the Red Guide to Temping (n.d.; hereafter, "Red Guide"). This is a website where temps can post reviews of their agencies. It has a standard review form, so that it is easy to compare different agencies with each other in a number of different categories (such as if they offer direct deposit, the average length of time between assignments, the average rate of pay). The evaluation form also has a space for temps to make recommendations about firms that other temps should seek out or avoid. Although this website focuses primarily on agencies doing business in New York and New Jersey, many of the firms are national agencies that do business in nearly every city in the United States.

When I read through the reviews, I quickly realized that I had grossly undersold my value with my own temp agency. Some of the temps on the Red Guide indicated they were being paid nearly three times the amount I was being offered for similar work. I felt taken! Before I had visited the website, I had assumed that the jobs and wages I was being offered were the best available. This is what my agent told me and I had no reason to doubt her. However, once I saw the wages that other temps were commanding, I immediately called my agency and raised my minimum asking price. Interestingly enough, I did not see a notable drop off in my assignments; just an increase in my paycheck.

This experience taught me that my willingness to please my agency and the fact that I could not easily discuss job-related issues with the other temps put me at a critical disadvantage in this industry. My agency was able to capitalize on my naiveté by paying me the minimum rate I had set for myself and taking a larger percentage of the fee they charged to the client for my services. It was at that moment that I realized my agency was not necessarily looking out for my best interests. I had entered the occupation assuming the agency was on my side because they were my employer—my agent. However, after comparing notes with the other temps on the Red Guide, I realized that I was wrong. This experience taught me my first important lesson about what it meant to be a successful temporary employee. Temps have to look out for themselves. The agency and the clients have no real incentive to develop a temp's skills or raise his or her wages because this will simply cut into agency profits. Rather than consider myself an employee of the agency, I needed to think of myself as a free agent and take a more active role in managing my own career.

Career Advice Websites

A second set of websites that define a unique occupational culture for temps are sites that help these workers pursue their individual career goals within the industry. Although the agency may be the temp's official employer, it is primarily concerned with serving the needs of its client firms and preserving its own economic advantage. As a result, agency representatives cannot afford to spend a great deal of time or effort trying to understand and meet the specific desires of every temporary employee. One agency representative I spoke with told me she had been reprimanded for spending too much time trying to place temps in jobs they would really like. She was instructed to instead focus on quickly filling positions with people who were easy to place (Gossett 2006).

Workers who plan to use the temporary help industry to develop new skills or try out a different type of career are not necessarily going to find a great deal of support within the agency environment. Temp agencies typically want to place people in jobs they already know how to do. However, workers can turn to temp-focused career advice websites to learn the tricks of the trade from other more experienced members of the industry. These websites function as a type of human resource office for the on-line temping community. They provide temps with a more sophisticated understanding of the industry and help them understand how temping differs from more traditional forms of employment. One example of this sort of website is www.Indeed.com. Indeed.com is a job search website that hosts a number of discussion forums, some of which are dedicated to temporary work. Temps use these forums to share information about particular agencies (e.g., Kelly, Manpower). For example, on Indeed.com's "Office Team" forum one temp noted that she signed up with "Office Team" but had not been placed on many assignments. She added that she had a lot of experience but was over 50 years old and was concerned that her age may be part of the reason she was not getting many job opportunities. Other temps followed this posting with similar concerns about age discrimination at this agency and within the industry as a whole. Several site participants posted specific career advice for older temps. One forum participant suggested:

> I would suggest staying away from agencies like Manpower, Office Team, Robert Half, Stivers, etc. I have had excellent luck with a small privately owned staffing firm in my city. The owner has great relationships with her clients and she has gotten me in with some great companies and the pay was market rate. [Indeed.com n.d.]

This discussion allowed the formerly isolated "Office Team" temp to feel connected to people who understood her situation and were willing to help her find ways to improve her experience in the industry.

On these career advice forums both agency representatives and temporary workers debate the best way to secure and keep desirable temporary assignments. For example, one agency placement manager cautioned temps against dressing too casually when coming into an agency to fill out paperwork. The agency representative argued that people who dressed professionally when they came into her office were more likely to be placed, regardless of how qualified the more casually dressed applicants might be. Taking this advice to heart, I made it a point to wear a suit or nice business outfit whenever I went into my agency office to pick up my paycheck. I might wear the same skirt and shirt three days in a row while actually working on a temp assignment, but always tried to look my best when I went into the agency. Although I am not sure if my dress code was the deciding factor, I will say that I seldom went without temporary assignment offers the entire summer, despite my modest typing skills and limited knowledge of business software programs.

What is particularly important about the information shared on these career advice sites is that it is practical in nature and designed to help workers get ahead in the temp industry. Temps use these sites to get information about particular agencies, learn strategies for working more effectively with their supervisors, and get suggestions for how to make themselves more attractive job candidates. These on-line communities also highlight the need for temps to stay proactive if they are going to remain steadily employed. A good temp needs to know how to market him or herself to both the client and to the agency. A temp is only as good as his or her last assignment and is always interviewing for the next job. To that end, career advice websites encourage temps to play the field and constantly look for new and better job opportunities. Temps who assume the agency or client will take care of them are temps who will soon be underpaid or unemployed.

Entertainment Websites

Finally, there are a number of websites designed to entertain members of the temporary worker community. These sites serve as the office break rooms and after-hours bars of the temping world. Temps visit these on-line groups to let off steam, gossip, and tell stories that only other members of the industry can fully appreciate. In a manner similar to the sensemaking and advice sites discussed above, these entertainment websites offer temps the ability to post their own stories and interact directly with each other on various discussion forums. However, these entertainment communities also provide a variety of other diversions for visitors to enjoy. For example, notmydesk.com provides tongue-in-cheek reviews of movies and books with temporary industry themes (e.g., "The Temp," "Clockwatchers"). This website also offers a satirical "field guide" for temps that includes recommendations for reading material that temps should and should not bring with them to a work assignment:

> Nothing says "go away" like a book . . . Stay away from popular genres, like legal thrillers or self-help books, because they will invite conversation. Stay away from books that are currently movies, because they will invite conversation. Stay away from *anything Oprah has recommended,* because they will invite *the worst conversation imaginable.* [Notmydesk.com n.d.]

Another entertainment website that I visited nearly every day while I was temping was Temp24-7.com. This website featured a video game ("Temps v. Suits") in which temporary workers used common office supplies (e.g., staplers, rubber bands) to wage war against permanent employees who attempted to give them extra work. This site also had a dictionary of "temp terms" designed to put an irreverent spin on some of the more common fixtures of the temp's work environment. Some examples of these terms include:

> *Pimp*: The temp's personal representative at the temp agency.
> *Solitaire confinement*: A lonely assignment in which the temp works alone with only a minimal workload to cope with, prompting marathon sessions of Solitaire to fill up the time. [Temp24-7.com n.d.]

I found these entertainment websites particularly valuable whenever I became frustrated with a task, unsure how to handle a problem coworker, or was just having a bad day. Reading other people's temp stories, laughing at the "temp term of the week" or taking out my frustrations by playing a quick game of "Temps v. Suits" was a fairly effective way to relieve any temp-induced stress I might be experiencing.

The mere existence of these entertainment websites also helped me to cope with difficult work assignments. If a job was going particularly badly, there was some peace of mind offered by the knowledge that I could always write up my story and post it to one of these on-line communities. For example, one day I was assigned to work as a receptionist at a small company. Unfortunately, everyone was out of the office the day I was scheduled to work, but no one had thought to call and cancel my assignment. I spent the majority of the day sitting in the front lobby of the building, repeatedly assured by my temp agency that the client's office manager (who was out of town) would find someone who could come down and let me in the building. At three in the afternoon, someone finally showed up to let me in the office and sign my time sheet.

Waiting all day to do a boring job for minimum wage is like being stood up by someone you did not really want to date anyway. You are happy to have the additional free time, while at the same time upset to realize that you are of such little importance that a company would rather let you sit on a bench all day like a house plant than just let you go home. Despite the ego-deflating nature of this experience, I took comfort in the knowledge that I could post this story to a temp entertainment website and get kudos from my fellow temps for how ridiculous the situation was and how well I handled it. Entertainment sites are important because they provide temps with a way to laugh at the little indignities they suffer on a regular basis and provide a much needed boost to their self-esteem. To survive and thrive as a temp, it is important to find a way to connect with other people who can help you cope with the ambiguities of the industry and put them in perspective.

Entertainment websites also enable temps to symbolically overturn the basic power structure of the industry. A temp may be the ultimate subordinate within their regular work environment; however the temp is often portrayed as superior to permanent workers on these websites. Most of the humor on these sites comes at the expense of the client firm and the agency. For example, the only person with a weapon in the "Temps v. Suits" game is the temp. Many of the items included in the temping "field guide" are tricks temps can play on the client firm or agency staff. Although the stories, jokes, and games shared on these entertainment websites may not change the material realities of a temp's work experience (e.g., pay, benefits, social status), these activities provide temps with a way to "challenge, in transformative ways, the emotional or 'psychic' normalcy of organizational life" (Fleming and Spicer 2002:66). In this way, entertainment websites provide temps with an alternative and perhaps more desirable way to define their experiences and occupational identity within the work environment.

THE SIGNIFICANCE OF THE ON-LINE CULTURE FOR TEMPORARY WORKERS

Temporary work has not typically been characterized as an occupation in and of itself, but rather as the lack of one. Temps are generic workers; organizational chameleons whose job is to fit in and function wherever they are placed, for however long they are needed. Organizational consultants and independent contractors may also struggle with some of these issues because of the remote and mobile nature of these occupations. However, contractors and consultants tend to be skilled knowledge workers within a distinct profession (such as accounting, law, and engineering). As a result, these workers often enjoy a higher social status and salary range than temporary employees. In contrast, temps typically occupy the lowest level in the organizational hierarchy because of their disposable and replaceable nature. Henson (1996) argues that temporary work has a social stigma attached to it that erodes the self-esteem of those who labor in the industry. Similarly, Padavic claims that temps suffer from a "spoiled identity" that requires them to continuously "confront the imputation of negative assumptions about their qualifications, abilities, and character" (2005:115). Some of the negative attitudes toward this profession may be because of the fact that temps often occupy low-skilled or entry-level positions in the work environment. However, the remote and mobile nature of temporary work may further limit the organizational and social status of these employees.

Although other occupations require employees to function independently or work without direct supervision, temping is a uniquely solitary profession. The structural and communicative nature of this industry ensures that temps are relatively isolated within their immediate work environments. However, there is a difference between working alone and being communicatively isolated. Occupational websites enable the members of this industry to forge a sense of community with one another. Even people who enjoy the somewhat detached nature of temporary employment may appreciate the ability to occasionally connect with others who understand the unique challenges of this transitory profession. These websites allow temps to share their stories and accomplishments with one another and create an occupational identity that transcends a single job assignment or agency relationship. Although temps still may be physically separated from each other, occupational websites ensure that these remote and mobile workers are never more than a mouse click away from their peers.

The various occupational websites discussed in this article provide a distinct set of resources for temps to draw on to be successful in this industry. For example, *collective sensemaking websites* remind temps to keep their eyes and ears open within the work environment and use this information to benefit themselves and their fellow temps. Agencies and client firms may attempt to restrict the negotiating power of temporary workers by limiting their access to information (pay rates, job opportunities, etc). However, collective sensemaking websites empower temps by providing these workers an easy way to share job-related information with each other. The information provided on these collective sensemaking websites allows temps to understand the value that they bring to particular organizational settings and enables them to feel connected to other workers in the industry. The *career advice websites* encourage temps to take responsibility for their own professional futures and not assume the agency or the client firm is going to take care of them. These sites also remind temps to constantly seek out new opportunities within the industry; they emphasize the importance of personal growth rather than value of organizational loyalty or commitment. Finally, a strong theme on the *entertainment websites* is the notion that temps need to be creative if they are to overcome the boredom and loneliness often associated with this occupation. Entertainment sites provide temps with a variety of games, reading material, and inventive suggestions for ways to pass the time while confined to a desk or cubicle. These sites can be vital occupational survival tools for temps working in particularly isolating, stressful, or demoralizing job assignments.

Although each type of website discussed in this article has a unique focus and set of resources, the theme that unites them together is the fact that they all remind temps that although they may often work by themselves, they are certainly not alone. These websites provide temps with a supportive community to "come home to" at the end of the day, comrades in arms who can validate a temp's worth and reframe bad client situations as something inherent in the industry and not the result of some personal failing. Beyond simply helping temps to cope with transitory nature of contingent employment, these occupational websites also have the potential to challenge the power dynamics underlying the entire industry. The remote and mobile nature of temporary employment no longer keeps the members of this industry communicatively isolated from one another. The practical importance of these on-line communities is that they allow temps to forge a collective sense of identity and a common culture outside the boundaries of any single agency, client firm, or geographic region. These sites might also provide temps with the ability to work together to campaign for higher wages, form a professional association, or engage in collective acts of resistance (e.g., strikes, protests). Any of these actions would provide temporary workers with more power in their immediate work environments and potentially increase the status of this occupation.

CONCLUSION

There are a number of websites that offer support, information, and resources for people involved in remote and mobile occupations. In this article I have identified three distinct on-line communities that are of particular interest to people working in the temporary help industry. However, this list is not meant to be exhaustive. Future research should examine other types of remote and mobile labor (e.g., telecommuters, consultants) to determine what additional websites may exist to meet the needs of these different work arrangements. Finally, scholars interested in remote and mobile forms of labor may want to consider examining these on-line communities to better understand how individuals make sense of their work environment and their identity within it. Occupational websites provide workers with an opportunity to discuss the unique nature of their labor arrangements and share information with others who are in similar situations. As such they are rich and important resources for organizational researchers and members alike.

NOTE

Acknowledgments. Loril Gossett would like to thank Julian Kilker, Linda Putnam, Tracy Meerwarth, Brigitte Jordan, and Julia Gluesing for all of their helpful suggestions and assistance with this article.

REFERENCES CITED

Aaronson, Daniel, Ellen R. Rissman, and Daniel G. Sullivan
2004 Assessing the Jobless Recovery. Economic Perspectives 28(2):2–21.
Berchem, Steven
2005 Rebound: ASA's Annual Economic Analysis of the Staffing Industry. Alexandria: American Staffing Association.
Bishop, Libby, and David I. Levine
1999 Computer-Mediated Communication as Employee Voice: A Case Study. Industrial and Labor Relations Review 52(2):213–233.
Bureau of Labor Statistics
2005 Contingent and Alternative Employment Arrangements. Electronic document, http://www.bls.gov/news.release/conemp.nro.htm, accessed September 1, 2005.

Daisey, Mike
2002 21 Dog Years: Doing Time @ Amazon.com. New York: Free Press.
Dundes, Alan, and Carl R. Pagter
1992 Work Hard and You Shall be Rewarded: Urban Folklore from the Paperwork Empire. Detroit: Wayne State University Press.
Fleming, Peter, and André Spicer
2002 Workers' Playtime?: Unravelling the Paradox of Covert Resistance in Organizations. *In* Management and Organization Paradoxes. Stewart Clegg, ed. Pp. 65–85. Amsterdam: John Benjamins.
Gossett, Loril
2002 Kept at Arm's Length: Questioning the Desirability of Organizational Identification. Communication Monographs 69(4):385–404.
2006 Falling Between the Cracks: Control Challenges of a Contingent Workforce. Management Communication Quarterly 19(3):376–415.
Gossett, Loril, and Julian Kilker
2006 My Job Sucks: Examining Counterinstitutional Websites as Locations for Organizational Member Voice, Dissent, and Resistance. Management Communication Quarterly 20(1):63–90.
Gottfried, Heidi
1991 Mechanisms of Control in the Temporary Help Service Industry. Sociological Forum 6(4):699–713.
Henson, Kevin D.
1996 Just a Temp. Philadelphia: Temple University Press.
Houseman, Susan, and Machiko Osawa
2003 Nonstandard Work in Developed Economies: Causes and Consequences. Kalamazoo: W. E. Upjohn Institute for Employment Research.
Indeed.com
N.d. Temp Agencies. Electronic document, http://www.indeed.com/forum/cmp/OfficeTeam/Temp-Agencies/t4570, accessed August 10, 2007.
Levine, Daniel
1998 Disgruntled: The Darker Side of the World of Work. New York: Berkley Books.
Mitra, Ananda
2001 Marginal Voices in Cyberspace. New Media and Society 3(1):29–48.
Notmydesk.com
N.d. Girding Your Loins. Electronic document, http://www.notmydesk.com/guide/loins.html, accessed August 10, 2007.
Padavic, Irene
2005 Laboring Under Uncertainty: Identity Renegotiation among Contingent Workers. Symbolic Interaction 28(1):111–134.
Parker, Robert E.
1994 Flesh Peddlers and Warm Bodies: The Temporary Help Industry and Its Workers. New Brunswick, NJ: Rutgers University Press.
Real, Kevin, and Linda Putnam
2005 Ironies in the Discursive Struggle of Pilots Defending the Profession. Management Communication Quarterly 19(1):91–119.
Red Guide to Temp Agencies
N.d. The Red Guide to Temp Agencies. Electronic document, http://www.panix.com/~grvsmth/redguide/, accessed October 1, 2008.
Rifkin, Jeremy
1995 The End of Work: The Decline of the Global Labor Force and the Dawn of the Post-Market Era. New York: G. P. Putnam's Sons.
Rogers, Jackie K., and Kevin D. Henson
1997 Hey, Why Don't You Wear a Shorter Skirt? Structural Vulnerability and the Organization of Sexual Harassment in Temporary Clerical Employment. Gender and Society 11(2):215–237.

Storrie, Donald
2002 Temporary Agency Work in the European Union. Dublin: European Foundation for the Improvement of Living and Working Conditions.
Taras, Daphne, and A. Gesser
2003 How New Lawyers Use E-Voice to Drive Firm Compensation: The "Greedy Associates" Phenomenon. Journal of Labor Research 24(1):9–29.
Temp24-7.com
N.d. Glossary of Temp Terms. Electronic document, http://web.archive.org/web/20010221200037/www.temp24-7.com/glossary/gloss_frames.html, accessed September 24, 2008.

IDENTITY IN A VIRTUAL WORLD: THE COEVOLUTION OF TECHNOLOGY, WORK, AND LIFECYCLE

Julia C. Gluesing
Research Professor, Department of Industrial and Manufacturing Engineering, Wayne State University, and President, Cultural Connections, Inc., Troy, Michigan

This article draws on personal experiences of remote work that is facilitated by virtual or on-line communication and collaboration technologies. This personal story illustrates how technology, work, and lifecycle coevolve and how the integration of work, family, and friends into the new, virtual workspaces can open up new conceptualizations of personal identity. An identity that is discretely bounded and that is dependent on physical surroundings can give way to one that more closely aligns with the lived experiences of mobile work and life. If we think of identity as multiple, as open to possibility, and as flexibly responsive to multiple cultures and contexts, we can alter our ideas about work and its relationship to our lives in ways that more closely align with today's hybridized, dematerialized and decontextualized world. Keywords: identity, coevolution, context, integration, virtual workspace

Looking back, it's not surprising how it all happened, how I have become who I am, and why I do what I do. My personal life and the way I work have evolved over the years to become well integrated to form a single fundamental philosophy that guides my daily activity. Technology, and by that I mean the now ubiquitous Internet, cell phone, laptop technologies, and all manner of gadgets designed and marketed to support mobile life and work, has made life as I now approach and live it possible.

This personal story of mobile work and life is, to me, a vivid illustration of the connection among the maturation process I have undergone as a person, the growth of my work in ever expanding and interlocking circles of interdependence, and the explosion of the information technology industry. My tale is one of coevolution and mutual shaping that crosses boundaries of many sorts, including the family–work boundary, the home–office boundary, disciplinary boundaries, generational boundaries, cultural and geographic boundaries, and gender boundaries to name a few. In my life's journey and through the coevolution of technology, work, and lifecycle, I have been cultivating an emergent conceptualization of identity that is flexible and multiple and is open to uncertainty and mystery.

I would like to tell you about this journey and what it has meant to me as well as frame my story in the concept of identity. Before telling the story, I provide an explanation of the identity concept by referring to Eisenberg's (2001) theory of identity as mystery. The story itself has three basic parts, the beginning, the middle, and (not the end!) the present

NAPA BULLETIN 30, pp. 70–88. ISSN: 1556-4789. DOI:10.1111/j.1556-4797.2008.00020.x together with the future as far as I can envision it with any measure of predictability. Following the story, I return to Eisenberg's model of identity as I have adapted it to my own life and circumstances and to provide a perspective on identity and mobile work. My account concludes with a discussion of what acceptance of identity as mystery has meant for me and what it could mean for others, personally, and in the pursuit of the anthropology of the technology-enabled, mobile work life.

I believe that sharing my journey can offer some insight to anyone who is interested in exploring what technology-enabled mobility and virtuality mean to their research or in their own lives. Bringing work, family, and friends into the virtual workspace (the on-line workspace enabled by communication and collaboration technologies) can open up new ways of thinking about personal identity and cultural identity. When I use the terms *virtual work* or *virtual workspace,* I do not mean that the work or the workspace is imagined. I simply mean that work and the spaces in which it takes place are enabled by the information technologies that decouple work from physical spaces and face-to-face interactions with coworkers and colleagues. A discrete, core sense of self that is grounded in physical surroundings can give way to an improvisational sense of self that more closely aligns with the lived experience of the hybridized, decontextualized, and dematerialized world enabled by virtual technologies. I have learned to think of identity as multiplicity, as possibility. My own identity has been shaped by and exists simultaneously in multiple locations, contexts, and cultures, and I now look at virtual work and its relationship to my own life in altered ways. However, the uncertainty this conceptualization of identity brings with it can also create anxiety and perpetuate a continuous feeling of living one's life in liminal spaces. In my story of coevolution, I will attempt to convey a sense of my own emergent, improvisational identity and its consequences and implications for life and work, both positive and negative, for me and potentially for others.

IDENTITY AS MYSTERY

I take the idea of identity as mystery from Eric Eisenberg (2001). Eisenberg, in his article entitled "Building a Mystery," has posited a new theory of communication and identity which is multiple and dynamic, and in my opinion, in line with the experience of living and working in a virtual world where boundaries are increasingly blurred and communities imagined (Gant and Kiesler 2001; Phillips 2002). In Eisenberg's conceptualization of identity, it is not a noun; it is a process that we create and in which we live. There is no attempt to seek clarity at all costs or to fix identity and its meaning once and for all. Instead, identity is viewed as a process that enables us to find meaning in interdependent, open systems in which we are challenged each day to know who we are and what we believe amidst an endless array of alternatives.

Eisenberg proposes a theory that connects the choices people make in how they communicate with their personal narratives, or their self-talk, and with how they emotionally experience their lives. All of this takes place within an environmental context, or "surround," that is available for the creation and sustenance of particular identities. People

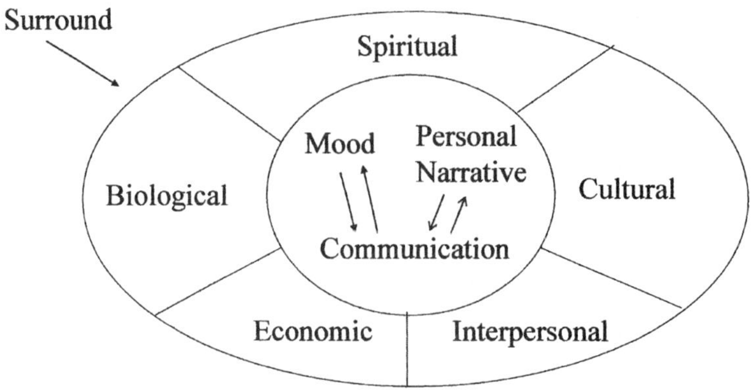

FIGURE 1. Model of the identity process (adapted from Eisenberg 2001:543).

draw from the surround, which includes culture as well as the physical environment, to make sense of their lives and construct their identities. The surround is a sort of information field that contains both symbolic and other raw material for sense making. For instance, the surround could be a physical environment (café, airport lounge, home or work office) located in the United States and a virtual environment with colleagues from multiple cultures in multiple locations simultaneously, characteristic of today's mobile work lives.

In Eisenberg's model, illustrated in Figure 1, there are three sensemaking processes that are mutually reinforcing. First, mood is the label for people's experiences of their body in the world. For example, we all have a physical presence which we feel and which others react to, that shapes our perceptions of who we are and how we think of ourselves. The physicality of one's identity is particularly influential if one stands out in some way. For example, if one is a person of color among a largely white population, or is someone who is very tall, or very beautiful, or physically abnormal or unusual in any way, one's experience in interacting with the world is likely to be shaped in a substantial way by these characteristics.

The second sensemaking process is the personal narrative, which takes account of the fact that people live according to stories, and that personal narrative is a primary tool for sensemaking. The stories we tell ourselves can heavily influence how we perceive of the world around us, how we give it meaning, and how we behave in it, particularly in relationships with others. Personal narrative and mood have a lot to do with one another. Self-talk about personal physical appearance (regardless of the particular physical attributes one possesses), for instance, can influence a person's mood positively or negatively and affect a person's experiences in the world, and therefore, a person's identity. The same could be said for self-talk about culture, with talk creating or reinforcing a particular cultural or occupational identity, for example, as an American anthropologist. The possibility inherent in narratives is central to the dynamic, flexible, and pluralistic view of identity. Storytelling, what we tell ourselves about ourselves and our experiences, as well as what we tell others, is important.

The third sensemaking process is communication with others, which is dialogic. When successful, it reinforces the competency of individuals as well as the power of the group. In dialogic communication each party to the process shares a commitment to both voice their experience and to be open to others. There are numerous complexities associated with the practical aspects of dialogue, including who gets to participate, and what effect existing power and status relations have on the resulting communicative encounters. For example, privilege often predisposes people to develop narratives of opportunity, while disadvantage can have the opposite effect and close people off from possibility. Identity is a complex process of drawing lists and stories from the surround that complement or otherwise inform one's mood, personal narrative, and communicative style. Changing communication is rarely enough to change social systems of relationships unless these changes can also be tied to altered moods, narratives, and elements of the surround.

Because the nature of work has changed in the past 30 years, largely enabled by the advancement of information technology, my identity has evolved in response to a world that is increasingly globally interconnected and technologically mediated, a virtual world in many respects. Through the past 30 years, I have altered my personal narrative about work, communicating and relating in new ways with the people in my social system. As the model implies, I have had to embrace uncertainty as a way to open up to possibilities and to change. This story of the coevolution of lifecycle, work, and technology is also the story of my evolving identity in a changing surround.

THE COEVOLUTION STORY

Because this story traces the coevolution of technology, work, and lifecycle, I begin not at the very beginning, but at the start of my working life in San Francisco in the 1970s.

In the Beginning . . . (1975–88)

Geography, workplace, and lifestyle are inextricably linked. Having completed my undergraduate education in the early 1970s, I embarked on a career in the hospitality industry in San Francisco, California, with the Hotel St. Francis, a Westin Hotel (Figure 2).

Anyone who has stayed in very large city hotels like this one knows that these hotels are almost like concentrated cities under one roof. They are filled with people from many different economic and social strata, diverse groups and nationalities, and reflect a cross-section of lifestyles and work. From the inside, as an employee, especially in a city like San Francisco, I had the opportunity to mingle with, make friends with, and work with many kinds of people from different stations in life and cultural groups. Interactions with Filipino maids, first generation Greek, Italian, and Irish bellmen (some of whom were 30-year veterans at the St. Francis) were part of my daily work. I worked side by side with gay desk clerks, French cooks, Japanese hostesses, Chinese room service waiters, and many other immigrants working as banquet waiters. I served

FIGURE 2. Hotel St. Francis, San Francisco. (Photo by Julia C. Gluesing.)

corporate executives working for the hotel or staying in it, regular hotel guests from the globe-trotting set. Fresh new managers just out of Cornell's hotel school, and Japanese tour directors became part of my cohort. It was the place itself, the St. Francis, that made this type of contact possible. We not only collaborated together inside the hotel walls but met for drinks, biking, walking, or other activities in off hours. People at the St. Francis, and in the hotel business in general, keep very odd hours, and befriending colleagues is commonplace because it is the only way to create or maintain a social life when everyone else who keeps regular hours of the "9 to 5" variety is working. The place, the St. Francis, was the center of my life. The geography of the workplace determined in large part the lifestyle I would keep and the friends and acquaintances with whom I would share it.

Boundaries are clear; roles are defined. Work itself took place in the "workplace" and did not spill over into my home or private life even though many of the people with whom I shared my off-work time and spaces were hotel colleagues or acquaintances. There was a definite line drawn between work and nonwork activities. Work was confined to the hotel spaces, which were always entered through the small, obscure door on the backside of the hotel. The start of the workday (or night) began immediately inside that door with punching-in at the time clock. It ended when I punched-out and emerged onto the street from that same door, no matter what time of the day or night it happened to be.

Socializing activities might begin at the Irish pub across the street, and we might gossip about work and colleagues as well as plot our survival in the current corporate climate of hotel management; however, we did not engage in work or "do" work, of any kind. We were paid, even those of us who were in the management track, or already among the management ranks, for the work we did inside the St. Francis. It was also physically impossible to do most of the hotel work without being in that space (e.g., making beds, checking people in, serving food and drink, resolving problems or taking care of requests for guests and coworkers, subordinates and superiors).

The nature of the work also required that roles be clearly defined to achieve a high level of customer service and meet the business objectives from a profitability and public relations standpoint. All of us, even if we rotated jobs, were well trained in the specific tasks required of each of the jobs we performed. We also knew what others in the hotel were responsible for accomplishing, and when and where certain tasks and people with specialized skills could be found. The hotel is located in a city characterized by its immigrant and transient population, and large hotel chains as a routine practice also move employees in managerial posts from property to property as part of the career development path (similar to the military). Therefore, roles and spans of responsibility were clearly defined, even among the managerial functions, to ensure stable, quality work performance. There was a certainty to work and its rhythms, while at the same time, the work was almost always exciting and unpredictable because the hotel was like a small city with all its attendant characters and surprises.

Communication technology is limited and narrowly focused on specific tasks. These early years in my work life occurred when the information technology revolution was just beginning. The Silicon Valley, where I used to visit my uncle and his family, had not yet received this label and was still a place of apricot orchards and small towns connected by two-lane roads. The introduction of the computer into the hotel business was just beginning in small ways. The St. Francis had used pneumatic tubes for many years to carry work-related messages between departments. The hotel received its first computers to manage housekeeping functions that could inform maids and front desk employees of the status of a room (occupied, checked-out, dirty, clean, etc.) to increase the efficiency of the turnaround for rooms and keep the guests moving in an out without "pile-ups" in the hotel lobby. By the time I left the St. Francis for a job transfer to another hotel in the chain, in Detroit at the Renaissance Center, the computerization of the hotel functions had proceeded only to manage the cashiering functions in the restaurants. There was no e-mail, nor was there any way to communicate regularly among employees in different departments, save for the still operational pneumatic tubes, the limited room status reporting and the occasional phone call, made primarily by the supervisors who generally took care of cross-departmental communication. Information technology certainly had not yet enabled employees to take work home with them, crossing this long-established boundary. Information technology was limited to the physical workplace.

Identity is tied to organization and physical space. To describe my identity as tied to the St. Francis does not do the strength of this tie justice. The physical space was my work and it contained all the work-related relationships that were networked within that space. While these networks spilled over to the private, nonwork sphere of my life in those years, they lost the work aspect of their nature when they moved beyond the walls of the hotel. I also identified strongly with the organization for which I worked, the Westin Corporation, because I was embarking on a career in the hospitality industry. I could see a future of work spaces like the St. Francis that would take me to various geographies around the world. The organization and the space largely defined the character of my working identity as well my personal identity.

Following these beginning years in the hospitality industry, I went back to school to receive my master's degree and doctorate, and I changed the direction of my work entirely to begin a career in communication and business anthropology. The middle episode of my life represents a transition in my work, my lifecycle, and the technology which helped to integrate the two.

In the Middle . . . (1989–2002)

Geography and physical space still matter but are more background than foreground. By 1989, I had completed my master's degree in organizational and intercultural communication at Michigan State University, had worked a few years with Sandy Corporation as a consultant to the auto industry, and had married a coworker at Sandy. I transitioned from the hotel industry where work was grounded in location, to research and consulting work, which was not tied to my physical surroundings. I also had two young daughters, four and six years old. My approach to life and work began to change to accommodate my desire to be with my children and to continue the pursuit of my Ph.D. in anthropology and my work as a consultant. For the first time in my adult life, I considered working from home as a means to accomplish all three of my objectives, not a completely unique choice in the 1990s for professional women who also wanted a family. With the establishment of J. K. Research, which I filed with the State of Michigan as a sole proprietorship business (commonly known as a "DBA" or "doing business as" company), I was able to set up shop at home. I still was tied to my local geography because of the constraints of family. However, unlike my early years in the hotel business, this new way of working did not require me actually to be in a specific physical space to accomplish my tasks. "Work" became detached from "workplace," and the physicality of the workplace moved to the background in my own idea of what work meant to me. I worked at home, at client locations, at the university, occasionally in hotels, at the homes of friends and family when we went to visit, and even abroad just a few times since I did my dissertation work in Paris, Boston, and Phoenix. I created a portable office containing the basic necessities like paper and notepads, a stapler and paper clips, floppy diskettes, a printer and fax, my laptop (as limited and cumbersome as it was in those early days), folders, electrical plugs and converters, et cetera which I housed in a standard roll-aboard suitcase that traveled with me everywhere.

Roles merge. Relationships altered as well, in a big way. Before long, my husband, Ken, joined me in the new business. He had continued to work at Sandy Corporation to maintain some stability in income while I got started in the home-based business. However, we had worked together before (in fact, a great work relationship actually enabled the personal one); we had enjoyed the experience and wanted to continuing working as a team. Once I had completed my Ph.D., and we had managed to find a large enough client to provide an adequate income to keep us going (not too difficult in the boom times of the 1990s), we incorporated and changed the name of the company to Cultural Connections, Inc. Any notion that there might be traditional roles related to gender or work or child rearing was completely abandoned. Ken and I shared in intermingled carpooling, housecleaning, proposal writing, client work, yard work, and all the rest that family and work relationships entail. Friends joined in from time to time, not just in the domestic aspects of our life, but in our work-related activities, too.

The workplace is flexible, and boundaries between work and home are blurring. The flexibility enabled by the separation of work and workplace led to a blurring of the boundaries between work and home. While the advantages garnered by operating our own business cannot be understated, especially in controlling our own time and activities, it was really the merging of life with work that was the most liberating for me. I enjoyed my work and did not see it as an intrusion into my life as mother, spouse, or friend or any of my other roles. Working took place over dinner preparations that Ken and I performed together or in late-night conversations over a glass of wine, interspersed with helping the children with their homework, chauffeuring them to dance classes, and washing clothes. We created a shared workspace together in the family room, which we continue to share to this day. Great ideas were hatched on early morning walks, or with clients on the plant floor. In fact, I began to view the work as an enabler of values I wanted to pass on to my daughters, of educational goals for them, of access to time with family and friends who were spread across the country, and even across the globe. Any practice of work as a "9 to 5" kind of thing at "the office" was completely eliminated from my daily life. Clients and subcontractors even met with me in my kitchen.

Communication technologies play a greater role. As I said earlier, I created a portable office in a suitcase that traveled with me everywhere. In the early 1990s, the concept of telework and virtual work was just beginning to really take off. The now ubiquitous terms *mobile work* or *mobile work life* had not yet been adopted by mainstream business. Yet my little laptop, with the black and white screen and 24K dial-up modem using CompuServe, made it possible for me to work in locations like my Paris hotel room for three weeks to a month at a time and stay in touch frequently with what was happening at home. I was able to receive scanned photographs of my daughters and of drawings they had made for me, and I maintained a running e-mail dialogue with Ken about everything. On the rare occasions that I actually placed a transatlantic phone call, it was not uncommon for Ken to call the girls to the phone to talk with me and have them respond, "We're busy. Can't she call back?" They were not exactly pining away for their mother! I did talk to them after some urging on Ken's part.

The point is that my daughters had become so accustomed to having me home and to having me accessible via computer connection on those rare occasions when I was away from them, that none of us really suffered too much when I did have to be gone for weeks at a time. Their ideas about work also were greatly influenced by these earlier mobile experiences. My daughters did not see mom or dad go off to work in the morning and come home in the evening. We were both around, in and out, all day, every day, almost. They brought us into their classrooms to talk about what we did, and tried to understand our work themselves, which was pretty difficult for them to explain to anyone else. When asked the question, "What do your parents do?" or "Where do your parents work," the children would say, "Work on the computer" or "Work at home and sometimes in the car or in the hotel."

The concept of mobile work had become not just the framework for my daily work practice, but also the focus of my work itself. I had decided to study global teams as my dissertation topic and to pursue research, education, and consulting in this area, seeing that these teams might become more prevalent in the years to come. What would this type of work mean for the future of the workplace, for collaboration in distributed work, for the lives of those who practiced it?

Identity is more flexible and plural. As mobility became more central to my work, I was faced with situations and feelings that I had not encountered previously and that fundamentally affected how I saw myself as an individual and how I conceptualized identity, both personal and cultural. The unstructured work day, and the uncertainties that come with the freedom (or burden) of defining one's own work, work day and work space, coupled with the need to continuously create new business to sustain a minimal level of income, produced anxieties I had not previously faced.

I had always been a person who coped well with uncertainty and embraced change in my life. I like variety and new adventures; but the mobile work situation threw me into such turmoil initially that I had a sense of being completely afloat, unattached to my surroundings, and unsure of who I was or how I should behave. While I continued to have people around me, my family and close friends, who imposed some role definition and concrete demands on my life, I had more room to move in defining who I was and would become than I had ever had in my life. As I increased my contact with people in other locations, bringing their ideas and practices into my daily interactions, my anxiety about my own identity multiplied. Others characterized me as a pretty open person who could "go with the flow;" however, mobile work had brought about so much change, so rapidly, that I was unsure whether I would be able to cope or to achieve a balance among the locations, cultures, diverse people and perspectives, and multiple workplaces that were continuously converging and diverging in my life.

It took me some time to create a structure for myself that would accommodate and help me make sense of my mobile work environment. I discovered that structure partly by accident and partly in a purposeful attempt to conceive of my own identity as plural, fluid, and flexible. I stopped searching for "my identity" in any sense of the word as permanent. Identity is commonly thought of as an essential self, the set of characteristics that a person recognizes as belonging uniquely to herself or himself and constituting her or his individual personality for life. To live the mobile life I had begun to create for myself and remain sane, I had to abandon this conceptualization of identity and adopt a new one. I tried on a view of identity that freed me to think of myself as possessing different characteristics and ways of thinking in different contexts with different people. I am not talking just about a changing presentation of self. I mean that I began to really see myself as plural, as having the ability to incorporate and enact multiple cultural frames that would enable me to adapt and change with the fluid circumstances of my mobile work and life.

In my virtual meetings with global team members, for example, I was able to listen to the other participants and to switch cultural frames, taking on a more "French-like" identity as I was listening to and talking with a French member of the team. I could code and encode the messages from a French frame and an American frame and make sense of what was being said from both perspectives, if not simultaneously, at least quickly enough for me to examine a topic from both frames. I knew that I was feeling both constrained by schedule as an American, but at the same time, free to circle back to an idea that had already been discussed and bring it up again, in interaction with my French colleague, for whom the circling back was the cultural norm. I could also think about how that topic and the interaction process might be perceived by the German and Chinese team members as they were listening to my interaction with our French colleagues, because I had learned enough about those cultures to "be in that cultural mindset," taking on that identity and putting myself in the others' shoes, so to speak, for a few moments.

In fact, as I grew more accustomed to this uncentered self-identity, I developed an easy and practical conceptualization of culture as a dynamic H.E.L.P. system (Habits or normative patterns of behaviors; Expectations for oneself and others; Language, both verbal and nonverbal; and Perspective on the world, or worldview). This model of culture enabled me to work as a consultant to global virtual teams, teaching these teams that a global mindset is one that includes multiple H.E.L.P. systems and a fluid and flexible cultural identity that draws on and integrates these multiple H.E.L.P. systems, often in the work of negotiating a new working culture at the intersections of the multiple H.E.L.P. systems salient to the team, whether occupational, organizational, or national.

A changing philosophy of identity enables an integrated life. With this changing philosophy of identity, I was able to reduce my anxiety somewhat and begin living what I have termed an integrated life. My family, friends, and colleagues moved in and out of my thoughts and activities throughout the day without the imposition of boundaries that defined the beginning or end of discrete segments that had previously defined my work day. I could not say when my personal life and my work life began or ended. I was working all the time, and I was also paying attention to domestic duties and important relationships in my life in ways that interspersed these activities with interactions with colleagues and with work tasks. I had not thought it possible to have this kind of integrated life. I had heard complaints often about the invasion of work into the private domain and home lives of friends and colleagues. I did not experience this feeling of intrusion. For me, the integrated life was enabled by my changed concept of identity and by the freedom both to fulfill my needs and also to take care of the needs of others and the requirements of my work by structuring daily activity in a flexible way, without the usual work–life boundaries. Integration was my way of solving the work–life balance dilemma.

Now and into the Future . . . (2003–?)

Travel dramatically increases. The year 2003 heralded another major life change for my family and me. My two daughters had graduated from high school. Both were attending university and had moved out on their own in another city. Of course, this transition to an "empty nest" is not new by any means; however, for me the transition meant the freedom to move into other spaces, not just virtually, but also physically. I began to travel more frequently as I moved into the academic work arena and took on the role of a global program developer for the Industrial and Manufacturing Engineering Department at Wayne State University. Here I was an anthropologist, an independent business owner, and now a research professor with global responsibility in an engineering college. I was able to expand and test my philosophy of identity even further. I worked hard to integrate my experience and background in communication, business, anthropology, and entrepreneurial ventures, into my work life in new ways that took me to India, China, Europe, Japan, Latin America, and many different locations within the United States where I was able to develop personal and professional relationships in new places while still maintaining connections with family and friends because of the explosion in new virtual communication technologies.

New virtual communication technologies are vital and central to my integrated and increasingly global life. The first decade of the new millennium has brought with it a revolution in information technologies, especially those that enable work that is accomplished virtually across distances. There are virtual collaboration tools, such as video conferencing, audio conferencing, and synchronous and asynchronous collaboration applications. Virtual team centers, and dynamic data sharing and visualization are popping up in businesses everywhere. These are technologies and tools that have made it possible for me to accomplish the integrated life I have been and still am seeking. These communication technologies have seemed to track my life stages and to be there as I needed them, facilitating the new ways of working and the exploration of identity in which I was engaged.

As I moved about the globe, sometimes with my husband or one of my daughters but most often on my own, I took advantage of the virtual technologies to maintain an integrated life, but I had to learn a new way of communicating. My own studies of virtual teams (Baba et al. 2004; Gluesing 1998; Gluesing et al. 2003) had taught me the importance of communicating about context in virtual work, both by making context explicit through sharing it in verbal and visual description, and in an interactive way if possible, and also by creating a virtual context and negotiating meaning and rules for interaction within this "imaginary" space. By context I mean a way of life and work in a specific geographic area with its own set of business conditions, cultural assumptions, and unique history, and not just the immediate surroundings or situation. I learned from my work and research with global virtual teams that I could not take for granted that other people shared my contextual knowledge or that they would have a common framework for working or living.

Crossing multiple boundaries, and identifying and integrating the different contexts this crossing entails, can have varying relevance and impact on work practices and daily living. It takes mindfulness and new ways of communicating to help people share context and create shared meaning and understanding. Like the team members I studied, I had to learn to communicate to my coworkers and to my friends and family about the features of my context, the subtle tacit elements as well as the physical features. Making context more explicit helped us all create a common understanding of our experiences and build a bridge across distance to bring us closer. I traveled with a laptop always, and I routinely used technologies like Skype to hold long conversations at little or no cost using Internet connections in hotels and public spaces. I obtained a phone number with my home area code so that neighbors and friends from home could call a local number and reach me at my computer or leave me voice mail on my computer at no cost to them. It really didn't matter where I was, to my home-based friends and family, I was never more than a local phone call away.

One interesting and unanticipated consequence of this mobile life was that I found myself advocating the adoption of virtual technologies to my friends and family as well as my work colleagues. I had to bring them all along with me, so to speak. I realized that I could not maintain my own conceptualization of an integrated mobile life and plural identity unless the important people in my life were also able to connect virtually. In E. M. Forster's novel *Howard's End* (1999), the phrase "Only connect . . . " is an imperative for making ties across obstacles, and these words became my mantra. I had to buy laptops or PC cameras for my mother (now 90 years old and virtually connected!), and my daughters (expensive, but worth it). I encouraged friends and other family members to get connected, too, and brought new technologies into my university workspace, successfully convincing my department chair and other faculty to also adopt. I had to become a change agent for mobile work and virtual technologies. While I met with some resistance, for the most part, I was successful in my diffusion efforts and it made all the difference.

For example, on one trip to China, I was able to videoconference quite easily with my husband in Michigan and my mother in San Francisco and chat about my day, showing both of them around the lounge in my hotel and the view from the window using my laptop camera (See Figure 3).

FIGURE 3. iChatting with mother, Urania, and husband, Ken. (Photo by Julia C. Gluesing.)

FIGURE 4. Mobile life in Mexico with friends. Julia is seated on the far right. (Photo by Kenneth R. Riopelle.)

My mother and husband also chatted with the Chinese girls in the lounge and with some of my colleagues, and I was able to show my family the purchases I had made. My husband and mother were able to share their news with me as well. By the conclusion of the video chat, we all had a feeling of renewed connection of each other's contexts. The boundaries of culture, geography, and time were blurred, if not completely eliminated.

On a trip to Mexico with friends, I took advantage of the opportunity to continue my work while engaging in leisure activities, but also to demonstrate the advantages of the virtual technologies as part of my efforts to "convert" my friends and bring them into my mobile life (Figure 4). My friends were able to connect to their own daughters and even do some of their own work in such a pleasurable way that they did adopt the technologies. One of my friends now uses Skype's videoconferencing capability to stay connected to her daughter in Japan. Sharing context is very much a part of their on-line ritual, and I am convinced that a semblance of "being there" is conveyed in ways that would not otherwise be possible.

Sharing context and creating virtual contexts where social and work activities can take place has become easier as the decade is nearing its end. There are many social networking spaces now available to the general public as well as an ever-burgeoning array of collaboration technologies to facilitate all kinds of work. Virtual spaces like Second Life are making it possible for people to actually create contexts and identities that allow them to explore possibilities and make connections in new ways, creating real innovation in ways of working and business models as well as enabling personal play and growth through interaction with new people and environments otherwise not possible. Of course, these technologies are not without their downsides. Alienation from the present physical world, as well as dangerous virtual liaisons that can have very real financial and personal negative consequences, are just two that quickly come to mind.

However, for me, the upside of the technologies as enablers of an integrated mobile life, outweigh the potential pitfalls.

Identity is a process, contextualized in multiple arenas, flexible, improvisational, and based in relationships facilitated by virtual technologies. As the decade closes, I am now convinced that my own identity is best viewed as a process. My life is taking place in multiple arenas. It spans geographies, contexts (physical and virtual, work and leisure), people, and time. I work with people in multiple countries on a weekly, if not daily, basis. I am an anthropologist and a woman with a full-time position in an all-male department in an engineering college. I have had to learn and internalize an occupational culture and professional identity different from my own primary professionally socialized identity while maintaining and nurturing my identity as an anthropologist. I interact in "virtual" worlds like Second Life to participate in "real" work interactions with "virtual humans," where work and play intersect and overlap. And I have learned to take on new cultural perspectives of my colleagues from China and from Germany, in particular, as I have interacted with them, crossing boundaries, cultural and geographic, to negotiate new working cultures. I have learned to be flexible in my approach to life and to manage the increased uncertainty and consequent anxiety created by the "ungrounding" of my life as I began this mobile work journey. I live in an improvisational space enabled by virtual communication technologies, yet I still have a sense of belonging. While I believe I have been fairly successful in changing my philosophy of identity to become more plural and fluid, I still have a need to belong. That is one of the most basic needs for me, and I expect for most people. How have I reconciled the need to belong with my uncentered identity and mobile life? I still have a "home base" which I call Turtle Island after a book of poetry by Gary Snyder (1974), the 1975 Pulitzer Prize winner for poetry. The introductory note in the book tells us that Turtle Island is Planet Earth on the back of the turtle. This image is common in creation myths that are shared around the world. These myths emphasize that we are all part of the same community on earth. To Snyder, place is an energy pathway that sustains life, and we are all caught up in the flow and swirl of living. We all have a special place on Turtle Island that gives us strength to reach out to each other in our common humanity.

The concept of Turtle Island, as Gary Snyder has stated so well, is focused on the work of "being together" no matter where we are, with the turtle's back to support us. My home space is my personal Turtle Island, the jumping off point for my travels and the primary connector in my mobile life. I also have become part of a virtual network of people with whom I work on almost a daily basis. I belong in the virtual context we have cocreated and in which we interact. Many of these people are also personal friends, real friends. We still meet face-to-face at least once or twice a year in various locations, and not all of us come together at any one time. These virtual connections are real relationships that enrich my daily life in an integrated way, yet they are not tied to any physical location. This group to which I belong "travels" with me and stays connected to me wherever I go.

DISCUSSION AND LESSONS LEARNED

Identity in a Virtual World . . .

As technology, work, and my own life have coevolved, I have developed my own philosophy of identity that incorporates the concept of mystery. My experiences with virtual communication technologies have been positive for the most part, and my narratives usually reinforce a sense of optimism and possibility. Not all has been rosy, and events could have influenced my experiences in a negative way (hard drive crashes, dropped connections, lost files, interrupted meals or sleep, etc.). However, interaction with others and my own self-talk kept the negative from prevailing, particularly in my encounters with technology. The point I want to make about technology and identity is directly related to personal narrative and the dialogic aspects of sensemaking. In my case, I have been interacting over the years with people who view virtual communication technologies as enabling even if at times these technologies are frustrating and disappointing. This notion of identity as mystery is one that I have observed team members enact in the virtual teams in which I have conducted research or taken part. My own narrative is similar to the stories team members have conveyed to me—that the experience with information technologies since the early 1980s has been supportive and liberating, and a mobile life has been incorporated as part of a philosophy about identity as multiplicity and possibility. The future of work is being facilitated by or constrained by information technology, depending on one's identity and position in the web of technology-enabled encounters.

As technology changes, culture changes and our conceptualizations of identity must evolve as well. To understand the relationship among technology, culture, and identity it is necessary to take a process approach to culture as well as to identity. If we view culture as a process we can understand the culture concept in new ways that are better suited to capturing the lived experience of a virtual, decontextualized, and dematerialized world and the mobile lives that many of us are now leading as globalization has proceeded. We should understand cultures in plural and diverse ways (Alvesson 2002) in the same way I have suggested we understand identity.

The culture concept dates to a time in the 1800s when demographic, economic, and political conditions were largely rooted in local geographies and nation-building grounded in history and were distinctive, bounded, with relatively stable, inherited, normative beliefs, values, and behaviors, and with limited cross-boundary interaction. The reality of society today is characterized as imperfectly bounded, with multiple and branching social alignments, in deterritorialized spaces led by multinational corporations and individuals facilitated by virtual communication technologies and the negotiation of the cultural experience is central (Kearney 1995). There is fluidity and permeability, complex and ambiguous interaction, new evaluations of old cultural forms (e.g., Islam, democracy, Christianity) borrowed forms (e.g., capitalism) and whole new forms (e.g., virtual communities) in changing circumstances. When we look at the complex connectivity of the human situation today, what we are concerned with is how globalization alters the context of meaning construction; how it affects people's sense of identity, the experience of place and of the self in relation to place; and how it impacts the shared understandings, values, desires, myths, hopes, and fears that have developed around locally situated life that is now connected with the vast systemic transformations, and transformations in our most local and intimate "worlds" of everyday experience, what Anthony Giddens has called "out-thereness" and the "in-hereness" of globalization (Giddens 1994).

Anthropologists have always engaged in processual thinking about human societies and cultures, as evolution, as diffusion, and as responses to the forces generated by modes of production in specific environments (Wolf 1997). I argue that we now need to theorize culture as process in context and focus attention on people's actions and interactions as people construct and reconstruct meaning and identity in response to the demands of multiple contexts if we are to reconceptualize culture in a meaningful way to capture the current reality of global and mobile life. A process view has guided my own research on global teams, and I expect that I will continue my work investigating the multiple identities and contexts that constitute the "surround" for global teams. While we can continue to recognize that there are historically based, distinct, and recognizable cultural forms that shape identity, we can at the same time focus on continually changing and emerging new forms of culture.

A process approach to culture means we view the edges of cultural groups as fuzzy and permeable. These edges are dynamic and are constructed and reconstructed continually and where identities, cultural or personal, are most fluid (Tomlinson 1999). One could say that culture is not either–or, but both–and, because multiple cultural forms can exist simultaneously in a single context when geographic and cultural boundaries are crossed to form new communities, such as the emergent open source community or more structured global virtual teams in multinational corporations. In this sense, too, culture is both being and becoming as people bring with them culturally shaped identities and are also part of shaping new ones. The intersections and overlapping cultural systems are where we can see the process of what I have termed *cultural hybridization* taking place in multiple contexts. Homi Bhabha (1990) has called this intersection a third space, and this is the starting point in the production of new hybrid cultural forms. As existing systems come together and intersect, often in virtual spaces, we can see how they flow into one another and hybridize, more rapidly than ever before. At the start of life on the Internet, Turkle (1995) told us that one of the reasons poststructuralist theories and postmodernism did not connect with many people was that there was a disjuncture between theories of the self as decentered and illusory and our lived experiences of everyday life, which pressures us to see the self as centralized and unitary. Now, however, Turkle says that in her computer-mediated worlds, the self is multiple, fluid, and constituted in interaction with both the technologies and other characters she meets in the virtual world. It is the interaction of people in spatial, temporal, and contextual mobility that requires the conceptualization of self and identity as mystery (Churchill and Munro 2001).

Seeing identity as mystery, an identity that readily incorporates technological and cultural change, enables me not only to cope with the demands of mobile life and work but also to thrive in this environment, in spite of frustrations and anxieties. I try to make sense of my experiences by thinking of my own identity as a process that enables me to find meaning in interdependent, open systems that are dynamic and in flux (e.g., educational relationships for global education with foreign universities, the global project teams in which I participate, and the global networked organizations I study). Boellstorff (2008:237) invites us all to think about old and new means for the virtual and the human and says that we could do well to imagine culture as incorporating the virtual, stating that we have been "virtually human" all along. I am challenged each day to know who I am and what I believe amidst an endless array of alternatives, but I have learned some lessons about identity as mystery and as possibility:

- Improvisation is an important skill. New technologies, work circumstances, and different relationships that are continually in flux require a great deal of on-the-spot adaptive action.
- Fluid circumstances can be empowering. While uncertainty can be uncomfortable, it also means that there are multiple alternative courses of action and potential outcomes that I can have a role in shaping.
- Anxiety is always an undercurrent. Where do I "belong," and what is the "correct" behavior, are often questions that I ask myself. I have had to learn to live with the anxiety that often accompanies mobile life and work.
- Mobile life and work is enriching. Moving across contexts and boundaries frees me to see alternatives I would not otherwise have considered. This movement leads to innovation as well as personal and professional growth.
- Circumstances are important but not as important as personal narrative and self-talk. How we interact with our surround and what we tell ourselves about our circumstances play a large role in identity formation.

A philosophy of identity as mystery has produced an unanticipated and welcome benefit for my work as an anthropologist as well. Mobile work has pushed me to see with new eyes, behave in new ways, and ask new questions such as: What are our digital or virtual identities and how are they culturally embedded, negotiated, or constructed? How are the processes of sociality and the mobile life, including technology, intertwined and with what consequences? These questions have become both a central focus of my work and my life.

CONCLUDING REMARKS

A Wrinkle in Time (L'Engle 1962), a children's book, has always been one of my favorite books, and I have returned to it many times whenever I have needed to refresh my capacity to dream. It has always inspired in me a sense of possibility and related science and technology to connections with others and with universal phenomena we don't necessarily understand. The book is a story of Meg and her friend Calvin's adventures in space and time. They discover that there is such a thing as a tesseract and that they can wrinkle time and space to move across universes. In the course of their adventures they not only discover that they are able to accomplish a dangerous mission but also to learn more about themselves and their own identities. For me, living the mobile life is not unlike the adventures of Calvin and Meg; this is the sense, the meaning I have constructed for myself.

REFERENCES CITED

Alvesson, Mats
2002 Understanding Organizational Culture. London: Sage.

Baba, Marietta, Julia Gluesing, Hilary Ratner, and Kimberly Wagner
2004 The Contexts of Knowing: Natural History of a Globally Distributed Team. Journal of Organizational Behavior 25(2):547–587.

Bhabha, Homi K.
1990 DissemiNation: Time, Narrative, and the Margins of the Modern Nation. *In* Nation and Narration. Homi K. Bhabha, ed. Pp. 291–322. New York: Routledge.

Boellstorff, Tom
2008 Coming of Age in Second Life: An Anthropologist Explores the Virtually Human. Princeton: Princeton University Press.

Churchill, Elizabeth F., and Alan J. Munro
2001 Work/Place: Mobile Technologies and Arenas of Activity. ACM SIGGROUP Bulletin 22(3):3–9.

Eisenberg, Eric M.
2001 Building a Mystery: Communication and the Development of Identity. Journal of Communication 51(3):534–552.

Forster, Edward Morgan (E. M.)
1999 [1910] Howard's End. New York: Random House.

Gant, Diana, and Sara Kiesler
2001 Blurring the Boundaries: Cell Phones, Mobility, and the Line between Work and Personal Life. *In* Wireless World: Social and Interactional Aspects of the Mobile Age. Pp. 121–131. New York: Springer-Verlag.

Giddens, Anthony
1994 Living in a Post-Traditional Society. *In* Reflexive Modernization: Politics, Tradition and Aesthetics in the Modern Social Order. Ulrich Beck, Anthony Giddens, and Scott Lash, eds. Pp. 56–109. Cambridge: Polity.

Gluesing, Julia
1998 Building Connections and Balancing Power in Global Teams: Toward a Reconceptualization of Culture as Composite. Anthropology of Work Review 18(2):18–30.

Gluesing, Julia, Tara Alcordo, Marietta Baba, David Britt, Willie McKether, Leslie Monplaisir, Hilary Ratner, Kenneth Riopelle, and Kimberly Wagner
2003 The Development of Global Virtual Teams. *In* Virtual Teams That Work: Creating Conditions for Effective Virtual Teams. Cristina Gibson and Susan Cohen, eds. Pp. 353–380. San Francisco: Jossey-Bass.

Kearney, Michael
1995 The Local and the Global: The Anthropology of Globalization and Transnationalism. Annual Review of Anthropology 24:547–565.

L'Engle, Madeleine
1962 A Wrinkle in Time. New York: Farrar, Straus and Giroux.

Phillips, Tim
2002 Imagined Communities and Self-identity: An Exploratory Quantitative Analysis. Sociology 36(3):597–617.

Snyder, Gary
1974 Turtle Island. New York: New Directions.

Tomlinson, John
1999 Globalization and Culture. Chicago: University of Chicago Press.
Turkle, Sherry
1995 Life on the Screen: Identity in the Age of the Internet. New York: Simon and Schuster.
Wolf, Eric R.
1997 [1982] Europe and the People without History. Berkeley: University of California Press.

REMOTE OR MOBILE WORK AS AN OCCASION FOR (RE)STRUCTURING PROFESSIONAL AND PERSONAL IDENTITIES

Perri Strawn
The Blue Company, Washington, D.C.

Writing from the perspective of both a remote and mobile worker, I explore the ways in which regular and frequent physical relocation challenges and redefines my relationship to home and work. This article explores questions surrounding how an employee who is "remote" is seen by others, including peers and senior management, and the role remote workers play in the culture of the firm. This article also discusses strategies to cope with the sense of fragmentation that results from constant relocations because of travel among work, home, and other locations, in other words, how to bridge the "there–not there," "seen–not seen" disjunctures that frame the experience of being a remote worker. Keywords: remote work, remote worker, mobile worker, fragmentation

Like more than ten percent of the some 950 employees at my company, a publicly traded firm in Washington, D.C., I am a remote worker—that is, I live farther than just a bad commute away from Washington and require special accommodations. However, most of us are in fact both remote and mobile because we regularly work in our home offices, spend significant time in the company's headquarters, and travel for client meetings, often all in the same week. We conduct ourselves in what has been described as "hybrid workspace" (Halford 2005).

Writing from the perspective of both a remote and mobile worker, I explore the ways in which regular and frequent physical relocations made necessary by job responsibilities challenge and redefine my relationship to both home and work. Working in multiple spaces creates a constant, dynamic engagement with the meanings of "home" and "work," both for the remote worker, family members, and colleagues. Similarly, the frequent crossing of home and work boundaries—and the blurring of the two—fosters a sense of fragmentation and disjuncture that pervades every sphere of life. This fragmentation is experienced at multiple sites as the physical body traverses social, professional, and home identities and is mediated by the conditions particular to each. These sites are not mutually exclusive, but together encompass the terrains where remote workers are challenged to forge new ways of understanding and meaning.

In this article, I will address the particular disjunctures made manifest in each context, and discuss strategies to cope with this fragmentation—how to bridge the "there–not

NAPA BULLETIN 30, pp. 89–101. ISSN: 1556-4789.
DOI:10.1111/j.1556-4797.2008.00021.x

there," "seen–not seen" disjunctures that characterize and shape the experience of being a remote worker.

PERSONAL CONTEXT AND TERRAIN

I joined the Blue Company,[1] located in Washington, D.C., in 1999 shortly after completing my Ph.D. in anthropology. In June 2005 I relocated to Philadelphia because of my husband's job and have officially been a remote–mobile worker since that time. No matter where I live, my job requires frequent travel for client meetings all over the United States. When not traveling elsewhere, I split my week between Washington (2 nights–3 days) and Philadelphia (3 nights–2 days).

Remote is a complex category at my company and elsewhere (Halford 2005). Employees at my firm defined as remote fall into two main groups. One category comprises roles whose primary focus is either sales or onsite client product delivery and therefore involve 80 percent travel (or more); the travel requirements of these jobs mean that no matter where the employees live they are unlikely to be able to be in the office much (and, in fact, are not expected to be). The second category includes people like me, responsible for creating and overseeing development of the services and products we sell; most have both tenure and senior roles. It is only in recent years that people in "content" roles (e.g., not sales or presenter roles, which all require nearly full-time travel) were allowed to "go remote." As the company has grown (and as explicit growth targets have become part of our focus, common with publicly traded firms) the pressure to recruit and retain talent has grown. Our work product and firm culture are idiosyncratic enough that tenured high performers are difficult to replace. Thus, over time, the company has become increasingly willing (although not eager) to allow at least some of us to relocate while remaining with the firm.

My focus here is on this latter category of employees (including myself). Literature about "working from home" typically has addressed the issues of home workers (often, migrants or other disadvantaged individuals forced to work at home for low wages; see for example Peake 1994); or of teleworkers, people who work full-time from home and the barriers they face technologically and otherwise (Brodt and Verburg 2007). Only in recent years has the issue of professional, even executive-level, individuals working a significant time away from the office (either in mobile settings or at home) become a focus of study (Baba et al. 2004; Wasson 2006), and it is to this body of work I hope to contribute.

What I have observed, and experienced, is that senior executives who "go remote" experience a particular set of challenges and tensions related to their professional and personal status. On the personal front, most of us are at a point in our lives in which we are ready to have something beyond work define us (e.g., children, or deeper participation in some aspect of our communities). Yet "going remote" challenges those personal desires acutely. It also highlights a thorny set of questions about work, most of which we had forgotten about in the years since we were new employees. For senior employees, these kinds of questions had long receded into the background because we are, by definition, successful (we are, after all, "senior"), and we presumably had figured out the answers. But, suddenly, with our bodies roaming around God only knows where outside of the office, we find ourselves confronted by such questions as: How much time in the office is "enough"? How much in-person time is required with peers and more senior leaders? How much in-person time is needed to manage teams (if we have direct management responsibilities)? How many hours is it necessary to work each day to prove we are really working enough?

These questions fall into what I think of as an "operational" category. Answers to them can, and must, be found for every remote worker, and the clearer the expectations set around time spent with each person and the preferred channels of communication, the better. I will address my own approaches to some of these issues throughout the article.

There is an additional category of questions which I have found more interesting, and also more provocative. Are we remote employees defined as "other," whether consciously or otherwise, by colleagues (and bosses)? Are we in fact "remote" in ways other than our home zip codes? Does that even matter? How much should we (can we) seek from the company for support? Should the company accommodate us more than it already does? And what is our role in participating in, transmitting, or challenging firm values and culture?

First, though: what does how I feel when I wake up have to do with this?

HOME IS WHERE THE HUSBAND IS—OR THE FRIENDLY FRONT-DESK CLERK

As noted above, the sense of fragmentation and disjuncture described as part of the remote–mobile worker experience manifests in multiple sites and contexts (physical, social, work, home). For me, where I am physically located at a specific time mediates my emotional or psychological response to events around me, and is often the trigger for feelings of fragmentation. An excellent example of this is what happens routinely to me during that liminal time between waking and sleeping. I regularly wake up in the middle of the night and either do not know where I am, or I mistake my location. Alone in the hotel room bed, I reach across for my husband, thinking I am at home; finding him absent makes me realize "oh, not at home." Conversely, when on the odd occasion he is in the hotel room bed, I mistake the hotel for home, and, disoriented, trip on furniture en route to the bathroom. But sometimes I wake up at home and do not know where I am. For a split second I believe myself to be in a hotel room, I know not where. I'm not sure which I find more disconcerting—the mistaking of hotel for home, or vice-versa.

With regard to my actual house and time spent there, I have developed what I believe to be a disproportionate passion for just being (t)here. I limit other leisure travel time to spend time at home, feeling that I can never "get enough." I plan vacation days, sometimes weeks, just to spend time at home. When traveling for leisure, if the time does not count as high-quality time (hiking in Maine with my husband versus fulfilling onerous family obligations), I find myself resenting the time away and literally counting the hours until I get back.

Among all the hotels where I do stay each year, the one that occupies "home away from home" status for me is the one in D.C. where I stay each week, literally a stone's throw from my firm's offices. Depending on the direction my hotel room faces, I can even see colleagues at their desks. I stay there two nights every week when in D.C.; the front desk clerk knows my name and habits and always tries to secure a larger room for me. This is also where the majority of remote workers from my company stay when in town; so, in spite of the fancy carpet, lighting, and flowers, it always feels a bit like a dormitory to me. We run into each other while working out in the gym, picking up carry-out Chinese in the lobby, or creeping around the lobby at dawn in search of coffee (this can become particularly tricky because our clients most often stay at this same hotel and early morning business meetings are often scheduled with them in the hotel restaurant; I have learned to be extremely mindful of what I say anywhere on the hotel property). We get together in each others' rooms to watch bad TV over a glass of wine.

On the one hand, seeing familiar faces in a hotel has a way of adding a certain degree of comfort and warmth to that commercial, not-home space. On the other hand, that work colleagues are making it feel "like home" seems somehow wrong or, at least, not quite right. Even as I experience the momentary pleasure of a familiar face, or a warm greeting, I simultaneously resist the feelings, not wanting to accept the implication—that work colleagues are providing a sense of "home." And that there is literally "no escape" from work even at hours when I feel I should get a respite.

ABSENCE MAKES THE HEART GROW FONDER

As to the Philadelphia community, my "home" in a larger sense, after two years as a resident here I am still distant. Our "key buddy" is our general contractor, with whom I have talked from all coasts and time zones as he has worked to get our house in living condition while my husband and I travel. When he installed a sump pump in the basement he insisted on including an extra battery, because "you two travel so much that I don't want you calling me from the road when it floods and telling me to go over there and turn on the sump!" Two years in, we still only have four (wonderful) friends here. With an extensive network of friends along the East Coast (many of whom find Pennsylvania an easier trip than D.C.), the fact of "four friends" bothers me less than the challenge of being able to sink myself into the community in a meaningful way. With three weeknights effectively "out" because of my regular travel schedule (not even counting irregular client travel), it limits my range of potential activities, whether a yoga class or sitting on the board of a local organization (what I had done in D.C., and for which weekly meetings after work were required). My main community involvement currently is with my local civic association, which meets once a month and much of whose work can be done via e-mail. I enjoy this work and am grateful to have the opportunity to do it.

But it makes me wonder about remote/mobile workers' loss of connection with their communities, and the associated costs to those communities.[2] Take voting as an example. How many remote–mobile workers vote? Growing up, my father hammered into me the importance of this civic ritual; as a result, for my entire life, no matter where I have lived—Taiwan, Hong Kong, Chicago, New Haven—I always ensured either that I was registered locally or that I had planned ahead for a timely arrival of an absentee ballot, so I could participate. This past fall, although the voting booth stood walking distance from my home, I had to vote absentee because I was traveling that day. Getting the ballot from Pennsylvania's arcane bureaucracy proved arduous (in fact more difficult and time-consuming than when I lived in Taiwan). I believe only the most persistent would-be voter could have done it, and that most would just give up.

On the other side of the equation, my ties in the Washington area remain strong. As I am physically present nearly every week, I have many opportunities to maintain them. I regularly see D.C. friends for dinner and occasionally can participate in family events involving my sisters, nieces, and nephew, all of whom live in the area. I missed the cherry blossoms in Philadelphia but had the chance to participate in that quintessential D.C. experience this spring, one evening after work just walking over to the National Mall from my hotel. Good, right? It was certainly memorable, especially shared with one of my closest friends. But in the past, in D.C. this was a spring ritual with my husband and one of the things I associated most deeply with living in that area; in ten years in the D.C area I had never once missed it. My sense of enjoyment this year was tinged with a bit of guilt for not having created a similar opportunity for myself in Philadelphia, and for "giving in" to my urge to continue to connect with D.C.

ABSENCE MAKES THE HEAD WORK HARDER

With regard to the office, I am acutely aware of the impact that being a remote employee has on how I spend my time in the office. On the one hand, I must ensure that I schedule time for certain critical meetings (with my direct reports; with my teams at key checkpoints; and with my boss). My personal management style is to have regular meetings with every team member on a weekly or biweekly basis, so I know how they are doing and so they feel they have "access to senior management" (a key indicator our human resources department is always eyeing on employee engagement surveys). This drives me to prioritize ruthlessly. I keep a hard watch on my calendar and will reschedule or put off people who are not at the top of my list for "in person" meetings.[3] If I need time with someone in person, I am relentless in pressing their assistant to find time for me for the hour I need. As a result of this (and of a meetings-heavy culture), I am typically scheduled in meetings back to back when in our D.C. office, sometimes for ten or twelve hours in a row. On the other hand, I try each week to create opportunities for that informal contact—"water cooler chat"—so critical both to finding out what is really going on in any office environment and also to providing a certain kind of glue to the office community. It is not unusual to find me taking the long way 'round to a meeting just to stop in at teammates' cubes, or poke my head into people's offices for a quick "what's up?"

I have found that "face time," especially with the boss and other senior executives, is more precious than ever, and that ensuring I get that time takes planning and, occasionally, more time away from home than I prefer. The truth is that, with the demands on our firm's senior leaders' travel schedules, I am physically present in the office as much or more than most of my peers who live in the D.C. area. But, for example, meetings of our senior management group (20 percent of whom are remote) are typically scheduled on Fridays—a day that mobile (but not remote) workers tend to be in the office. So at times I have traveled to D.C. just for these meetings—calling in just is not good enough. I know from experience I need to be "seen" for it to "count."

I was surprised when I first went remote to find that my boss of many years preferred not to schedule certain meetings or have certain kinds of conversations by phone. And I was likewise surprised to discover his penchant for leaving me lengthy voicemails, and occasionally sending e-mails, about things I would much prefer to have talked about in person. Over time this abated significantly, with my boss—aware that I am nearly always on e-mail—growing accustomed to sending me messages with "can you talk for a minute?" in the subject line. If available I would always call immediately. I know how much he would prefer to have been able to walk down to my office for that chat—but I appreciated the willingness to adopt a practice that enabled us to get that "real-time" interaction. (Observing his conversing with his children via "instant-messaging," or live text-messaging, I considered asking if he would be willing to set up an instant-message chat with me but never did.) Having now just started a new role with a new boss, my challenge (I have learned) is to "train" him to understand that even when I am not physically in the office, I am working full-time. (When we started working together he asked me directly, "Tell me again what days you are full-time?")

In a place with 950 people and growing, it is hard to know everyone and see everyone on a regular basis. So I should not care whether random people I only ever see in the elevator know if I am remote. But I do! I have realized that I feel a tiny prick of pride every time someone spots me in the elevator with my suitcase and says "where to today?" and I explain "back home to Philadelphia" and they respond with surprise: "Really? I had no idea you were remote. It seems you are always here." Secretly I'm thinking, "Ha! Fooled them."

But why the need to fool them? As no doubt it is apparent to the reader, I feel defensive about my remote status, and a strong need to prove that I am spending sufficient time in the office. And, I also feel a need to prove I am spending my time usefully when at home, too. In this, I am not alone; this urge is, in fact, the norm among professionals who spend any time working from home, especially so among females. Susan Halford describes this phenomenon among workers from Insurance Co. (who split their time between headquarters and working from home):

> These individuals were acutely aware of the symbolism that the domestic carries—as a place of rest, pleasure and private activities—and have readily responded to a perceived need to

> prove themselves far more than they would do within organisational space. In organisational space, bodily presence implies a working body. Bodily absence, and especially location in the domestic, is intrinsically subject to suspicion, something that these respondents took evasive action to avoid. [2005:26]

Thus, while the literature about teleworkers and "homeworkers" describes problems with motivation and productivity, this is not the norm among professionals who work remotely. However, as demonstrated in the quote above, it turns out my neurotic need to prove myself is.

THE BOUNDARY BLUR OF HOME-WORK

The quote above provides context for discussion about the issue of work done at home. For many people, working at home presents a challenge of keeping the two spheres separate. There is the issue of physical space and of carving out time from family responsibilities for work. And the issue of simply working too much because people have a hard time "shutting work down" when it is right down the hall:

> Working from home means you tend to put in far more hours than you would if you were working in an office. You may also lose track of time without colleagues around you to remind you its lunch or home time, and you may not be able to resist "just checking my emails" in the evening or at weekends, and bang, there goes another three hours. [Burdett 2007]

I am fortunate to have a specific place in my home that is "the office." I do not have to set up a desk in the living room or dining room as some people do, and, as it turns out, I rarely work in places other than my office when at home. But it is my home office too—materials related to my job commingle on the desk with grocery lists, notes to the plumber, and the flower seeds I plan to plant who knows when. I have become uncomfortably accustomed to hearing colleagues' voices through the same phone routinely used to call my mother-in-law; in fact, call waiting might cause me to be on the phone with both of them at once. It is one thing to do work at home; it is another to welcome people to join you at home-work via phone, fax, and videoconferencing. Hearing the boss's voice wafting over the speaker phone where a few moments before the cat perched is humorous, but disconcerting. In this way, the physical space of office work has merged with (at least part of) my home space. Is it an invasion? An infection? Suzanne Tietze and Gill Musson use strong language to discuss this phenomenon: "the private sphere has the potential to become colonized by the more dominant vocabulary and practices of industry" (2005:1337). Colonization, invasion, infection—for me, these words fail to capture the reality of the experience because, in truth, I both want and indeed seek the intrusion. I want the office to know I am "on;" I am not sitting here gazing out the window or worse. I am working!

ROUTINES CREATE AN ILLUSION OF CONTROL—BUT THEN THERE'S TONY

A coping strategy I have developed in response to the fragmentation (and that I believe most "successful" mobile workers do) is a series of routines for both home and travel.

People who travel infrequently typically express astonishment at the many little routines we regular travelers have. My suitcase is ever packed with airplane-friendly liquid containers and a few extra quart bags, boarding pass or Acela ticket printed in advance; all I need is to throw in the latest clothes back from the dry cleaner and I am off. At the office I replicate as much about home routines as I can—work out every day (gym shoes live there); cereal for breakfast; a complete replica of my home pharmacy stashed in my desk drawer. Routines make the chaos of travel feel controlled—if I just follow the routine, I will not forget something. I will have what I need. I will not feel stressed out. The need to stick to routine is now a craving, a crutch to stave off the sense of dislocation that otherwise might pervade my mental space. By now, my "remote" routine is set—to D.C. Monday on the 7:15 a.m. Acela train; two nights at the hotel; back to Philly Wednesday on the 6:00 p.m. Acela. But add the reality of the mobile work requirements, such as travel for client meetings, and it can push me too far—wake up in too many unique beds in one week, and the routines falter. Clothes are forgotten in hotel room closets, phone chargers left who knows where. And did I forget my niece's birthday? Sure. (Every time I hear an ad for one of those "virtual assistant" services I make a mental note to sign up for just this reason—but never get around to it.) Liminal night time provides yet another challenge to routine; superego's message of "exercise, dinner, early to bed" struggles against the pull of a colleague's suggestion of dinner out; or of my TV pal Tony Soprano, from the TV show *The Sopranos,* beckoning to join my room service dinner.

At home, I take care to make sure that the things of most importance do not get taken over by the urge "to just keep on working a few more minutes." I block my calendar for the hours I plan to attend a gym class, even though it occurs during regular work hours; I compensate on my days home by starting work especially early. If a teammate (or boss) suggests a phone meeting starting at 5 p.m. on Friday (not unusual, unfortunately), I politely try to push them to an early morning time instead; if that fails, I let them know ahead of time I have a "hard stop" at 5:30 (because of a weekly appointment my husband and I have with our ballroom dance teacher). I confess to feeling a bit odd about what I prioritize (the gym and ballroom dancing), but both are necessary to help me manage stress, feel good physically, and have fun with my husband—all of which are, in fact, incredibly important to me.

THE CHALLENGE OF FORGING, AND SUSTAINING, CULTURAL TIES THAT BIND

Earlier I proposed that as a remote–mobile worker I face a set of more abstract questions about my relationship to the firm as a whole. Specifically:

1. What role can, and should, the remote–mobile worker play in bearing and transmitting organizational culture? What is a realistic expectation for the firm to have? Is there room to expand the locations, times, and opportunities for culture transmission (from face-to-face interactions to the virtual workspace, for example)?
2. To what extent does the remote–mobile worker become excluded from the corporate events and rituals that reinforce, invigorate and evolve corporate culture? Can or should they take steps to avoid this? Related to this is the "identity" remote workers occupy in the collective consciousness of their "regular" colleagues. Do local colleagues perceive remote colleagues as receiving special treatment? Less able to "climb the corporate ladder"?
3. Can, or should, remote–mobile workers evolve their own subculture? If a subculture develops of its own accord, should the firm support or discourage this?

I have realized that my own position brings these questions particularly to the foreground. As someone whose profession by definition is to explore culture (as well as a skeptic by nature of all things "group"), I rarely am able to disengage the urge to critique and analyze the norms and values around me, and this at times has made me the most unhappy of corporate citizens. But as one of the managers responsible for both transmitting a specific corporate culture as well as being a standard-bearer for it, I feel responsible to engage these questions and find answers that will satisfy both me and the firm. I have wrestled with these issues since I first joined the firm, and particularly so since becoming a member of the firm's elected management group. This is not to say I do not support my firm's values; in fact I am, perhaps surprisingly so, one of the firm culture's most avid supporters and defenders. But now, with the added challenge that being a remote employee brings to the mix, I find that pursuing these answers has a new urgency and importance for both me, and the company as a whole.

For my company, the issue of culture and whether remote employees can "get it" and "keep it" has been of central concern as we have begun to expand our remote ranks. In fact, we typically will not hire someone who lives remotely into a "content" role—only people who have worked at headquarters and proven themselves over time are allowed to then go remote. For full-time mobile workers, the situation is different; as mentioned earlier, their roles keep them on the road most of the time anyway, so where they live is of less consequence. For all employees, the human resources department conducts an extensive orientation to the company and its culture, including a two-hour speech by our lead national speaker, videos, and an extensive review of the company's founding and history. In addition to participating in this program of orientation, most mobile employees are required to spend all of their first two months in the office, in hopes that they will "attach" to the culture and soak up enough to sustain them once they go on the road.

I cannot presume to assess the role or importance of "culture" at other firms, but I can say with certainty that "culture" is extremely important where I work. It is also a site of active engagement and, sometimes, struggle. The culture and values are referenced by new hires ("I was attracted by the values you have stated on the public website"), by us in debate with each other ("That just isn't who we are"), and in assessing new products and services ("Given who we are, is that what our clients would expect from us?").

Our culture, brought to life through our values and our behavior to each other and our clients, is integral to our value proposition in the marketplace. The concept of service, which runs throughout the firm principles and values, pervades the language of every interaction we have with clients and influences our colleague and peer interactions. We try to hire for this quality, but it is only through constant observation and interaction with key culture bearers (e.g., senior leaders) that more junior staff can see these values in action and receive feedback on their own efforts to master the language and behaviors associated with our culture.

As a remote–mobile worker I struggle with my role in this effort. Returning to the three questions I posed above, one issue is the ability to fulfill my responsibility to my junior staff to make sure they know what it means to work at our firm. To address this I use formal channels as much as possible, scheduling regular check-in meetings for days I am in the office; sitting in on client interviews led by junior staff and giving them immediate feedback; and taking time to explicitly talk with them about our standards for communication and behavior with each other and clients. I have found this works best when I have a trusted "number two" whom I can rely on to run interference if needed, to check in on people when I am absent, and to help reinforce the messages we both agree need to be communicated. Currently, working with an entirely new team, I have no such person (yet).

The second question relates to finding my place in the larger culture. I have already discussed some of the scheduling challenges related to the senior management team meetings. Additionally, there are firmwide events, participation in which I naturally resist (see above, re: natural skeptic) but at which it "counts to be seen." I have also found that in spite of myself, in the end I enjoy and value these large gatherings, if only because it is fascinating to see how we re-present ourselves to ourselves each time we convene as a whole. These events are natural watersheds in our evolution in meaning-making. Time and schedule are, as ever for the remote worker, the issue—is this valuable enough for me to spend another precious night at home away? Does my attendance mean I will have to push other work to the night or weekend? Will anyone even know I attended?

Beyond that is the role of our firm in the local community of Washington, D.C. Our firm has an exceptional commitment both to supporting individual volunteer work and to encouraging the entire firm's participation in a number of major service events a year. Recently I filled out a survey from the internal group whose job is to support all of our volunteer activities (and that tracks our participation, then awarding a certain number of hours or even days off, at the end of the year, in recognition of our efforts). Filling the survey out made me realize that I have never participated in one of the firm-wide service events; the majority of them occur on weekends, and I have not been willing to give up a weekend at home for it, even though in the weeks before these events each year the CEO personally implores each of us to "come out and join in" and though there are prizes for the division inside the firm with the highest participation rate. I have already discussed here my own challenges in finding meaningful local volunteer work in my new home community. This ideal is so important to the firm's identity it is committed to paper in the firm values ("In Service to Our Community"). Yet with my work life and home life dispersed across two zip codes, fulfilling this ideal has been hard.

And then there are all of those other smaller events which contribute to the interstitial glue that holds the group together. These events also provide chances for informal conversations and networking that are important in a 360-degree sort of way (junior staff relish a chance to see me "let my hair down" with a drink or at the bowling alley after hours; for myself, I relish the chance for informal chats with some rarely seen peers around the firm; and, then, we are all always trying to network with the higher-ups, even if we are, in a sense, one of them. There is always someone higher.) But, once again, the remote worker's schedule interferes with and often prevents these interactions. Firmwide happy hours for example, happen twice a month—only on Fridays, a day remote folks are almost never in the office (or if they are, they have left for home by earlier than 5:30 p.m. so they can arrive home with at least a bit of Friday night remaining).

Finally, how to define what goes on among remote workers and how others perceive them at the firm? Above, I asked whether remote workers can, or should, develop their own "subculture." At my firm, I could imagine, for example, a working group of remote employees trading best practices in staff management, lobbying for purchase of videoconferencing equipment, and ensuring that our typical schedules are taken into consideration when firm-wide events are scheduled. This would be, then, more of an advocacy group, not a "subculture." But should remote workers have an "advocacy group"? Does that not just serve to highlight our otherness, and maybe even our "specialness"? Also it would imply a level of support for remote employees that perhaps the human resources department would prefer to keep quiet, not wishing to further encourage employees to "go remote."

In my own situation I have noticed the development of a sense of "us" among a group of very close colleagues who are remote. For this small group, there is occasional kvetching about the challenges we experience because of being remote. I also find myself having a greater number of private, although work-related, conversations with my remote colleagues; we seem more comfortable talking about work away from the physical, official workspace and take advantage of the out-of-office time to deal with matters we might find uncomfortable talking about in the office (see Halford 2005, for a discussion of this phenomenon). When talking with other remote colleagues from across the firm (not in my specific division), discussions tend to be more around management strategies for our teams. But all of these conversations form or strengthen connections among a particular group, a group which transcends formal organizational hierarchies and divisions, and which creates an "other" inside the totality of the firm. Although I cherish the connections with like-minded colleagues, I question whether this sense of otherness is good for the firm as a whole.

CONCLUSION

Through an exploration of the sites across which my physical body travels between home and work, I have highlighted the sense of disjuncture I routinely experience both at home and at work, investigated some of the reasons behind that experience, and described responses and strategies I have developed as a consequence of my situation. The exploration has caused me to delve much deeper into a number of issues I now am aware I had ignored with regard to my personal situation for some time. For example, in rereading this essay I was struck by the theme of "sufficiency." On the one hand, I am unable ever to "get enough" of home time; on the other, I fret over whether I am working enough either at home or in the office. The theme of course is not unusual in people trying to balance work and life overall—but suggests that remote work is not an antidote to that challenge. This work also heightened my curiosity about the larger community both at my firm, and beyond, of remote workers. As a result, I have already proposed to our human resources executive a wider research study at my firm among our remote workers to test the hypotheses brought forward here.

Seeking to understand "what is happening to me" and "where I fit in," I have read widely in the literature about remote workers, teleworkers, and homeworkers. One chief conclusion is that much remains to be done in advancing and clarifying the definitions of these categories, all of which seem to be in nearly constant evolution at the moment. As well, the boundaries of class, role, ethnicity, and gender are implicated heavily in this work and bear further investigation. However, in reading the literature, the description I found which best described my response to my own situation at this moment on the cusp of the 21st century, as I struggle (still) with 19th-century ideas about home and work, came from Frederic Jameson (1991).[4] Jameson's idea of "postmodern hyperspace" strikes me as particularly apt in describing the situation of us remote workers who are conducting our business in "hybrid space." He used the term *postmodern hyperspace* as a way of describing spaces which have "transcend[ed] the capacities of the individual human body to locate itself, to organize its immediate surroundings perceptually, and cognitively to map its position in a mappable external world" (1991:44). Although Jameson drew the idea from a description of a physical structure, the idea describes perfectly the physical sensation of having work and home dispersed across multiple physical locations: an inability to determine a fixed mapping of one's self to the external world, a constant effort to locate, to situate, to position, to say definitively "this is where I am."

NOTES

1. The Blue Company is a pseudonym.

2. The "lack of engagement" in a remote physical community is a well-known artifact of modern work patterns in the larger context of globalization. That said, I would argue that while there is some similarity to what I describe here, to try to claim that my situation relates to (or is caused by) globalization would be inaccurate.

3. As an aside, I believe that doing this since I became a remote employee has significantly improved my time management skills; I try hard to adhere to Stephen Covey's (1990) directive that we should focus most

of our time on "quadrant 2" activities, those that are important but that we continually put off because they are not an immediate crisis, instead of the daily crises that force themselves on us.

4. I am indebted to the work of Claudia Strauss (1997) for stimulating my thinking about fragmentation and the relevance of Jameson's work to my understanding about the impact of being a remote–mobile worker on my own subjectivity.

REFERENCES CITED

Baba, Marietta, Julia Gluesing, Hilary Ratner, and Kimberly H. Wagner

2004 The Contexts of Knowing: Natural History of a Globally Distributed Team. Journal of Organizational Behavior 25(5):547–587.

Brodt, Torsten, and Robert Verburg

2007 Managing Mobile Work—Insights from European Practice. New Technology, Work and Employment 22(1):52–65.

Burdett, Claire

2007 The Home Working Revolution. Electronic document, http://www.ecademy.com/node.php?id=84521, accessed August 18.

Covey, Stephen R.

1990 The Seven Habits of Highly Effective People. New York: Free Press.

Halford, Susan

2005 Hybrid Workspace: Re-Spatialisations of Work, Organisation and Management. New Technology, Work and Employment 20(1):19–33.

Jameson, Frederic

1991 Postmodernism, or, The Cultural Logic of Late Capitalism. Durham, NC: Duke University Press.

Peake, Linda

1994 Engendering Change: Women's Work and the Development of Urban–Social Theory. *In* Women, Work, and Place. Audrey Kobayashi, ed., Pp. 3–26. Montreal: McGill-Queen's University Press.

Strauss, Claudia

1997 Partly Fragmented, Partly Integrated: An Anthropological Examination of "Postmodern Fragmented Subjects." Cultural Anthropology 12(3):362–404.

Tietze, Susanne, and Gill Musson

2005 Recasting the Home-Work Relationship: A Case of Mutual Adjustment? Organization Studies 26(9):1331–1352.

Wasson, Christina

2006 Being in Two Spaces at Once: Virtual Meetings and Their Representation. Journal of Linguistic Anthropology 16(1):103–130.

DISENTANGLING PATTERNS OF A NOMADIC LIFE

TRACY L. MEERWARTH
Cultural Anthropologist and Contract Researcher, General Motors Corporation, Detroit, Michigan and Owner, Consolidated Bearings Company, Cedar Knolls, New Jersey

As a corporate anthropologist who studies how work gets accomplished in the spaces and places workers inhabit, I have become keenly aware of the patterns of behaviors and emotions that arise from my experience as a nomadic worker. The term nomadic comprehends the multiple and geographically distributed sites across a landscape where work gets accomplished. The term suggests a rhythm of movement during which time workers are enabled by technology to pull away from a centralized core and travel across the landscape with homes and work on their backs. In this article, I explore reconceptualizations of physical space (e.g., home, away, and transitional) and the shifting changes in relationships (e.g., with communities, friends), which emerge with my increased mobility. I argue that although the media illustrates the seamlessness and ease of social integration and mobility that technology offers, it is often a distortion of a nomadic worker's reality. Personal conflict and tension often arise when trying to manage culturally valued concepts such as integration and mobility simultaneously. I deconstruct my conflict and identify areas for growth in my experience as a nomadic worker.
Keywords: nomadic worker, mobility, integration, cultural conflict, distributed work

Walking through Newark International Airport en route to my gate, I am bombarded with advertisements heralding images of popular mobile handhelds and new network devices. They are products that claim to increase my efficiency, protect my privacy, and boost my speed of data transfer. They also tout that I can work from almost anywhere with ease and peace (see Figure 1). Technology and the products that span our vast ubiquitous computing universe are advertised as fun and effective tools for getting work done and staying connected with others.

Born from large capital investments in science and innovation, our society embraces devices that enable us to be mobile while staying connected with others. For example, BlackBerry, the wireless, handheld device introduced in the United States in 1999 integrates e-mail, acts as a mobile telephone, offers text messaging, and allows you to browse the web. Similarly, Apple Computer earned the spotlight more recently with its July 2007 debut of the iPhone, which sold 270,000 units in the United States in the first 30 hours it was on the market! Mobile workers can thank much of their ability to receive consolidated information as they roam freely in part to developments in technology innovation.

I am part of a growing number of knowledge workers that are taking advantage of these new technologies and opting to work in unconventional spaces and away from the

NAPA BULLETIN 30, pp. 102–117. ISSN: 1556-4789.
DOI:10.1111/j.1556-4797.2008.00022.x

FIGURE 1. Advertising ubiquitous computing. (Photo by Tracy L. Meerwarth.)

traditional workplace.[1] For the past six years I have worked as a contract researcher for General Motors Research and Development (GM R and D). By choice, and with the support of my coworkers, I am not tied to a specific geographic location for very long. I conduct my work at a distance from GM R and D located in Warren, Michigan. There are several terms used to describe people who are mobile and work in nontraditional work settings, including remote, distributed, and independent. I associate most closely with the term *nomadic worker* because it is more representative of my experiences.[2] It comprehends the multiple and geographically distributed sites across a landscape where people are able to accomplish work. The term reaches beyond the image of a worker at home or on frequent business trips and captures the dynamic of that worker traveling down similar paths and grounding themselves in familiar places for long periods of time. It also suggests a rhythm of patterned movement where the worker is enabled by technology to pull away from a centralized core and roam across the landscape with home and work on their backs.

The reality is that workers such as myself are largely faced with figuring out how to manage mobility on their own. By managing I mean working through a variety of logistical and emotional challenges including how to collaborate with colleagues at a distance and how to stay present (e.g., socially and emotionally involved and connected) in the lives of friends and loved ones. There are no guidelines for behavior or advice columns that address the complexities of the mobile experience; thus, I have learned about mobility generally by pairing my experiences with observations of the world around me. Specifically, I have taken note of how mobility is being advertised in public commuter areas such as airport terminals, airport lounges, on highway billboards, and in train stations. Because these advertisements suggest what the product, lifestyle, or experience (in this case, mobility) is "supposed" to be like, they are tools that can be used to compare one's personal experience. In general, I have found that advertisers build specific assumptions into the mobile experience thereby distorting the challenging process of leading an integrated life while simultaneously being mobile. I came to realize these representations of experiences and assumptions about our social environment oversimplify the surrounding context of what a mobile worker is like. I use these examples, not to criticize the advertising companies, but as a point of departure for the patterns I have begun to disentangle in my life as a nomadic worker.

Some characteristics of nomadic work are constant movement and circling back to familiar places. This repetition of patterned behavior has allowed me to analyze the patterns of my lived experiences. In this article, I argue that two highly valued cultural concepts, mobility and integration, are not as seamless as advertised by some. I illustrate with examples, how managing mobility and integration involves a process of experiencing and resolving tension and conflict as a nomadic worker. I deconstruct this conflict and identify areas for growth in my experience as a nomadic worker. In conclusion, I argue that anthropologists are well-suited for understanding and contributing valuable insights into this type of work.

CULTURAL VALUES AND ILLUSIONS OF MOBILITY

Although advertisements often target a specific commodity, some advertisements are trying to sell a commodity paired with a particular "lifestyle" (Goldman 1992; Williamson 1978). Advertisements carry assumptions about what life can "be" and "feel" like when purchasing or consuming the product (Goldman 1992; Marchand 1985; Messaris 1997). For example, the choice of colors in advertisements, the way people look, are dressed, and the behaviors they exhibit often convey a particular ideology or point of view (Fowles 1996). Thus, advertisements are the product of taking assumptions about our culture and producing artful social texts (Fowles 1996; Goldman 1992) that resonate with consumers.

EASE AND SEAMLESSNESS

I have found that the media largely portray romantic, social depictions of workers' mobile experiences. Typically in an advertisement involving this type of worker, technology is enabling a successful execution of work, data transfer, and interaction with others while that individual is away from a centralized workspace, coworkers, and boss. For example, we see no struggle with technology or with family relationships in Figure 2.

In fact, the mother and child each appear to be at ease and having fun. The social text from this advertisement suggests that mobile technology and the act of being mobile

FIGURE 2. An illusion of ease.

is serving to reinforce highly regarded U.S. cultural values such as self-reliance (Hsu 1961), independence (Trice and Beyer 1993), and freedom (Mirchandani 2000) for both the mother and child. It also suggests that the technology being used is helping to support highly held organizational values of availability, responsiveness, and commitment (Hochschild 1997; Middleton 2007; Perlow 1997; Williams 1970) by allowing the mother to be "on" and available, even at the beach! Technology is easily and effectively enabling the mother to simultaneously enjoy her vacation, her child, and the satisfaction of completing her work. This feeling of being "integrated" with family and work is affirmed by the lines of text in the advertisement that convey a sense that she is ticking items off her mental list and accomplishing each one with success.

Figure 3 is similar in that the advertisement for this phone exemplifies the smooth transition from work to play that is so often portrayed as part of the mobile experience.

FIGURE 3. An illusion of seamlessness.

The task of emailing a senior coworker (e.g., CEO) via a mobile device while roaming around the golf course is accomplished without a glitch.

Ideally, the owner of this device can experience freedom of movement through recreation and uphold the organizational cultural value of productivity while being away from the confines of their physical office.

Based on my observations of print media, integration and mobility appear to be strongly held cultural values in North America.[3] They are often advertised as supporting one another with the implied claim that mobility leads to contact and integration (e.g., feeling and being connected to a group) whether it is with family, friends, work, or other communities of which we are a part. The process of integration via mobility suggests that barriers such as distance and time are eliminated—bringing people together in unrestricted and equal association. For example, in Figure 4, the telecommunications company is advertising the ease of their network interfacing with a woman's mobile phone. The network supports the woman's desire and need to be connected with "home" (e.g., friends, family, and the like) while at a distance. Although the woman in this advertisement is probably a college student or young professional, she could easily be substituted with a colleague, partner, boss, or coworker trying to touch base with the office.

Thus, it is clear that the cultural values of mobility and integration are reaffirmed at the individual and organizational levels. My experiences suggest, however, that the process of achieving these two cultural values is more difficult than illustrated by the media, particularly when one is nomadic. What the advertisements do not comprehend

FIGURE 4. Advertising the ease of mobility and social integration. (Photo by Tracy L. Meerwarth.)

is the struggle associated with trying to be integrated in a variety of ways while on the move and accomplishing work.

THE JOURNEY TOWARD MOBILITY

I conceptualize my journey toward mobility in four stages. In general, there was a progression away from a centralized place of work, thereby opening up a multiplicity of places from which work could be accomplished. Similarly, relationships, both personal and professional, shifted from being collocated to being distributed across vast geographical distances. A more formal, structured workday gave way to a lifestyle that entertained the comingling of work and nonrelated work tasks.

Working for Consolidated Bearings Company

My work experience began in a traditional setting after college. I worked as an inside sales representative at my family business, Consolidated Bearings Company (Consolidated). I answered phone calls from customers, helped resolve product questions, and checked product availability. Our corporate sales office and warehouse were collocated in New Jersey. Consequently, all of the sales tools we needed to accomplish work, including daily inventory runs, engineering manuals, product interchanges, and coworkers' expertise were located within our physical reach. The culture was one in which formal and informal information was transmitted between employees and managers just by being there.

The workday at Consolidated had a visible structure. The hours of business were 8:30 a.m. to 5:30 p.m. Monday through Friday. Although orders were processed after hours and on the weekends, it did not require the entire organization to be open 24 hours a day, seven days a week. Because my job in sales did not require me to work beyond the allotted working hours, my time after work and on weekends was predictable and my own. Most of my friends and family were collocated in New Jersey, and my ties to them were easily maintained by frequent visits and planned events.

Pursuing Graduate School in Applied Anthropology

In 2000, I took a leave from my family business in New Jersey to pursue my master's degree in anthropology at Northern Arizona University in Flagstaff, Arizona. My time, the type of work, and my work style changed dramatically. Rather than being forced into set times and spaces within which to do work, I had the choice of when, how, and where to study (e.g., graduate lab, coffeehouse, apartment, library). I was also working differently than when I was at Consolidated. Instead of processing orders and problem solving for customers, I was engaged in independent, analytical tasks such as conducting data analysis, developing research designs, and preparing presentations. I was largely engaged in heads-down work,[4] activities such as writing and reading that reflect the characteristics of a knowledge worker.

The increased flexibility associated with time and space enabled me to design a lifestyle where I was able to balance nonwork related activities with work tasks. For example, my apartment was situated near a golf course and hiking trails, which allowed me to take a break from writing, meet with friends, exercise for a few hours, and then get back to work again. This type of lifestyle in which activities were interspersed with work throughout the day was something I could not take advantage of in a traditional job setting.

Shifting from a collaborative sales position to working on individual research projects in graduate school did have an impact on my relationships. Although I did meet up with friends in classes several times a week, much of our work was done individually and at different field sites. In addition, we chose to study in different venues and some of us had accepted jobs off campus. Consequently, there were days and weeks that would go by without seeing any classmates at all. The more we were dispersed, the greater the motivation we had to reconnect. When we did plan to get together, these events were generally used as a forum for venting about class work and reaffirming that you were not going through the graduate school experience alone!

During graduate school I was fortunate to work as a summer intern at GM R and D in Warren, Michigan. I began my work with GM in a traditional work setting and gradually became more mobile and remote. I was hired as a cultural anthropologist to work on a team that would study organizational issues and offer recommendations to internal GM business units such as R and D and manufacturing. Traveling to different locations was particularly critical to getting work done because our interviews and observations were done in situ with study participants. Thus, most of the fieldwork we conducted occurred at different sites, while the analysis and writing was done in our individual offices in Warren.

When I returned to graduate school I remained connected with my GM colleagues through the continuation of our research project. Project discussions, planning, and writing were all done at a distance. I believe that successfully working at a distance from my colleagues in Warren set the stage for working more remotely when I was hired into a full-time contract researcher position following my graduation in 2002.

Beginning a Professional Research Career at GM R and D

I recognized that I faced a difficult decision when accepting a position at GM R and D in 2002. Although I was passionate about working at R and D and excited about being a researcher alongside other accomplished anthropologists, I had to negotiate strong ties to New Jersey, including my family and my family business. I considered leaving New Jersey and moving to Michigan. However, that did not feel very good in terms of nurturing my relationship with Consolidated, and that option was eliminated. I also considered not taking the position in Michigan and remaining in New Jersey, but reconsidered that option based on the excitement to finally be able to pursue my passion for anthropology in an applied business setting.

In the end, I decided that I would propose to my manager and project principal investigator (PI) that I would commute to Michigan every few weeks from New Jersey. They agreed to the proposal on the condition that there would be no issues with my performance and that I would shoulder the expenses of travel. From my perspective, remaining connected to both GM R and D and Consolidated made sense and was worth the increased financial burden. For several years this meant splitting time between an apartment that I rented in Michigan and a condominium that I owned in New Jersey. I spent two weeks of every month in Michigan because we were conducting fieldwork and needed to be physically present in the research locations (e.g., automotive plants, research facilities). Traveling between New Jersey and Michigan enabled me to be part of my work team (while located in Michigan) and close to my friends and family at home (while located in New Jersey), although it became increasingly difficult to "feel" as if I was truly connected and integrated with both. It was hard to be tightly connected to the team while also being regarded as a "dependable" friend and family member, given my desire to belong and be present in two places at once. Being "neither here nor there" created a sense of discomfort because often there was interesting and exciting work that I would miss out on in Michigan, or I would have to forgo social events in New Jersey because I was always in the process of moving or had already left.

Transitioning to a Nomadic Worker at GM R and D

Mobility and the distribution of researchers continue to characterize our team at GM R and D to this day. The composition of our team has changed, but at our height, three out of six of us were working remotely from Arizona, Colorado, and New Jersey. The only person living and working in Michigan as a salaried GM employee was and currently is our PI. This makes attending annual professional anthropology conferences (e.g., Society for Applied Anthropology, American Anthropological Association) and scheduling trips to Michigan critical to upholding a sense of team and continuity of work.

My physical time at GM R and D has decreased over the past several years, but I continue to work at a distance. I also attribute this shift in "presence" away from Michigan to the nature of our current work tasks (e.g., writing research reports, patents) and a change in fieldwork sites. We have fieldwork projects now that require travel to Bangalore, India for example. Although these sites are not located in Michigan, they are GM R and D satellite organizations. I also attribute my increase in mobility to the excitement that results from experiencing and investigating new ways of working from different vantage points around the world. All in all, given the ebb and flow of coming together and breaking apart, I feel we have maintained a highly successful distributed research team.[5]

One of the initial patterns I recognized while being nomadic was thinking in new ways about home space and away space. I began with set ideas of what "away" and "home" space meant and watched as these ideas shifted in unexpected ways. Home was in New Jersey, a symbolic and emotional place made up of material culture (e.g., pictures, clothing, or furniture), vivid memories, and certain roles. Home was also not confined necessarily to a physical house, but included the surrounding local areas where my family, friends, work, and community activities were located. I was socialized by the significant events that took place there and the memories that were built from these experiences. My parents had a business located in New Jersey and had established themselves in the community. In contrast, "away" was largely associated with temporary places and shorter stays. I was less "vested" in places that I would visit, compared to the energy and attention I would give to friends and family members at home. Up until the time I left for graduate school, home and away spaces were largely distinct.

Part of my attempt to create a stable work and social life in Michigan involved duplicating aspects of my "home" space from New Jersey in Michigan. Consequently, "away" space (the apartment in Michigan) became reshaped as "home" to me. Personal effects such as clothes, pictures, recipes, and work materials were split between the apartment in Michigan (away) and the condo in New Jersey (home). I developed memberships at gyms and yoga studios in both locations to streamline workouts. I frequented the same grocery store chain to ensure that I could continue to cook the way I wanted to in each place. I could depend on regular routines and activities from place-to-place. Similar patterns developed with my work habits. I was given a shared office with our PI and there I left duplicated copies of field notes, books, research files, and other personal items such as photographs and team awards. Work related files and personal effects were set in their place and I was ready to pick up and work when I arrived. Duplication made the transitions to and from Michigan and New Jersey easier. Thus, increased mobility brought about a process of creating and shaping two home spaces through material culture.

However valiant my attempts to construct two home spaces, I still felt awkward and tried my best to avoid answering the question, "Where do you consider home with all of the traveling you do?" My hesitancy and avoidance of this question indicated a discomfort with the new reshaping of home space. What kept cropping up in my mind in Michigan were concerns that I was not meeting expectations as an owner of a small business while being at a distance from New Jersey. I was regularly calling and checking in with our CEO and Sales Manager, but I thought "Does calling to check in 'count' as work and convey a 'legitimate' interest in the role as owner?" Likewise, in New Jersey I worried that an unoccupied desk in Michigan would signal lack of commitment to my team, given that the majority of GM R and D employees spend their time on site in traditional offices and laboratories. After all, I was given a desk, my name was on the door, and I should probably occupy it, right? So although there was an attempt to transfer material culture, the thought of not "appropriately" meeting role expectations made life complicated.

As a nomadic worker, I also used "away" space much differently than I had while working at my family business. As I became more mobile I took advantage of working at "in between" locations and in between different activities. Much has been written about the rise of mobile work done in third spaces such as coffeehouses and libraries.[6] Although I did take advantage of spaces like these, my mobility stimulated an increase in use of what I call "transitional spaces." By transitional spaces I mean the places that you occupy en route to a destination. For example, I found myself verbally recording research ideas into my tape recorder while driving in the car, writing in my note pad during long walks, and reviewing interview transcripts on domestic and international airline flights. I also noticed that I reconfigured public transitional "away" spaces such as airport lounges. I would put on headphones, as is illustrated in Figure 5, hunt down an electric plug, and lay out work material around me.

Stacks of paper, my laptop, and the occasional glass of wine would act as insulators to the outside world and define the space as "my working territory." Being able to control the outcome of my nomadic experience, by reconfiguring the physical spaces that I occupied while in transition from one place to another, provided relief that there would be very few interruptions, disappointments, and surprises. Continually traveling through and occupying these transitional spaces also left me with the knowledge of where the best places for food were, where the cleanest bathrooms were located, and where I could find the most helpful employees in airport lounges. These transitional spaces developed into dependable places of refuge for me—places of calm amid chaos as I moved from place to place.

FIGURE 5. Reconfiguring transitional spaces. (Photo by Tracy L. Meerwarth.)

Patterns such as the reshaping of home and multiple use of away and in between spaces are somewhat a function of the type of work I do as a nomadic knowledge worker. At Consolidated there was linearity to work that was structured by place, time, and the work tasks required. In contrast, some of our work as anthropologists requires linking ideas, patterns, concepts, and theory together to derive understanding. Work can be "carried" with us, which fits nicely with the requirements of a mobile worker. As knowledge workers, our best creative moments and insights are not necessarily associated with any particular space and time. Thus, my mobility, coupled with knowledge work, opened up new opportunities for thought, work, and reasoning in the "in between" spaces.

MANAGING LOCAL AND DISTRIBUTED RELATIONSHIPS

The changes that I experienced as a mobile worker were not confined to space and material culture. Moving back and forth between my two homes in Michigan and New Jersey generated new challenges to "local" and "distributed" relationships. For example, when I was working in Michigan I established "local" relationships and also maintained more remote, distributed relationships from New Jersey. This was different than in the past because my friends, family, and some of the communities of which I was a part in New Jersey had to adjust to the periodic nature of my visits and communicate with me at a distance.

My desire to work through these changes in relationships did not necessarily match the expectations of others. For example, when I was in Michigan I was anxious to meet people with similar interests, and I did not want to spend all of my downtime working. In reality, these friendships turned out to be "pseudo local" relationships. I use the term *pseudo* because even though my visits were occurring at relatively predictable two-week intervals, I was still perceived by many as temporary. Not everyone in Michigan was interested in hearing, "Sorry, I can't come to your get-together, I'll be in New Jersey" (for the third time in a row). Consequently, the sporadic nature of my time in Michigan certainly limited my ability to pursue close friendships outside of our team and maintain them in the most ideal way. This "pseudo locality" was something that I had not given much thought to in the past. When I was in a permanent location, I had always been able to provide face-to-face support to my friends and family by planning events or being available to get together spontaneously. Establishing "local" friends in Michigan was a hard adjustment to make because in some cases I was not around, and therefore, I was not meeting others' socialized expectations for friendship.

I had to make other adjustments in relationships with my friends, family, and communities in New Jersey as well. Whenever I returned to New Jersey, I spent a considerable amount of time reestablishing connections with friends and community organizations, even though they were long-standing relationships. I was often the one contacting others because friends did not know my exact schedule or know if I was around or not. I would call people one to two weeks ahead of time to let them know the dates I would be in town. "Scheduling" time with people rather than letting casual get-togethers happen more naturally felt awkward, as it was not something I was used to doing. I found keeping commitments was important, more so than if I were around on a regular basis, so that friends and community members could recognize that I was vested in them and interested in maintaining relationships. This was particularly important with a community volunteer organization of which I am a member. Planning what volunteer activities I could participate in many months in advance, and staying committed to these events, enabled me to volunteer in spite of my time limitations. Meeting volunteer requirements also helped build up a sense of my accountability and dependability with other members of the organization, in spite of my frequent absences.

My focus on actively managing local and distributed relationships stems from my need to mediate feelings of liminality and retain a sense of community (Varenne 1977) and a role in that community while being mobile.[7] Being neither here nor there, coupled with a shifting sense of roles from place to place, contributed to this sense of placelessness. Mobile workers, particularly nomadic workers, are simultaneously managing both relationships and roles at a distance and those that exist locally, wherever they may be physically. Even if there is a strong base of friendships, I found that these relationships and roles require time and work to maintain, especially while traveling. In a sense, the mobile worker is neither here nor there and this sense of being "in-between" often results in a sense of being dislocated from a group. When I was not always constantly present in a particular place I felt that others perceived an indeterminacy and an ambiguity about my role, regardless of whether or not this was the true reality.

WHAT CAN WE LEARN FROM THE NOMADIC WORK EXPERIENCE?

The term *nomadic* captures the dynamic of workers traveling down similar paths and grounding themselves in familiar places for periods of time. It involves workers traveling down multiple and geographically distributed sites across a landscape where they are able to accomplish work. Nomadic workers' movements are repetitive, thereby constituting a particular structure and pattern. It is clear to me through my own personal observations that patterned movement amplifies nomadic workers' experiences. This is not to say that other traditional workers who travel a great deal or work remotely from an office do not experience similar feelings and anecdotes comparable to what I have described. It is just that being nomadic predisposes workers to face issues of integration and mobility more often, and at shorter intervals.

Being nomadic provides an opportunity, if you are observant, to interpret the repetition of your movement and identify specific areas for growth and conflict that form at the interface of mobility and integration. Nomadic workers are one group of mobile workers, perhaps at the end of a continuum because of the degree to which they travel and are uprooted. If one aspires to understand mobility more deeply, and specifically mobile work culture, there are cultural learnings that abound at the interface of nomadic workers' behavior and technology. One of many questions that emerged during this reflexive process is: What opportunities for growth exist for the worker in terms of work style and social interaction? Another obvious question that follows is: What challenges exist for the worker at this interface?

Adapting to Relationships and Physical Surroundings

One area of growth for me as a nomadic worker was an increased ability to adapt more quickly to the changing expectations for relationships and my physical surroundings. Once my mobility increased, original models of how I maintained relationships prior to my more mobile lifestyle were not necessarily transferable. For example, I soon recognized that friends in Michigan and New Jersey were operating from strong, socially constructed notions of how friendships were maintained. Knowing this, I was not going to risk them assuming that more worthwhile relationships existed with people that were collocated with them, rather than at a distance. As a result, I tried new ways of maintaining involvement in their lives such as scheduling formal times to meet, or making an extra effort to call two weeks ahead to plan events. I also began to educate them on what my work and personal experiences were like as a nomadic worker. This proactive communication helped bridge the distance between my friends, who lead more traditional lives and myself, who was more mobile.

Another way I learned to adapt as a nomadic worker was to prioritize certain relationships. Rather than trying to develop strong allegiances with everyone in the places I lived and worked, I managed to come to terms with the notion that different contexts can yield different types of relationships—all of which do not need to be my strongest and most important. As a result, I grew more attentive to prioritizing those relationships that played important roles in my life including my colleagues, my boyfriend, and my closest friends. Over time these groups of people were able to sense my commitment to balancing work and relationships and in turn I feel I garnered their support.

I also feel that my ability to adapt to my changing physical surroundings as I traveled across different landscapes was an additional area of growth. As a mobile worker, I was accustomed to taking advantage of the spaces I would "leave" (homes) and "get to" (workplaces). However, I recognized through experience that there were opportunities in the spaces that lie in between where we are, and where we are going. These spaces that were once silenced and unnoticeable in my role as a traditional worker, took on important roles in my life as a nomadic worker. I learned that transitional spaces are intellectually and emotionally useful when nomadic. Transitional spaces not only provide a new physical space where I can work and think but they offer a place for me to recharge my batteries. In this way, they offer "breathing room," comfort, and a chance for clarity.

Negotiating the Transfer of Roles

Although there are opportunities for growth that I identified as a nomadic worker, there are challenges as well. Material culture such as books, photographs, clothes, and data are easily transferable from place to place given some effort. Likewise, I could substitute gym memberships and grocery stores, given some minor differences. What emerged as challenging to me were the multiple roles that I had to carry with me and negotiate from place to place as a nomadic worker. These roles include friend, daughter, researcher, and owner. To me, physical presence and active involvement reaffirm these roles. Personal conflict arises when mobility begins to undermine the ability to uphold roles from place to place. This is caused by the inability to maintain simultaneous physical presence and simultaneous involvement—something that is unique to the nomadic experience.

For example, when I was in Detroit, I was occupying my desk and completing work on site, which sent a message that I was present and committed in my role as a "researcher." However, I was well aware that by not being located in New Jersey during that time, I could be perceivably undermining my role as "owner" of Consolidated and compromising my role as "friend" with missed events and activities. This situation easily flip-flops while located in New Jersey. I think that a function of this conflict stems from the perception of the mobile worker that roles are somewhat bound by socially constructed expectations about what you should be doing in your role and where you are. It is easy to justify, for example, that when I am in Michigan, I should dedicate myself solely to research work and activities done there. However, it has been my experience that those who lead more mobile lives carry roles with them that are not as easily silenced or temporarily abandoned. The conflict that the transferal and upholding of roles across boundaries and space creates is something that I am continually aware of being a nomadic worker.

CONCLUSION

Interestingly, in deconstructing my nomadicity, I have given little attention to the details of the work I actually do on a daily basis. Rather, I was inspired, probably because of my training in anthropology, to learn from the surrounding context—the circumstances, feelings, events, and behaviors of life as a nomadic worker. The priority I give to the broader context within which mobile work falls is a critical insight that I have gained from my experience. In other words, I have come to realize that being flexible and mobile has as much to do with the challenges of spanning distances with material culture and relationships as it does with the complexities of negotiating and transferring different roles across spaces and boundaries.

Nomadic workers offer a richness of experience because of their patterned behavior across the landscape. Anthropologists are in a unique position to propose research agendas and apply theory in their investigations to help advance our understanding of the interface between mobility and social integration. This is a very different approach to understanding mobility because the focus is on the worker rather than solely on the advances in technology. What we begin to understand is that the cultural conflict that one experiences as a mobile worker as a result of balancing two simultaneously, culturally important themes is an area of worthwhile investigation. I suggest that anthropological research that targets the social and behavioral components of mobile workers can complement the current product and technological focus (e.g., effectiveness of product, network, or service) of research on mobility. Perhaps an investigation of this kind in workplaces will inform current work related to cultural conflict. The outcome of this will yield a more holistic, comprehensive view of mobile workers, specifically how they live their mobile lives.

NOTES

Acknowledgments. I would like to thank my colleagues at GM R and D, particularly Elizabeth Briody for supporting my work at a distance. I would also like to thank Gitte Jordan, Julia Gluesing, Scott Pester, Robert Trotter, and Marietta Baba for encouraging me to pursue my role as lead editor of this bulletin.

1. *Knowledge worker* is a term first used by Peter Drucker in his 1959 book, *The Landmarks of Tomorrow.* Knowledge workers include those in the information technology fields, such as programmers, systems analysts, technical writers, as well as engineering designers and others using new knowledge to perform creative tasks. It also includes academic professionals and researchers, among others, who are creating that knowledge in the first place.

2. This term is most often used to describe computing capabilities where one is able to have a consistent computing experience wherever one roams. Leonard Kleinrock (1995) has written about the technology aspects of the nomadic computing. I expand the term by taking into consideration what we can learn from one's physical and social distribution across a landscape.

3. I limit my observations to North America, because my observations are largely based in that area.

4. *Heads-down time* is a term that emerged from our GM work with researchers and R and D workspace (Meerwarth et al. 2008). The term was used by researchers to describe times when concentration, privacy, and quiet were required during the workday.

5. A discussion of keys to a successful distributed team is not the focus of the article, however, I do feel that there are a few very important components, which have made our GM R and D team successful including a locally based PI, clear and frequent communication between team members regarding personal and professional expectations, frequent face-to-face contact, a diverse contribution of skills, and a general respect for one another.

6. In contrast to first places (homes) and second places (workplaces), third places offer an informal atmosphere to be with others. Ray Oldenburg wrote about third places in his 1999 (3rd edition), *The Great Good Place: Cafes, Coffee Shops, Bookstores, Bars, Hair Salons, and Other Hangouts at the Heart of a Community.*

7. I use the term *liminal* to highlight the pressure it exudes on relationships rather than using this term to identify a process (e.g., rite of passage) that is traditionally associated with anthropology (Turner 1967).

REFERENCES CITED

Drucker, Peter
1959 The Landmarks of Tomorrow. New York: Harper and Row.

Fowles, Jib
1996 Advertising and Popular Culture. Thousand Oaks, CA: Sage.

Goldman, Robert
1992 Reading Ads Socially. London: Routledge.

Hochschild, Arlie R.
1997 The Time Bind: When Work Become Home and Home Becomes Work. New York: Henry Holt.

Hsu, Francis L.K., ed.
1961 American Core Values and National Character. *In* Psychological Anthropology: Approaches to Culture and Personality. Francis L. K. Hsu, ed. Pp. 209–233. Homewood, IL: Dorsey Press.

Kleinrock, Leonard
1995 Nomadic Computing—An Opportunity. Computer Communication Review 25(1):36–40.

Marchand, Roland
1985 Advertising the American Dream: Making Way for Modernity 1920–1940. Berkeley: University of California Press.

Meerwarth, Tracy L., Robert T. Trotter, and Elizabeth K. Briody
2008 The Knowledge Organization: Cultural Priorities and Workspace Design. Space and Culture 11(4), November.
Messaris, Paul
1997 Visual Persuasion: The Role of Images in Advertising. Thousand Oaks, CA: Sage.
Middleton, Catherine A.
2007 Illusions of Balance and Control in an Always-On Environment: A Case Study of BlackBerry Users. Continuum: Journal of Media and Cultural Studies 21(2):165–178.
Mirchandani, Kiran
2000 "The Best of Both Worlds" and "Cutting My Own Throat": Contradictory Images of Home-Based Work. Qualitative Sociology 23(2):159–182.
Oldenburg, Roy
1999 The Great Good Place: Cafes, Coffee Shops, Bookstores, Bars, Hair Salons, and Other Hangouts at the Heart of a Community. 3rd edition. New York: Marlowe.
Perlow, Leslie A.
1997 Finding Time: How Corporations, Individuals, and Families Can Benefit from New Work Practices. New York: Cornell University Press.
Trice, Harrison M., and Janice M. Beyer
1993 The Cultures of Work Organizations. New Jersey: Prentice Hall.
Turner, Victor
1967 Betwixt and Between: The Liminal Period in Rites de Passage. *In* The Forest of Symbols: Aspects of Ndembu Ritual. Ithaca, NY: Cornell University Press.
Varenne, Hervé
1977 Americans Together: Structured Diversity in a Midwestern Town. New York: Teachers College Press.
Williams, Robin M., Jr.
1970 American Society: A Sociological Interpretation, 3rd edition. New York: Knopf.
Williamson, Judith
1978 Decoding Advertisements: Ideology and Meaning in Advertising. London: Marion Boyars.

LOCATED MOBILITY: LIVING AND WORKING IN MULTIPLE PLACES

AMY GOLDMACHER
Wayne State University

The phenomenon of working away from a traditional office space is broadly called remote or mobile work. When work takes one away from a primary residence for an extended period of time, home and work take on new meanings. Working and living from a distance requires personal, social, and emotional flexibility. I use the term located mobility *to refer to simultaneously living and working in more than one space. This was the case when I relocated for a three-and-a-half-month internship in San Francisco, California, and simultaneously managed the logistical and emotional aspects of my home and work lives in Detroit, Michigan. This article illustrates by way of personal examples a traditional work setting, a remote work setting, and my lived experience of located mobility. I discuss the emotional and practical demands of living and working away from a primary residence for an extended period of time and offer insight into managing the challenges associated with located mobility.* Keywords: remote work, mobile work, located mobility, flexibility, emotion

The phenomenon of working away from a traditional office space is broadly called "remote" or "mobile work." The range of remote or mobile work arrangements includes working from home or from other locations that are not in one's permanent home or primary work spaces. This article posits that another type of mobile work, located mobility, exists where workers may both live and work away from a primary residence and traditional office space. Unlike owning a second home, where one has physical and emotional attachments to two living spaces, and unlike a vacation, where one has a temporary emotional and physical relationship with another space, the phenomenon of living and working away from primary home and work spaces requires flexible emotional and physical attachment to spaces and relationships. The term *located mobility* is taken from Kat Jungnickel's (2007) work on the use of computers and wireless Internet access in Australian homes. She defines *located mobility* as the outcome of

> the increasing incidence of wireless enabled devices in the home, (such as laptop computers and hand held devices) and the changing nature of broadband Internet access which can be wirelessly broadcast throughout the home or in a myriad of 'hotspots' across major metropolitan areas . . . on a basic level these changes mean that people no longer have to move to locations where these interfaces are fixed in place. These technology interfaces can now move with people wherever they choose to use them in and outside the home. [Jungnickel 2007]

NAPA BULLETIN 30, pp. 118–127. ISSN: 1556-4789.
DOI:10.1111/j.1556-4797.2008.00023.x

My use of the term *located mobility* expands this definition to include the personal, social, and emotional aspects of mobile technology use when living and working from a distance. Technologies enable people to transcend locations, but when people use mobile technologies to live and work remotely, they also must find ways to manage feelings of distance and presence. I am adapting the term *located mobility* to specifically refer to the phenomenon of simultaneously living and working in more than one location and managing its associated emotional challenges. By emotional challenges, I refer to feelings of presence and distance in home and work lives.

In "The Idea of a Home: A Kind of Space," Mary Douglas (1991) discusses the qualities of the idea of home. Douglas discussed the fact that the very definition of *home* is widely contested: it can be a house, or a community; it can be virtual or real; it refers to space, time, location, and resources. Home has strong and varied emotional connotations. Home's relationship to work has changed over time; for some, work and home are two entirely separate domains, and, for others, boundaries between work and home are less defined and are, in fact, permeable.

This article describes my personal history in a traditional work setting, a remote work setting, and my lived experience of located mobility. I discuss the emotional and practical aspects of living and working away from home for an extended period of time, and offer strategies for managing the challenges associated with located mobility. I use Christena Nippert-Eng's (1996a, 1996b) concept of *boundary work* as a way of managing the experience of located mobility. Finally, my conclusion will summarize how the experience of located mobility requires different emotional work and boundary management than other types of mobile work.

In the next section, I describe my own career trajectory as an example of a range of lived experiences in managing home and work boundaries, including what it means to experience located mobility.

TRADITIONAL WORK

My first traditional job post-college was with an academic college textbook publisher. I use the term *traditional* to describe this job because it was a 40-hour-a-week salaried position with benefits, including my own assigned cubicle in an office building. I was hired as an editorial assistant and later worked as a marketing coordinator in an office building in a suburb of Boston, Massachusetts. My job was rigidly structured and my responsibilities never required me to work outside of the office. I did not fill out a time sheet, but I was expected to be at my desk during normal working hours, that is, approximately 9 a.m. to 5 p.m. I did not own a personal computer at this time, nor did I have a cell phone (this was just about the time that personal cell phones were becoming affordable and popular), so I never took work home with me, and I was not expected to communicate with anyone from the office during off hours. I recall, in the three years that I had this work arrangement, going into the office on a weekend to check my personal e-mail only one time. Overall, the boundaries between work and home were perfectly clear: work was accomplished at work, and though personal communication via telephone and e-mail could also be accomplished at work, the reverse was not true. Home was distinctly work-free.

REMOTE WORK

There was a striking contrast between the office-based job in which work and home were completely segmented, and my next position in sales where work and home were fully integrated. I was relocated from Boston to California to be one of the two representatives responsible for college textbook sales in the greater Los Angeles area. My territory consisted of 13 area colleges and universities. My responsibility was to visit the campuses and talk to social science and humanities professors about the books and materials they used to teach their courses and, ultimately, to get them to use my company's texts. Being a sales representative meant I reported to a district manager who reported to a regional manager. I was responsible for achieving a certain percentage increase in sales over last year's sales in my territory. The expectations were that I would be on campuses making sales calls during business hours, but my hours spent on campus were not monitored in any official way. My district manager was very hands-off; he told me to treat my territory as if it was my own company, and he expected me to manage my time and tasks as I saw fit. As long as the sales results indicated I was doing my job, I was left to do my job with little supervision.

The company did use several communication tools to track and monitor sales to determine whether each territory would reach its goal. These methods included mandatory telephone conversations with regional and district managers, voice mail updates, e-mail messaging, and a database on my work-provided laptop computer to be synchronized with the home office at least weekly. Occasional on-site visits from senior management demonstrated the remote methods of monitoring sales progress. In addition, I made myself available to my customers through a home telephone, a cell phone, and an e-mail address printed on my business cards. A customer once called me on my home line at 6:30 a.m. on a Sunday, illustrating to me that there were no distinctions between my home and my work.

In this remote work arrangement, I found that my home and work boundaries blurred, and I was working more hours than ever before, even though I had more personal flexibility. Early on in this position, I would spend eight or nine hours a day on a college campus and then return home with hours of follow-up work to do. This included responding to e-mails and voice mails, entering all product requests into the database, estimating sales based on calls with customers, and preparing for the next day. As I spent more time managing my territory, I learned how to better manage my time by setting appointments with professors, understanding that professors stayed in their offices mostly before and after their class times, and rarely came to campus on Fridays. I stored books and marketing materials in my car as a mobile office. I conducted personal and work-related calls while traveling. In addition, my home was my office. I set up a desk in between my kitchen and my living room to create an office space where I could sit and work on a computer and spread my papers and books out around me. My bookcases had several shelves dedicated to work materials. My home was my office, my car was my office, and my offices were my home.

LOCATED MOBILITY

My experiences as a sales representative (finding professors in their native settings, providing business solutions to their needs) inspired me to look at graduate schools for anthropology. I decided to attend Wayne State University in Detroit, Michigan, because it offered the only Ph.D. in anthropology in the United States with a specialization in business anthropology. From this program I hoped to get a set of specific skills that would allow me to return to industry with the credentials and experience to provide services and solutions in organizational settings.

After passing my qualifying exams, I struggled to focus my interests on a dissertation topic and decided that gaining some industry experience would assist my career trajectory and provide the inspiration for the dissertation. I wanted to find a paid position for the summer months because I would need to be earning income while I was gaining experience, and the summer was the best time to be away from my university job in Detroit. I applied to an innovation and design company known for its human-centered approach to product design.

The position required I relocate to San Francisco from Detroit for the duration of the internship. Although the company would have preferred a six-month commitment to fully teach their corporate culture and allow for exposure to multiple projects, I preferred a three-month contract. Any longer felt like I would be gone too long from Detroit to be able to maintain an apartment and have a job waiting for me when I got back. Eventually the intern recruiter and I compromised on 15 weeks, which seemed to meet the company's needs to have me for the length of time required to learn from the internship opportunity, and met my needs of not being away from my primary home and work situation for what I felt was too long.

Once the start and end dates were agreed on, I began to plan out the practical aspects and demands of living and working away from a primary residence for an extended period of time. There were issues related to living and working in San Francisco, and there were separate but related issues of maintaining my living and working situation in Detroit while I was gone. All of these issues were critical for me in developing a sense of belonging at home and at work in a new place while maintaining those related to my primary residence.

While still in Detroit, I needed to find a furnished place in San Francisco to live that was safe, affordable, and close enough to the office to be commutable by public transportation because I was not going to take my car with me. I found a room in an apartment in a great neighborhood 15 minutes away from the office by public transportation. One of the other roommates in this living arrangement was also an employee of this company, so I had a good resource for work-related questions while I was there. I talked on the phone with the other roommates in an informal interview to make sure I would fit comfortably in their living arrangement. This living situation was only for two months, so I would need to find housing for the second half of my internship once I was in San Francisco. I was confident that I would be able to find something once I had established myself in San Francisco and had a feel for neighborhoods and knew how to make my way around the city. In fact, I met a friend of a friend who graciously offered me her second bedroom for a small amount of rent for the remainder of my time in the city, which I gratefully accepted. Although packing up and moving apartments in the middle of my time in San Francisco was unappealing, I felt that I was able to intimately experience multiple parts of the city by living in two very different parts of town. On the Detroit side, I did not find someone to sublet my apartment, which was a financial burden, but it was a relief to leave it unoccupied because I would not have to worry about a stranger living unsupervised in my place.

My work situation in Detroit was supportive of my internship plan, and my employer agreed to hold my position for me until I returned. They agreed to continue my health insurance while I was away, and I was responsible for finding a way to make sure my tuition was paid so that I could receive financial aid. These things were essential for me to be able to undertake the internship. I would not have been able to go to San Francisco without uninterrupted insurance coverage because I would have been unable to pay medical bills if something happened to my health. Similarly, I needed to make sure my tuition and financial aid were maintained so that I would not miss a whole semester. Finally, I needed to have a job when I returned to be able to afford the costs associated with living and going to school. If any of these things had not been sustainable during my absence, I literally would not have been able to afford the internship experience.

With two suitcases in hand and a box of books and papers on its way to me, I arrived in San Francisco with a full day to get acclimated before starting my internship. At the apartment, I quickly unpacked my belongings into the space left for me. Because my new roommates were all out of town, I relied on using my laptop computer and Internet access to find a supermarket in my neighborhood for some food and directions to work Monday morning. I wondered how much food to buy because I didn't want to stock the apartment with food until I knew how much time I would be spending in the apartment or traveling for work. As I put away my groceries, I wondered where to place my stuff in the pantry and the refrigerator. Whereas I had made arrangements prior to arriving about which towels I was to use and which drawers were available to me, putting my food items on the shelves felt like I was marking my territory, drawing a boundary that stated "this is mine, and it fits in here." As a result, I ate out a lot, which was much more expensive than buying groceries and preparing my own meals. Although it was never discussed explicitly with my new roommates, I always felt that though I was welcomed into this home, I could not get too relaxed about spreading my belongings around because my stay was temporary. The living situation felt more like a home than a hotel room would, but I felt like it was not "my home." Rather, it was "my home for now." I had the sense of being in a place that was neither home nor away but a new hybrid.

I wondered how close I could or should get to my new roommates. Would they be interested in developing a friendship with me, knowing at some point in the near future I would no longer be there? I did not think the terms of friendship could be negotiated ahead of time, so I decided to do my best to make friends but let them know ahead of time the duration of my stay. When introducing myself to new people, I always framed my introduction with the information that I was in San Francisco for a summer internship. By providing this boundary information, I felt that I made public the temporariness of my situation, allowing others to determine whether they wanted to engage in a provisional relationship.

Once I learned a little about the neighborhoods in which I was living and working, I found a boxing studio that would let me join for a six-week membership. Being able to work out enabled me to feel like I was using my free time like I would if I were at home. I borrowed a friend's boxing gloves and was able to participate without using my own gear, which was back in Detroit. I also found people from work who participated in running and other group sport events, so I joined them whenever I could. Realizing that living in San Francisco provided the opportunity to run outside in beautiful weather almost all year round, I was inspired by a roommate's commitment to run a half marathon toward the end of my stay, even though it was double the distance I had ever run before. I figured that this event was a unique opportunity I would not get in Detroit, so I should take advantage of it while I could. Working out was essential to my well-being, and being able to do the activities and hobbies I enjoyed in Detroit while located in San Francisco gave me a feeling of continuity.

I worried about how to maintain my personal relationships in Detroit while I was away for the duration of the internship. I figured that regular e-mail updates would keep family and friends apprised of the details of my daily life, so they could, to some extent, experience what I was experiencing. It seemed to me that the San Francisco experience was worthy of mass-e-mailed descriptions to friends and family, whereas my Detroit experiences were not communicated in the same manner. It was important to me to go beyond e-mail when communicating with my boyfriend because I wanted to feel that we were as close as we could possibly be, despite being 2,400 miles apart. Daily text message exchanges with occasional phone calls, e-mails, postcards, and gifts through the mail mitigated some of the effects of geographic distance, but both of us missed the feeling of being in the same time zone and the ability to see each other in person on a regular basis.

During the timeframe of the internship, I made two quick weekend trips to Detroit and he came to San Francisco for five days, so that we were able to see each other once a month. I felt that I was trying to be present in multiple places at once; I needed to be physically and mentally focused on the work in San Francisco, but I also felt that I needed to demonstrate a presence in Detroit. Maintaining this relationship took considerable time and energy on both our parts, and impacted how immersed I felt in San Francisco. Sometimes, when work was busy and I had a routine established, I felt fully integrated in San Francisco work–life, and aspects of my work and life in Detroit felt more remote. Other times, when I was not entirely focused on work and life in San Francisco, I felt closer to my work and life in Detroit but frustrated by my lack of focus here and my longing to be physically present in Detroit. Managing the feeling of being simultaneously here and there was an ongoing challenge.

Finding a place to belong in the San Francisco office was also a challenge. The office space was organized to promote interaction among colleagues and allow for temporary group spaces. Long rows of tables created workstations for people to sit and plug in laptop computers. Although most people had an assigned workspace at a table, people would take up residence in a project space when they were assigned to a project. Project spaces were enclosed rooms along the walls of the office, and project team members would spend the duration of their project time in these spaces. At the end of a project, the spaces would be emptied out and new project teams would move in. When I first arrived at the office, I was bounced from workstation to workstation, depending on who needed that space for the day. After two weeks, I was assigned to a project and therefore a project space, but the first few weeks of not knowing where to go once I was in the office was disconcerting and led to a feeling of not belonging.

Once assigned to a project, my life became busy. My work hours became longer, and there was travel to different sites around the country. There were instances where I felt that my separate existences were overlapping. In addition to my boyfriend's visit to San Francisco, other visitors were able to see where I was working, what I was doing, and experience some of the details of San Francisco life. On a visit to San Francisco, two of my Wayne State advisers came to my office to talk about developing a recruiting relationship between the company and the university. In addition, my brother visited for a weekend and together we experienced making our way around on public transportation and doing some of the more touristy activities in San Francisco. Sharing San Francisco experiences with friends and family made me feel closer to them and validated my own experience of being in San Francisco.

Around the two-and-a-half-month mark, I noticed a shift in my thinking. It felt like my time in San Francisco was coming to an end. I started to acknowledge that there were many restaurants I would not have the chance to eat at, museums I would not get to go to, and events I would not get to attend. In fact, time was marching on without me: I started to get e-mails at work in California about future events and projects that would occur in my absence after I left. In addition, I was starting to think ahead to things I needed to do back in Detroit: plan meetings, draft papers, scope out projects. Perhaps it would soon feel as if I were never in San Francisco and had never left Detroit.[1]

DISCUSSION

How I managed the boundaries between home and work spaces differed with my experiences of traditional work, remote work, and located mobility. Nippert-Eng (1996a, 1996b) uses the term *boundary work* to describe the ongoing mental and physical processes of classification and categorization, specifically in home and work spheres. Boundary work can refer to either the placement of boundaries or the management of boundaries. How each of us segments or meshes our home and work lives is, according to Nippert-Eng, marked by physical symbols and mental processes.

Nippert-Eng provides examples such as calendars, keys, pictures, the clothes we wear or change into, what we carry in our wallets and purses, and what we eat and drink as ways we differentiate, make similar, or transition between our home and work lives. For example, one may only drink coffee while in the work environment and tea at home, because coffee signals participation in a group's culture or remind one of work. One may keep separate calendars for work and home tasks, or one may keep an integrated calendar for both home and work items. In this case, how people choose to use a calendar is a strategy to help manage the boundaries or make them permeable between home and work lives. Nippert-Eng primarily discusses boundary work strategies of traditional office workers and telecommuters but acknowledges that telecommuting, and by extension mobile work, raises interesting questions. In traditional work arrangements, boundary work is very personal and reflects one person's management of boundaries, whereas in telecommuting and mobile work arrangements, boundary work requires input from and acceptance by other parties, including employers and families. Therefore, the experience of located mobility offers a news lens through which to view boundary management strategies for mobile work arrangements.

During my traditional work arrangement, work and home experiences were completely segmented: my work hours were spent in the office, and there was no crossing of that boundary, as I never brought work home. When working remotely as a sales representative, my work and home experiences were completely integrated. Because my home space was also my work space, I often felt as though I was always working. My car was both a personal space and a work space, so there was little chance to escape one for the other. Although my remote work experience afforded me flexibility in my schedule, I missed the social interaction and the ability to create a boundary between work time and non-work time. There were a few ways to separate work from my home life. Often, I would have the television on in the evenings while I took care of the office tasks of the day so that I could try to keep up with my favorite shows while working. Even if I changed from work clothes into more comfortable casual clothes when at home, I still had difficulty creating strict boundaries between work and not-work.

Trying to manage boundaries was even more complex in my experience of located mobility. For example, Nippert-Eng says keys symbolically and physically represent access to home and work spaces. When I arrived in San Francisco, I took my Detroit keys off my key ring and put them in a drawer, because I knew I didn't need to carry them around while I was 2,400 miles away. According to Nippert-Eng, I was managing my classification of where I consider home by keeping San Francisco keys with me at all times and putting away my Detroit keys. It seems as though I would have to carry my Detroit keys with me while in San Francisco to feel close to my home and work life in Detroit. However, I had a home space and a work space in both San Francisco and Detroit at the same time. Regardless of where I was physically and geographically, I could be and feel present in any or several of the places at the same time through information and communication technologies. For example, while on a business trip to

Seattle, I communicated via e-mail and phone with coworkers in San Francisco, friends and coworkers in Detroit, friends and family across the country, and the people with whom I was living in San Francisco. I was also working on this article, reading materials associated with my dissertation research, and planning future activities in both Detroit and San Francisco. Each activity made me feel as though I was establishing my presence in and emotional connection to multiple spaces. I was trying to accomplish personal and work-related tasks as I would at home or at work, even though I was simultaneously neither and both.

While using information and communication technologies to stay connected to others is not uncommon for anyone who works in the 21st century, I posit that not everyone is both living and working in multiple places at the same time. This is where the concept of located mobility may be useful for mobile workers because of the very nature of our work: located mobility includes a sense of obligation and belonging to more than one place at the same time, of trying to demonstrate a presence and feeling of connection while geographically distant. Located mobility also goes beyond identifying what the work and home realms are; it requires more permeability between work and home. One's sense of what home and work is becomes flexible. This is accomplished in part by using information and communication technologies to manage boundaries between work and home spaces, as I did when trying to maintain a feeling of closeness and to keep my presence alive with my friends, family, and employers. Another aspect of located mobility is having the emotional flexibility to make connections that are temporary, and being able to disengage when necessary. Flexibility with emotional connections allows for fluidity in multiple home and work spaces.

I echo Nippert-Eng's assertion that "the more successful we are at transition work, the more permeable we make the boundary" (1996b:288). *Boundary work* provides insights that any worker can draw on. I would go further to suggest that, as mobile workers, we can make our home and work boundaries more flexible through emotional boundary work. For those new to mobile work or for those looking to achieve a greater sense of success while working remotely, recognizing the objects (such as keys, purses, or the talk associated with one sphere rather than another) and cognitive areas (such as transition times, rituals, and acts associated with both home and work realms) in our home and work lives will start the process of negotiating hard boundaries into permeable areas for change. Emotional boundary work alleviates the discomfort of trying to be here and there at the same time. Nippert-Eng's *boundary work* provides insights that any worker can draw on. Recognizing emotional boundaries may help those of us who do not have traditional work arrangements feel that we are successfully managing the personal challenges associated with mobile work, including the experience of located mobility.

CONCLUSION

Drawing on my personal experience living and working in San Francisco while trying to maintain a presence in and connection to my primary living and working spaces in Detroit, I found I was attempting to be emotionally present in multiple places at once. Nippert-Eng's *boundary work,* although primarily based on traditional work arrangements, offers insights that can be applied to mobile work situations, including the experience of located mobility. When there are multiple home and work spaces to consider, ideas of home and work become more flexible and take on new forms and new meanings. Managing flexible home and work boundaries requires emotional flexibility as well, as attachments to people and spaces may be temporally or geographically bounded or both. The experience of trying to be emotionally connected to multiple home and work spaces simultaneously shaped my relationships with people and places, affected how I thought about duration and objects, and required me to become more emotionally flexible to feel as though I was managing my experience successfully. I suggest that the concept of "located mobility" will be helpful to those who need to successfully manage multiple home and work spaces simultaneously and their concomitant feelings of presence, distance, and emotional attachment.

NOTES

Acknowledgments. More than anyone, mobile workers appreciate the challenges of and insights from that type of work. I am grateful to Tracy Meerwarth, Gitte Jordan, and Julia Gluesing for applying their experience to create this volume, and for their many helpful suggestions on earlier versions of this article.

1. The editorial process allows me to reflect on my experience eight months after this article was originally written. Contact with friends and colleagues I met in San Francisco has trickled away to infrequent instant messages or emails; and though I still feel that these people are important to me, I do not feel the need to maintain a presence with them, and I assume the same is true with them.

REFERENCES CITED

Douglas, Mary
1991 The Idea of a Home: A Kind of Space. Social Research 58(1):287–307.
Jungnickel, Kat
2007 Domestic Space and Interfaces for Located Mobility. Electronic document, http://www.studioincite.com/locatedmobility/intro.htm, accessed August 19, 2007.
Nippert-Eng, Christena
1996a Calendars and Keys: The Classification of "Home" and "Work." Special issue, "Lumping and Splitting," Sociological Forum 11(3):563–582.
1996b Home and Work. Chicago: University of Chicago Press.

INTERRUPTIONS AND INTERTASKING IN DISTRIBUTED KNOWLEDGE WORK

PATRICIA G. LANGE
Postdoctoral Fellow, School of Cinematic Arts, University of Southern California

I analyze ethnographic practices in a distributed, on-line research project. Through self-reflexive investigation of interactions with family and interviewees, I discuss challenges that I faced when doing distributed work from home and I problematize assumed benefits of "multitasking" and "flexible" home-based work. By examining remote work (such as interviewing people on-line), I show that "multitasking" inaccurately describes certain work processes which are not actually executed simultaneously. I propose the term intertasking *to describe activities that are interleaved in short intervals to satisfy multiple and often-conflicting work demands. I explore whether multitasking and intertasking are gendered or smuggle in moralistic judgments and conclude that multitasking and intertasking may be effaced or judged differently by people with different work styles. I reveal these dynamics so that members of distributed projects and teams can design processes, tasks, and tools that accommodate different dispositions with regard to doing several things in a short amount of time.* Keywords: reflexivity, distributed work, multitasking, on-line field sites, gender

This article analyzes ethnographic practices in a distributed on-line research project that began when I was a Ph.D. student in anthropology and continues today.[1] The analysis focuses on distributed work experiences that occurred while I investigated two on-line communities that I call Mining MUD and Learning World.[2] This analysis begins with a discussion of some of the challenges I faced when doing distributed work conducted from home. It highlights specific issues related to the difficulty of sharing home workspace with family, and it problematizes common assumptions about automatic benefits of "flexible" homecentric work environments and "multitasking." Through self-reflexive investigation of interactions with family and with interviewees, I explore the meanings and ramifications of "interruptions" on work.

This article explores questions such as: How does conducting a remote research project change ideas about what constitutes ethnographic research? What factors influence the successful execution of a remote ethnographic work project? What insights emerge from seeing the distributed work project not as a field site to be visited but, rather, as a dispersed team in which the ethnographer is also a member who merits observation and study? What can be learned about multitasking and its effects on productivity? Given the merging of work-life activities, is it necessary or possible to have a room of one's own

NAPA BULLETIN 30, pp. 128–147. ISSN: 1556-4789.
DOI:10.1111/j.1556-4797.2008.00024.x

today? How can examination of one's own experiences and work processes illuminate larger concepts about human behavior?

Despite the widespread incorporation of self-reflexivity into ethnographic study, such observations receive criticism in the academy as potentially solipsistic, reification of vague memories that can turn "the self into the field site" at the expense of the cultural "other" (Robertson 2002; Rosaldo 1993). Such critics argue that self-reflexive exercises succumb to their own ideologies, although they are different from those that motivated the objectively driven ethnographic studies that reflexivity sought to critique (Stockton 2002). Self-reflexivity contains its own pitfalls, such as invoking myths "in which selective experiences are remembered—that is, re-membered, as in reconstituted—for the purposes of a 'real-time' argument or interpretation" (Robertson 2002:787).

The present analysis argues that if the objections to self-examination within research mainly concern relevance and rigor, then it is clearly possible for contemporary studies of distributed work to achieve both ends. In fact, it is necessary to incorporate meaningful self-reflexive analysis into research about distributed work processes because distributed work is crucial to much contemporary anthropological work-life. In a distributed work project, participants are not "virtual"[3] others but, rather, ourselves and other human beings who participate remotely in our research projects. A case could be made that every ethnographic project could benefit from systematic capture of self-experiences and interactions.

Incorporating rigorous ethnographic methods on the researcher's personal interactions can yield key insights into how work practices are accomplished and negotiated both remotely and at home. Field notes, transcripts, and logs of on-line interviewing become tangible connections to (although certainly not holistic representations of) certain complexities of interaction. If we trust these materials as helpful for studying others, why should they be ignored for understanding the researcher's role in distributed work? The anthropologist can examine artifacts such as field notes and logs of interaction and develop theoretical insights about distributed work as a result of studying these encounters. For instance, during my MUD research project, I often wrote in field notes about my frustration over what felt to be a lack of "presence" I felt from interviewees in certain on-line interviews. I could not always tell if they were still attending to our interview. Interview transcripts and field notes offer evidence as to how I handled these and other telecommuting problems, and I use these self-observations to uncover insights about remote work processes.

By focusing partly on my own experiences, I found that, contrary to previous literature, multitasking is not the automatic purview of women but, rather, is also influenced by other factors such as individual dispositions. While some people seek to incorporate so-called multitasking in their work routines, others strive to reduce instances of perceived interruption and maintain a focused work environment. I analyze personal data on distributed work negotiations to propose a new term called *intertasking*, which refers to interleaving activities in sequence, rather than assuming that tasks requiring similar skills can be accomplished at the exact same time. I argue that multitasking often smuggles in notions of morality (e.g., what is perceived as good versus bad, or what is considered virtuous in conducting work), which deem people who routinely multitask as more productive than are those who prefer "focused immersion" (Rutkowski et al. 2007) work styles. Conversely, people preferring focused work dispositions may erroneously assume a lack of discipline in people predisposed to intertask and multitask.

Bringing to light differences between intertasking and multitasking opens a space with which to reevaluate and encourage the construction of more productive and amenable collaborative work environments that are sensitive to different dispositions while reducing unreflective moral judgments. Notably, these theoretical insights emerged by closely attending to the results of interactions not only between myself and participant-interviewees in a distributed work environment but also through exploring encounters between my family and me. Finally, the analysis concludes by revisiting the reflexive critique of self-observation and discusses how the literature on "multitasking" has been influenced by particular research agendas, possibly at the expense of understanding multitasking, or in some cases, intertasking, in wider perspective.

THE IMPORTANCE OF ONE'S OWN ROOM

I first bought Virginia Woolf's *A Room of One's Own* (1929) because I thought it would be useful for my fieldwork. I was fascinated by how the two on-line communities I studied used words to represent spatial descriptions of their on-line worlds. In both communities, participants could design their own room, all described in text. They could invite people in or metaphorically "close the door" and be alone. I originally thought that Woolf's book would provide insight on what it means to have a room of one's own on-line. What importance did each person's room have for them in their on-line space? Instead, Woolf's book threw into sharp relief why it was important for me to have a room of my own in which I could conduct research, think, and write.

Originally, I believed that having a distributed project that I could access through a computer would make things easier for me than for other anthropologists who must travel to their field sites. I anticipated eventual marriage and children and believed that a field site I could access from home would enable me to work from any location and, thus, offer flexibility that would be synergistic with family life. To some extent my original prediction came true. Rather than uprooting family to go to a field site or having to forgo fieldwork, I could stay at home and collect data on-line. However, my project also had certain disadvantages that expose how common assumptions about distributed work, such as seamless flexibility, do not always bear out in practice.

Computing is assumed to be mobile and offer ultimate work flexibility. Many technologists are enthusiastic about devices that "free" the user from needing a permanent workstation because they supposedly can accomplish work from anywhere. Yet, reviewing my field notes from those days, I frequently wrote about how hard it was to "feel flexible" when I did not have access to e-mail one day because the service was down or I could not read files off a transported disk that became corrupted. When the Internet was down at home, I had to go to one of the school's computer centers to accomplish work. I wrote in my field notes that even though the university had several computing centers, I had definite preferences over which one to use. Such a preference belies the fantasy of perfect work mobility from any location. For instance, while some centers were social magnets for boisterous students, others were quiet and sported more ergonomic furnishings, which are crucial for those of us who spend the better part of a waking day sitting behind a desk.

My field notes record one instance that illustrates these challenges. One day my Internet connection was down, and I proceeded to my favorite computer center on campus (which took commute time out of my normal work day). I liked the big purple chairs that were vastly more comfortable than other workspaces on campus. The work tables were wide, and the air conditioning cooled the room nicely in the hot Ann Arbor summer. On arriving at the center I found that most of the computers had frozen up. It was, of course, a Sunday, and there were no technicians around to help out. I finally found a computer that worked and sat down. The network was up and running at the university. But then I remembered that the computers there did not have the MUD client programs that I needed to record my on-line research activities. The computing lab at the university had a policy against playing games and going on MUDs in public computer centers, even if you are an anthropologist with a distributed research site. So I went back home.

The Internet connection was back up when I arrived, but I logged in only to find that my particular field site was down. The MUD's administrator promised to send an instant message when the world returned. But if I could not get my MUD client program to work or the Internet was down when the world reopened, then I would miss important data, anthropologically speaking. I realized that I would lose all the data that I would have gotten had everything worked properly from home in the first place. In my field notes, I write about how my husband Andrew says I concentrated on the problems and not alternatives when these disruptions occurred. He had a point. I acknowledged in my field notes that there was a lot I could do while the Internet and my field sites were down. I could write more detailed field notes about these events, for example.

The interactions I have with family, such as the exchange above, influence how work in a home-based, distributed project is conducted. A number of factors, including things such as physical layout of work spaces as well as expectations about what our work schedules should be, impact our productivity, and affect the general ambiance of the work–home atmosphere. For example, Andrew and I have sometimes been fortunate enough to have our own home offices. Other times we have had to share a home office, especially after the birth of our first child. It is not always easy for me to share an office. I remember one incident in which his computer was humming especially loudly right behind me in our small, shared room. I continue with my work. Eventually, I feel swept up in on-line events. Andrew and I argue because I want to keep working and he wants us to take a break. He tells me that I should get off the computer and write more field notes. I get annoyed and tell him that he'll have to trust me; I am well aware of how to balance observations and field notes. I am in an anthropology Ph.D. program, after all.

Another time, I try to work. He is working in the office too. I get engrossed in a task. He tries to interest me in something he finds on the Internet. This time, it is not something related to my work or our home technology infrastructure but, rather, something amusing. I miss the first part of what he said because I am reading. My train of thought is disturbed. I am annoyed and snap. It happens another time as I try to observe an on-line event. I can barely focus on what he said. He accuses me of being a poor multitasker. I am irritated. I no longer feel that I am appearing as attentive or "present" to other participants on-line.

Problems were not always solved when we lived in places that allowed us to have our own home offices. Despite having rooms of our own, similar issues about interruptions emerged when we found ourselves working at home at the same time. I might be working at my computer, and I want to ask him a question about something that is not working right. It is helpful having a professional network engineer at home. I go to his office next door. I want help right away. He stops what he is doing to help me diagnose and fix my network problem. Later, I pass by his office as he is working to develop next-generation Internet architectures. I feel social and decide to tell him something fascinating about my work. He is interested in it, too. It was very important, of course, that I tell him my observations just at that moment. Did I interrupt him? Did he consider that an interruption?

WHAT CONSTITUTES AN INTERRUPTION?

An interruption is anything that causes a break in the continuity or uniformity of a process or condition (McFarlane 1998). But when is something an interruption, and from whose perspective is it an interruption? The literature on conversational interruption is extremely complicated. Some linguists argue that interruption is not always "done to" someone else, but that it is negotiated and people must signal "being interrupted" for an actual interruption to occur (Bilmes 1997; James and Clarke 1993). Given interruption's negotiated aspects, it is apparent that there is a relationship between interruption and multitasking. The *Concise Oxford Dictionary, Ninth Edition* defines *multitasking* as "the execution of a number of tasks at the same time." If one multitasks effectively, how can researchers determine when an interruption occurs? Is an interruption a break in work, or is it part of effective multitasking?

I wish I had read Daniel McFarlane's dissertation, "Interruption of People in Human-Computer Interaction" before Andrew and I had argued, so that I could have defended my poor "multitasking" abilities. McFarlane argues that "multitasking" only really applies when people do tasks requiring different skills at the same time. He quotes research that states, "People can perform actions in parallel along three dimensions—perceptual, cognitive, and motor, but within each of these three dimensions people must perform actions sequentially" (1998:32). For instance, you can make a sandwich (motor skill) and think great thoughts (cognitive skill) at the same time, but it is hard to make a sandwich and juggle knives.

McFarlane, paraphrasing Edmondson, points out that when people do several things at once, they actually accomplish this by working on one thing at a time while "interleaving the execution of all the different activities (asynchronism)" (McFarlane 1998:37). The computer realm offers a useful analogy. Multitasking is used to refer to instances in which a single processor executes tasks simultaneously. In fact, what often happens is that the processor is actually "time-slicing" and swapping activities in and out to such a fine degree that it only appears to be multitasking (English 2000; Intermec, Inc. n.d.; Learning Services Web Team 2008; Monmouth University Department of Mathematics 1997).[4] A more accurate definition for computer multitasking in many cases is, "The process of switching from one operation to another quickly. This results in the *appearance* that several programs are running at the same time" (Intermec, Inc. n.d., emphasis added).[5]

When a distraction is associated with an interruption or unwelcome break in a task, unfortunate consequences may occur. For instance, when a person is interrupted, they must typically recover from the interruption to return to their work. McFarlane notes that "people become prone to make serious memory errors when attempting to resume interrupted tasks" (McFarlane 1998:36). Bolstering my argument that interruptions impair my work is the fact that the literature is filled with unfortunate examples of how interruption impacts the successful completion of a task (Bailey et al. 2001; Latorella 1998; Trafton et al. 2003). While the impact of interrupting a scholar is typically not as severe as interrupting an airline pilot, over time interruptions nevertheless have an impact in that they make concentration and quality of work–home life challenging. That I am not a "good multitasker" is not surprising given that humans are not expected to be able to do multiple tasks of the same type at the same time.

I propose that a better term for interleaving activities of the same type with others is *intertasking,* which connotes doing something in between doing other things. Multitasking often has a positive connotation (Priola 2004; Wasson 2004). Yet in some cases, it is actually a misnomer that sets up unrealistic expectations on the person who is socially expected to multitask effectively. Intertasking reveals the sequential nature of the work that is involved in trying to satisfy the demands of accomplishing several tasks within a finite period of time. Sharing the prefix "inter," the term *intertasking* retains a similar connotation to the term interruption because it emphasizes doing something between other things. It is something that breaks the action, is potentially unwelcome, and places a certain burden on the human processing system. Recognized as intertasking, does doing several things in rapid succession have the same positive connotation as does multitasking? How does intertasking affect remote and home-based work productivity? I found that intertasking and multitasking could have negative effects, for example, when I had to compete with other demands on a remote interviewee's time in a distributed research study.

ADVANTAGES AND DISADVANTAGES OF ON-LINE INTERVIEWING

I have often interviewed people on-line via a chat program about their on-line experiences. Interviewing someone in a distributed fashion on-line rather than in person is beneficial, especially in text chat mode. The chat transcript provides a ready-made document with the interviewee's own words that can be analyzed without requiring the time and cost of travel or the cost of long-distance telephone conversations. In addition, interviewing via on-line chat does not require the tedious, painstaking hours and cost of transcription that are required for in-person or telephone interviews. Chat-based interviews also reduce the risk of traveling to unfamiliar places to meet unknown persons. Finally, they facilitate interweaving doing several things during the interview. Conducting tasks such as briefly checking messages, chatting with a family member, or sending an e-mail during the research interview enables both the researcher and the interviewee to be "flexible."

However, flexibility often has a price (Martin 1994). There are downsides to on-line chat interviews. Both intertasking and multitasking could divert attention away from the interview. Silences on the chat line were ambiguous and required interpretation. Was someone slow to answer a question because they were "thinking," because they did not understand it, or because they were doing something else such as debugging code? Distributed interviewing, as opposed to in-person or phone interviews, had a different rhythm requiring negotiation. Should I prompt them for more information? How many prompts become obnoxious? During several interviews I sensed that people seemed not to be "present" for our conversation. Transcripts and field notes reveal that my main tactic in handling these silences was mostly to go at their pace, even if I could sense that they were not all there. After all, they were doing me a courtesy by helping me with my project with no immediate gain for themselves. The interview could be interrupting their normal routine. Typically, if I could sense that they were no longer as attentive or mentally "present," I would ask at the end of the interview if they had been "multitasking" during our session. Below are two examples:

Example (1) Learning World–April 2001

Patricia says, "So as we wind down here, I like to ask, were you multi-tasking during the interview?"

Lori laughs. "Of course."

Patricia says, "What kinds of things?"

Lori hopes you're not offended by that.

Patricia says, "Not at all."
Patricia smiles.

Lori has 8 characters in various mu*'s connected. 1 is RP'ing. Most are idling. And I'm working on a paper that needs to be submitted on Friday.

Lori giggles, "And I just went to the bathroom and came back."

Patricia says, "Heh."[6]

Example (2) Learning World–February 2001

> Patricia says, "So you have so much going on on-line. Did you find yourself multi-tasking during our interview?"
>
> Mary says, "Let's see . . ."
>
> Mary says, "I fed my son, gave peanuts to the 2 year old, helped my older girls through some math problems, had a stimulating argument about Pennsylvania politics, hired a staffer here, looked at some [code] submitted for [—], told [—] that the mods to the MUX channel code were [an] affront to the Gods and why, razzed 3 other people because they were simply there and answered 5 emails . . . is that a 'yes'?"
>
> Patricia says, "Wow!"

I did not lie to Lori, because I was not offended, just disappointed. What would our conversation have been like without the lapses? How much more information could I have obtained? I had similar feelings while interviewing Mary. She characterized her "multitasking" in a way that connoted pride in her ability to intertask and multitask during the interview. I wanted to be grateful and appreciative of her time, but I was also disheartened. I could tell that she wasn't all there, and although she might be able to multitask activities requiring different skills, such as giving a peanut to her son (motor skill) and formulating interview answers (cognitive skills), I suspect she was intertasking when trying to accomplish multiple cognitive tasks such as answering my questions while debating Pennsylvania politics.

On the one hand, it is arguably true that the distributed nature of the chat-based interview most likely enabled active participants like Mary to talk to me in the first place. She was obviously very busy and engaged in many activities and a phone conversation might have been too difficult to fit into her routine. On the other hand, that she was engaged in so many things detracted from my goal, which was to understand in her own words her on-line experiences. It also made the task of interviewing her more difficult and less pleasant as I sat at my computer waiting for responses while unsure of whether she needed more prodding or was thinking. I do not feel I obtained as much information as I usually do in chat sessions where the person feels more "present" to me. Of course, that I saw her intertasking and multitasking on-line and experienced their effects are themselves insights that are just as important as having her own words about her on-line experiences, because they revealed key distributed work patterns in my study.

The contention here is not that multitasking does not exist because, as McFarlane (1998) argues, it is possible to do tasks requiring different skills at the same time. As Table 1 below indicates,[7] it is possible to do tasks that require motor skills at the exact same time as tasks that predominantly require cognitive skills. However, multitasking is not an accurate characterization of all types of multiple work tasks. McFarlane argues that tasks requiring the same skills are interleaved, whereas tasks requiring different types of skills may occur at the exact same time. Some tasks are more appropriately labeled "intertasking" because they involve interleaving activities requiring the same type of skill.

TABLE 1. Tasking Categorizations According to Required Skill Types

	Perceptual (Look at computer code)	**Cognitive** (Develop a political argument)	**Motor** (Feed son peanuts)
Perceptual (Look at an interview question)	**Intertasking**	Multitasking	Multitasking
Cognitive (Develop a response to interview question)	Multitasking	**Intertasking**	Multitasking
Motor (Type a message)	Multitasking	Multitasking	**Intertasking**

Using Mary's example as a case study is helpful because it delineates what kinds of tasking she was accomplishing and helps pinpoint when certain combinations of tasks likely resulted in intertasking rather than actual multitasking. When Mary fed her son a peanut (a predominantly motor task), she could simultaneously look at an interview question (a predominantly cognitive task) on her computer screen. When conducting these types of tasks, which require different types of skills, she could multitask and accomplish them at the exact same time. However, when Mary attempted to formulate an argument during a debate about politics (a cognitive task), McFarlane argues it would be quite difficult—if not impossible—for her to develop a response to an interview question (also a cognitive task) at the exact same time. When doing these tasks, she would need to interleave portions of the task, or accomplish what I call intertasking. In another example, two tasks that both require motor skills would need to be interleaved (barring special circumstances, such as being able to feed her son a peanut with her foot while typing a message with her hands).[8] Most of us would need to interleave feeding someone peanuts and typing a message using both hands! This type of interleaving of activities requiring the same type of skill is what I refer to here as intertasking.

Identifying different types of tasking is of theoretical and practical value. These differences illustrate constraints on task execution and provide information about whether social expectations about work styles are realistic. For example, I was accused of poor multitasking because I could not look at a funny Internet comic while looking at my computer screen. Yet this demand was unrealistic, according to experts in human perceptual and cognitive processing. It is not possible to "multitask" two perceptual tasks if by multitask we mean executing them at the exactly same time.

MORAL IMPLICATIONS OF MULTITASKING AND INTERTASKING

Mary expressed pride that she was able to execute what I was then calling "multitasking" but that was actually a combination of intertasking and multitasking. Andrew expressed disappointment with me in not being able to multitask, whereas he prided himself on his ability to get several things done at once. Similar connotations of efficiency, virtuousness, and morality appear in the scholarly literature on multitasking. Wasson calls multitasking "positive" because employees who multitask are "putting in an extra level of effort, not wasting time" (Wasson 2004:48).[9] There is a sense of virtue and morality associated with being productive in certain social groups in the United States. Wasting time, either one's own or someone else's, is seen as bad. Similarly, research indicates that U.K. women managers' narratives included pride at having the ability to multitask (Priola 2004).

On the other side of the coin, Lori could sense by my question about her "multitasking" that I potentially ascribed a negative judgment to her choice of focus. She asked whether or not I was "offended" by her "multitasking." Being offended carries the connotation of judging someone else's actions as morally wrong or bad. Whereas some people view multitasking with a sense of pride and accomplishment, I tend to see it during interviews or focused writing as interruptive. I also tend to see it as potentially signaling an inability to focus or concentrate intensively on work. The literature on children's time management and media use takes on similar evaluative and moralistic tones by describing children's multitasking as unfairly burdensome, morally wrong, or a threat to human creativity (Brooks 2001; Steptoe 2003). These observations contrast to the literature that celebrates multitasking in work teams. In sum, some scholarly literature praises intertasking and multitasking as morally right while others condemn it as morally wrong.

In a more neutral vein, Anne-Francoise Rutkowski et al. (2007) propose that some people have certain dispositions toward focused work whereas others thrive on being stimulated and interweaving activities in rapid succession. When researching "virtual teams,"[10] Rutkowski et al. (2007) noted that individuals could exhibit different dispositions with regard to preferring "focused immersion" or executing multiple tasks. They noted that, "If a person is highly focused on a single task, then that person may be said to have a high level of focus immersion" (Rutkowski et al. 2007:102). Such "focused immersion" individuals may find themselves pressured while doing teamwork to meet the demands of others, such as communicating with them. Rutkowski et al. (2007) suggest that focused immersion people thus tend to prefer to use asynchronous communication media such as email or bulletin boards, so that they can deal with conflicting demands at a "more convenient time." Rather than being morally lacking if one enjoys or eschews intertasking and multitasking, it may be that such preferences are related to varieties in human work dispositions.[11] Unfortunate judgments and social expectations may be made on certain individuals or groups to execute or avoid intertasking, potentially at the expense of a person's productivity or self-actualization in particular cultural contexts.

ON THE DEMOGRAPHIC DIMENSIONS OF "MULTITASKING"

When reacting to earlier versions of this article, several women suggested that women were generally more prone to multitasking than men. I found this reaction to my article interesting yet a little irritating because my own case study belied the idea that women are inherently better suited to or typically accomplish intertasking and multitasking more than men. After all, Andrew felt that he was quite good at multitasking and accused me, a woman, of being a poor multitasker. While one female interviewee expressed pride at multitasking, my reaction was not congratulatory but, rather, dismay at her "lack of focus" on the task at hand (as defined by me, of course). Assumptions about women being more frequent or better multitaskers prompted additional reflection on my part. A number of important theoretical questions emerged, such as: Do women "multitask" more than men? Are there cultural or demographic dimensions of so-called multitasking?

A certain body of literature initially confirms the assumption that women around the world multitask.[12] Maria Floro's (1995) survey of the literature in peasant societies and in home-based and informal work sectors shows that overlapping activities have been found to be prevalent in the working lives of women from Mexico, Costa Rica, Kenya, India, and Spain, "particularly among poor or working-class women" (Floro 1995:5). Yet multitasking does not appear to be limited to poor or working-class women. Research on women managers in the United Kingdom similarly showed a prevalence to characterize pride in multitasking and attributed preferences of working with women over men to the idea that women were better multitaskers (Deem 2003; Priola 2004).[13]

However, a large body of research challenges the assumption that only women intertask and multitask (McMahon and Pospisil 2005; Pendleton 2004; Rutkowski et al. 2007; Wasson 2004). Many studies show that people in different demographic groups—based on characteristics such as age (McMahon and Pospisil 2005; Pendleton 2004), choice of computer hardware (Jameson and Klöckner 2004), work tasks (Wasson 2004) or disposition (Rutkowski et al. 2007)—tend to multitask or might need to multitask more than others. For instance, Mark McMahon and Romana Pospisil (2005) claim that the so-called millennial generation of children born after 1982 are more highly skilled at multitasking than are people in other age groups. Jameson and Klöckner argue that people using handheld computers are "not as strongly associated with multitasking" as people who use wearable computers because handheld devices are used in "stationary settings" (Jameson and Klöckner 2004:1). Wasson's study of dispersed meetings did not identify gendered multitasking but rather argued that workers could be more productive by multitasking according to the type of meeting in which they were engaged. Workers could increase productivity in informational meetings if they could multitask whereas problem-solving meetings required more attention from participants (Wasson 2004).

That so many groups are engaging in multitasking belies the notion that it is the exclusive purview of women, or that women are generally better at multitasking than are men. Floro's observations about the difficulties in seeing and measuring multitasking are extremely helpful in this regard (1995). Floro insightfully details how difficult it is for researchers to obtain accurate information about multitasking, partly because of how researchers have traditionally framed time-diary questions that focus on specific activities "thereby precluding the possibility of [describing] overlapping activities" (Floro 1995:5). Floro argues that "The omission of overlapping activities tends to create a systematic bias in the data; time devoted to certain activities such as child care, for example, tends to be underestimated" (Floro 1995:5).

It may be difficult for researchers to "see" actual intertasking or multitasking that is going on in certain settings according to their presuppositions and research agendas. I would extend Floro's analysis and assert that a researcher's bias might cloud an ability to see actual intertasking and multitasking practices beyond what the researcher expects to see. For instance, if researchers are predisposed to assume that women are superior multitaskers and intertaskers, how might such a disposition interfere with an ability to see how men multitask? The women who read my analysis and yet still claimed that women do more multitasking seemed to have more difficulty "seeing" that it was Andrew, a male, and not myself who was the self-identified expert multitasker in the family. Further, although Mary (a female) expressed pride at multitasking, I (also a female) did not share her assessment. To cite another example, it is possible that my bias in priding myself as having a "focused immersive" disposition elides how I too intertask and multitask in everyday work practices. While it is true that reflexive investigation may be laden with dispositions and research agendas, it is also true that a reflexive investigation may help identify certain biases and broaden the lens of data collection. In the example here, it was only through careful cataloguing of my own conflict with people having other work styles and needs that led to the observation of how morality is often associated with intertasking and multitasking and how those moral connotations impact collaborative work. Rather than seeing one style as more virtuous and productive than another, perhaps a more fruitful approach is to consider how such contrasting styles may be successfully negotiated.

NEGOTIATING INTERRUPTIONS

Janet Salaff (2002) rightly argues that the full impact of teleworking cannot be known by asking an employee alone. Rather, one must interview family members to understand their role in helping an employee achieve certain professional goals. I certainly cannot compare myself to the women in the post-Fordist teleworking arrangements that Salaff discusses. In these instances, women balance work and home life by intertasking dull, repetitive work throughout their waking hours. My children are in school and I am doing something that is highly privileged in terms of knowledge work that I often find to be self-actualizing.[14]

Nevertheless, many of the themes that Salaff talks about in her article have surfaced and influence my distributed work projects in the anthropology of media studies in academe. My job allows for flexibility, but as Emily Martin (1994) points out, flexibility is a social concept in that who is flexible and under what circumstances they are allowed to be flexible is socially negotiated. Even though flexibility has a positive connotation for many people, there are certain negative consequences when viewed from a particular point of view. For instance, when Andrew and I work at home, he often assists me with solving network problems in ways that may disrupt his routine in developing better ways to design Internets. We balance home and work life, but there are always tradeoffs.

Having a room of one's own is still shockingly complicated today, even given the multiplicity of rather amazing technical tools that are available to do distributed work. People can be in the same house and still have constant interruptions and distractions that demand intertasking. Examples from my current project include distractions and interruptions from my family and now interviewees from the field who instant message me unexpectedly to chat. Is there a way to handle not having a room of one's own in distributed, knowledge work environments? Jerry Franke et al. (2002) provide some suggestions to help manage human–computer interruptions. It is a worthwhile exercise to explore whether their proposed solutions are applicable to the human–human interruption conundrum as well. They suggest four possible solutions to dealing with interruption:

1. Interrupt immediately and get it over with.
2. Provide negotiation support so that the user controls the timing and exact context of switching between tasks.
3. Provide intelligent mediation that brokers the onset of interruption tasks on behalf of the user.
4. [Use] scheduled interruption time cycles so that the interruptions only occur during set times or contexts.

In the case of emergencies, such as needing to take children to the hospital, it is safe to say that strategy number one is the way to go. But it is not a desirable strategy at all when my husband and I interrupt each other with mundane questions such as, "What do you want for lunch?" In addition, strategy number one is not likely to be very useful for the many scenarios that fall between these extremes.

Personally, I have tried very hard during the course of my distributed work to apply strategy number four. In this strategy, specific time is marked off for me to think and write in an uninterrupted fashion. It is understood that I am not interruptible during these times. Is this a gendered practice? My husband also sometimes works at home, and my children and I must not interrupt. Strategy four, although often useful, is not foolproof. When I was a graduate student at the University of Michigan, we were all issued little yellow signs that we could hang on the doorknob to our work space (at least those of use who had an office space with a door). The sign said that graduate work was underway, and the person was not to be disturbed. It was a do-not-disturb sign for our roommates and families. That it was designed as a doorknob hanger is interesting because it presupposes that there is a physical door or barrier to a room where someone works, as opposed to working at a desk or other mobile space that lacks physically bounded separations.

Graduate students were given these signs because administrators understood that it can be difficult to balance home life with completing a Ph.D. This kind of sign enacts strategy number four above, which aims to schedule interruptions so that they cannot occur while someone is engrossed in a project. I tried hanging my yellow sign on the door to our shared office during a time in which my husband and I agreed I would work uninterrupted. But the sign can irritate family members. It can seem rather rude to other people in the household who may see it as an insensitive and cold form of social manipulation. Needless to say, I did not ultimately use the sign.

Strategy number three implies that automated systems will decide when and how interruptions occur. Because we are far away from the design of intelligent, commercially available, purely automated systems that can broker family negotiations such as what the children will have for lunch and when, it is safe to say that strategy number two—giving the user some control to negotiate interruptions—is perhaps the most realistic near-term solution. As Franke et al. point out:

> Of these four solutions, negotiation was measurably the best approach for all kinds of user performance, except in cases where . . . the current task is too important to allow distraction by the negotiation process or the interrupting task is too important to wait for the negotiation to be completed. [2002:2]

In other words, all parties in the home would ideally discuss when it is okay to interrupt and, each time, the importance of the interruption will have to be weighed against the importance of the work that is being conducted. Rather than expect a physical room of one's own as Woolf suggested, many of us are facing situations where negotiation helps carve out mental and social spaces where people can accomplish their work.

Of particular importance for Franke et al. is not only finding ways to help the user negotiate the time and place of interruption but also to recover context when they switch back to their original task. In other words, they want to find ways to help the user negotiate questions such as "Where was I?" and "What was I last working on?" after the interruption has been handled. Their work acknowledges that an interruption by itself is not the only problem. Another issue involves determining where you were when you left off and how you can recover your place and remember the "amazing insights" you were about to impart to the world before the interruption took place. The words have potentially disappeared forever, or perhaps you will be able to recall them with persistent prodding. Even if they are not world-changing insights, at least they are one's own, and it becomes frustrating if one is frequently unable to complete one's thoughts.

I conclude with another personal vignette. It is late Sunday morning, October 22, 2006. I realize that I have to leave our shared office to get something from the other room. I sit in my chair for a moment before stepping out. I do not want to open the door nor emerge from the room. My husband and children are on the other side of the door, playing and having a good time. But if I leave, they might want to interact with me, and my article is not finished. I want to have the psychological completion of finishing this article today, not to mention meeting the demands of the conference panel organizers. My article is almost finished, but not quite. I decide to leave the room for a moment. On my way back my son is running down the hallway. My husband walks toward me. I enter the room and begin closing the door to our shared office. My husband follows and asks what I am feeding the children for lunch. "You are making us all grilled cheese sandwiches!" I yell. "Me?" he responds, "You've been working for three hours!" I shout back, "What do you mean? I fed the kids breakfast. I've only been working since 9:30." "Okay," he says, "But we've given you two solid hours without any interruptions." I throw my head back onto my chair and look up at the ceiling in an almost mocking, pained fashion. "It's all going into the paper!" I shout. My husband shoots back, "Come on, I'm kidding. Can't I kid?" They go off to the other room. I realize as he leaves that I just bought myself a few more minutes until lunch time. I don't know at this point who is going to make the grilled cheese sandwiches. My husband closes the door on his way out. Back to my article. Now where was I? Is this the kind of negotiation Franke et al. suggested?

DISCUSSION

Characterizing the ethnographer not as a person going to a "virtual field site" but, rather, as one participant in a dispersed team yields insight about the execution of remote work conducted from home. By systematically cataloguing my own personal experiences both at home and on-line, I was able to explore deeper theoretical understanding of multitasking, or in some cases, intertasking, to understand conflicting demands on a worker's time.[15] Although having a room of one's own may not be physically possible, it may be important for people working from home to carve out time for focused work that may require ongoing family negotiations.

Requiring focused work time has several implications. Identifying differences between intertasking and multitasking sheds light on whether expectations about so-called multi-tasking in collaborative work are realistic. While it may be possible to expect workers to execute tasks requiring different skills at the same time, it may be difficult or impossible to demand that they multitask when performing tasks requiring the same types of skills. Managers and team members should be alert to instances in which they are requiring multitasking when this may not be easy or even possible to achieve from a human processing perspective.

It is also important for members of collaborative work teams to understand that people may have different dispositions with respect to intertasking and multitasking. If people with different dispositions must work together, conflict may ensue if people have unrealistic expectations of other workers' ability to intertask and multitask. Demanding that people who prefer to multitask cease doing so may be problematic. Similarly, judging people who prefer focused immersion as morally bereft and unproductive if they do not intertask and multitask may also be problematic. Making such unrealistic intertasking and multitasking demands risks failing to achieve optimal levels of group productivity and basic human respect. One potential solution is to explore accommodating different dispositions in ways—both technical and social—that maximize the potential of people with different work styles and perspectives on intertasking and multitasking.

The analysis also revealed that identifying actual intertasking and multitasking practices can be difficult, especially when a researcher's immediate sphere of interest tends to influence what intertasking and multitasking activities they can actually "see" and record. For example, I tend to pride myself on being "focused," but is this judgment clouding my ability to see how I routinely intertask and multitask? Is it true that intertasking and multitasking are limited to people with different preferences or to different demographic groups? Or are researchers' agendas leading to the identification of some multitasking activities while effacing or missing others? Self-reflexivity can help identify biases in which one is predisposed to seeing or eliding such practices.

It may be illuminating, although highly invasive, to investigate behavior using combinations of videotape and screen capture devices to more systematically study whether people are intertasking or multitasking in particular situations.[16] It would be advantageous to understand more closely what the effects of such practices are on work processes and human creativity. Systematic capture of what researchers and study participants are doing during the research process could be quite productive and useful. If numerous studies have already identified different demographic groups who intertask and multitask, is it possible that demographic characteristics have little to do with determining the likelihood of intertasking and multitasking? Is it possible that instances of multitasking increase according to the demands of specific tasks at hand within specific personal and cultural contexts? Future explorations could compare which tasks are likely to yield more demands for intertasking and multitasking and suggest how to craft more customized work routines according to different tasking requirements. Future studies might also address to what extent intertasking versus actual multitasking goes on, and whether a variety of social groups perceive such activities as more gendered or moral in specific contexts.

CONCLUSION

Distributed interaction is a crucial part of many people's contemporary social and work-life. Reflexivity in ethnographic work-life is not a solipsistic luxury but is necessary to understand, from a holistic perspective, dynamics in distributed research projects that include the ethnographer as a team member. In addition to identifying certain biases in research, systematic data collection of the ethnographer as team member is crucial for analyzing how home, family, and participant work styles influence the course of research and determine what counts as valid data under study. As research projects become increasingly dispersed, including researcher data at a fine level of detail will be critical for understanding certain research questions, such as the dynamics of holistic work processes.

Much of what is called "multitasking" is perhaps better called "intertasking," in which certain activities are not accomplished at the same time but rather are interleaved within a finite period. Such a distinction is important for understanding whether or not certain work expectations about multitasking are realistic because it may not always be possible to accomplish tasks requiring the same skills at the exact same time. Further, understanding that intertasking and multitasking demands may differ according to specific work requirements and individual work dispositions is helpful for managing teams with people who may have different attitudes about the advantages and disadvantages of conducting multiple tasks within a finite period of time. Rather than seeing intertasking or multitasking in gendered or moral terms (such as being more productive or signaling a lack of focus), it is more fruitful to consider how different individuals accomplish work in different ways and design work spaces and protocols accordingly.

NOTES

Acknowledgments. I would like to thank the people of MiningMUD and Learning World for their generous cooperation in helping me with my research study. I would also like to thank Tracy Meerwarth, Brigitte Jordan, and Julia Gluesing for their insightful comments and suggestions on earlier versions of this article. I am also particularly grateful to Andrew Lange for his continued support and feedback on my work.

1. I am currently a Postdoctoral Fellow at the School of Cinematic Arts at the University of Southern California where I research digital youth and how they share on-line videos on sites such as YouTube.

2. LearningWorld is an on-line group called a MUSH (which stands for multiuser shared hallucination). MUSHes are similar to MUDs (or multiuser dimensions) in terms of being persistent on-line worlds displayed only through text. In MUSHes and MUDs, people can come together on-line to interact and chat via text. However, the focus on LearningWorld was not on gaming (as is more common in MUDs such as MiningMUD). Nor was the social emphasis on role-play and multiuser creation of stories and characters (which is common in MUSHes). Both Learning World and MiningMUD contained numerous discussions of offline themes such as mentoring, work, technology, and popular culture rather than only in-game topics or fantasy role play.

3. Much terminology in the social science literature on computer-based work revolves around the term *virtual.* This term emerged from technical explorations of computer-generated environments that were meant to simulate offline experiences. The term is often applied whenever a researcher is describing interaction or research conducted in an on-line or "distributed" environment. Yet as Christine Hine (2000) notes, the term *virtual* carries with it the connotation of being not quite real. In fact, distributed work teams and their end goals are real, as are the ethnographers who study such processes. The term *virtual* obfuscates observable realities and has led to inaccurate conclusions about human interaction. In most cases it should be eliminated in favor of a more empirically accurate term, such as *dispersed* work terms (Lange 2008).

4. See for instance: English 2000; Intermec, Inc. n.d.; Learning Services Web Team 2008; Monmouth University Department of Mathematics 1997.

5. See Intermec, Inc. n.d.

6. Role playing, as in to take on a character and engage in an interactive story with another person playing a character on-line.

7. This chart is meant for illustration purposes only. The tasks described are actually complex in that they would likely involve multiple types of skills. For instance, typing a message requires motor and cognitive skills. The chart provided here merely tries to describe how intertasking compares to multitasking.

8. More research would be needed to understand which, if any, motor skill-based tasks could be done at the exact same time, such as tapping one's head and stomach simultaneously.

9. I find this interesting because it potentially shifts the burden of dealing with an unproductive or poorly run meeting onto the meeting participant. One interpretation of these remarks is that if the meeting is a time waster, meeting participants should be doing something else during it. Before my current position in which it is de rigueur to bring computers into meetings, I generally preferred not to bring a computer into a meeting. I felt that the people running the meeting and my participation required and deserved my full attention. Yet I also have the expectation that my time will not be violated by unfocused meetings filled with personal ephemera and wandering tangents. Am I therefore a "time waster" by attending a poorly run meeting and not intertasking during it?

10. Despite the use of the term *virtual*, this research describes actual teams of people trying to write a real book chapter on-line, rather than characters fantasizing about writing an imaginary book chapter.

11. The observations from my study raise an interesting line of future research, which has to do with variations in work disposition. Future studies may be targeted to understand a more nuanced range of dispositions and to investigate systematically instances in which expectations based on different dispositions may conflict and may have to be negotiated.

12. Of course, we do not have the data to know if they are actually intertasking rather than multitasking because previous literature uses the term multitasking to apply to tasks that are interleaved as well as tasks conducted at the exact same time. Future studies could begin to address this by systematically examining when women are multitasking and when they are intertasking.

13. Another interesting area of research could investigate whether and how interview and discourse-based data on women's multitasking deliberately invoke certain terms to craft virtuous "feminine" identities, such that more successful women workers are those who say they can multitask. Such research could observe the extent to which claims in interviews map to observed practices. It could also study to what extent identity discourses of virtuous, multitasking femininities adhere to a dominant, assumed universal stereotype (that certainly did not bear out in my case study in multiple ways) that women multitask and men do not.

14. Knowledge work is generally contrasted to skilled and unskilled manual labor. Knowledge work involves forms of employment with primary responsibility of using analytical approaches to produce new knowledge (Drucker 1973).

15. The incidents with family mentioned in this study are anecdotal. But if it is important to study from a holistic perspective how family impacts remote work, then systematic data collection and thus human subjects issues are important to consider. As work and family life increasingly merge for many anthropologists and ethnographers, then understanding complexities in intertasking and multitasking will likely require more systematic study of all participants—including family—that impact how work is done. Such an observation raises the uncomfortable but important question of how to balance self-expression of one's own life while considering the effects on others' lives. I am grateful that Andrew took the time to intertask and read and comment on earlier versions of this draft. I felt more comfortable that he could preview my remarks. At the same time, I do believe that on some level people should be able to express themselves in certain personal ways without asking legal permission.

16. On the one hand, such an exercise can all too quickly lead to an oppressive form of socialized control at work or during work–home life. On the other hand, from a theoretical perspective, it may be difficult to understand actual intertasking and multitasking practices, given that they can occur in such finely sliced time intervals and in such rapid succession that they may lie below levels of immediate awareness. In addition, interviewees' self-portrayals of productive multitasking or focused-immersion abilities are often influenced by moral lenses that characterize their behavior in ways that may not map to actual practices in fine detail.

REFERENCES CITED

Bailey, Brian P., Joseph A. Konstan, and John V. Carlis

2001 The Effects of Interruptions on Task Performance, Annoyance, and Anxiety in the User Interface. Electronic document, http://www.cse.unr.edu/~sushil/class/ps/papers/EffectInterruptions-interact-2001.pdf, accessed June 19, 2008.

Bilmes, Jack

1997 Being Interrupted. Language in Society 26:507–532.

Brooks, David

2001 Time to Do Everything Except Think. Newsweek April 30:71.

Deem, Rosemary

2003 Gender, Organizational Cultures and the Practices of Manager-Academics in UK Universities. Gender, Work and Organization 10(2):239–259.

Drucker, Peter F.

1973 Management: Tasks, Responsibilities, Practices. New York: Harper and Row.

English, John
2000 Glossary. In Ada 95: The Craft of Object Oriented Programming. Electronic document, http://www.it.bton.ac.uk/staff/je/adacraft/glossary.htm, accessed September 23, 2008.
Floro, Maria Sagrario
1995 Women's Well-Being, Poverty, and Work Intensity. Feminist Economics 1(3):1–25.
Franke, Jerry L., Jody J. Daniels, and Daniel C. McFarlane
2002 Recovering Context after Interruption. Paper presented at the 24th Annual Meeting of the Cognitive Science Society, CogSci 2002, Fairfax, August 8. Electronic document, http://interruptions.net/literature/Franke-CSS02–1096.pdf, accessed June 20, 2008.
Hine, Christine
2000 Virtual Ethnography. London: Sage.
Intermec, Inc.
N.d. Multitasking. *In* Intermec Glossary. Electronic document, http://www.intermec.com.au/learning/glossary/a.aspx, accessed September 22, 2008.
James, Deborah, and Sandra Clarke
1993 Women, Men, and Interruptions: A Critical Review. *In* Gender and Conversational Interaction. Deborah Tannen, ed. Pp. 231–280. New York: Oxford University Press.
Jameson, Anthony, and Kerstin Klöckner
2004 Analyzing User Multitasking With Mobile Systems. Electronic document, http://www-users.cs.york.ac.uk/hilde/time_design/contrib/jameson_analyzing_user_multitasking_with_mobile_systems.pdf, accessed March 15, 2008.
Lange, Patricia G.
2008 Terminological Obfuscation in On-line Research. *In* Handbook of Research on Computer Mediated Communication. Sigrid Kelsey and Kirk St. Amant, eds. Pp. 436–450. Hershey, PA: IGI Global.
Latorella, Kara A.
1998 Effects of Modality on Interrupted Flight Deck Performance: Implications For Data Link. Electronic document, http://techreports.larc.nasa.gov/ltrs/PDF/1998/mtg/NASA-98–42hfes-kal.pdf, accessed June 20, 2008.
Learning Services Web Team
2008 Useful Definitions. Electronic document, http://www.learningservices.gcal.ac.uk/it/staff/definitions.html, accessed September 23, 2008.
Martin, Emily
1994 Flexible Bodies: Tracking Immunity in American Culture from the Days of Polio to the Age of AIDS. Boston: Beacon.
McFarlane, Daniel C.
1998 Interruption of People in Human-Computer Interaction. Ph.D. dissertation, The School of Engineering and Applied Science, The George Washington University. Electronic document, http://www.interruptions.net/literature/McFarlane-Dissertation-98.pdf, accessed June 20, 2008.
McMahon, Mark, and Romana Pospisil
2005 Laptops for a Digital Lifestyle: Millennial Students and Wireless Mobile Technologies. *In* Proceedings of ASCILITE 2005. Pp. 421–431. Electronic document, http://www.ascilite.org.au/conferences/brisbane05/blogs/proceedings/49_McMahon%20&%20Pospisil.pdf, accessed June 20, 2008.
Monmouth University Department of Mathematics
1997 Glossary of Internet Jargon. Electronic document, http://mathserv.monmouth.edu/coursenotes/jargon.htm, accessed September 23, 2008.
Pendleton, Jennifer
2004 Multitaskers: Kids Quick to Master Myriad Choices in Media but Marketers Question Effectiveness and Ad Impact in Their Fast-paced Lives. Advertising Age March 29(s-1):8.
Priola, Vincenza
2004 Gender and Feminine Identities: Women as Managers in a UK Academic Institution. Women in Management Review 19(8):421–430.

Robertson, Jennifer
2002 Reflexivity Redux: A Pithy Polemic on "Positionality." Anthropological Quarterly 75(4):785–792.
Rosaldo, Renato
1993 Culture and Truth: The Remaking of Social Analysis. Boston: Beacon.
Rutkowski, Anne-Francoise, Carol Saunders, Douglas Vogel, and Michiel van Genuchten
2007 Is It Already 4 a.m. in Your Time Zone? Focus Immersion and Temporal Dissociation in Virtual Teams. Small Group Research 38(1):98–129.
Salaff, Janet W.
2002 Where Home Is the Office: The New Form of Flexible Work. *In* The Internet in Everyday Life. Barry Wellman and Carolyn Haythornthwaite, eds. Pp. 464–495. Oxford: Blackwell.
Steptoe, Sonja
2003 Ready, Set, RELAX! Fed Up with the Fast Track, People Are Banding Together to Find Ways to Slow Things Down. Time, Oct. 27:38.
Stockton, Sharon
2002 The Multiple Discourses of Anthropology. American Behavioral Scientist 45(7):1103–1124.
Trafton, J. Gregory, Erik M. Altmann, Derek P. Brock, and Farilee E. Mintz
2003 Preparing to Resume an Interrupted Task: Effects of Prospective Goal Encoding and Retrospective Rehearsal. International Journal of Human-Computer Studies 58(5):583–603.
Wasson, Christina
2004 Multitasking During Virtual Meetings. Human Resource Planning 27(4):47–60.
Woolf, Virginia
1929 A Room of One's Own. Orlando: Harcourt, Inc.

CONCLUSION: PATTERNS OF MOBILE WORK AND LIFE

Julia C. Gluesing
Wayne State University and Cultural Connections
Tracy L. Meerwarth
General Motors Corporation and Consolidated Bearings Company
Brigitte Jordan
Palo Alto Research Center (PARC)

In this concluding chapter, we articulate four salient patterns that emerge from the contributors' eight narratives about mobile work and life: (1) the performance, presentation, and meaning of work, when activities are interwoven in personal, relational, and work spheres across contexts; (2) the multiplicity in identity and self-presentation; (3) the context and the decontextualization and recontextualization of meaning in changing spaces; and (4) the technological change and dexterity as well as the centrality of communication technologies in defining and redefining what it means to be a mobile worker. We explore each of these themes by referencing examples from the narratives to illustrate how mobile work is redefining the very meaning of work and its place in our lives. We conclude by suggesting directions for further research on mobility in the workplace. Keywords: performance, identity, context, technological change, mobile work

EMERGING PATTERNS

The eight articles in this volume offer new insights into the lived experiences of mobile and remote workers and the strategies these workers employ to manage their work and life responsibilities in the increasingly flexible global labor economy, largely enabled by new information and communication technologies. The patterns of mobility illustrated in this volume are transforming the meaning of work and how work is positioned with respect to the rest of life. Technology has brought about flexible work by way of a lengthening work day and a blurring of the boundaries between work and personal life for workers of all types in traditional and local workplace contexts. However, globalization and the rapid flow of goods, people, and information across geography, particularly the increased mobility in knowledge work, have added complexity by seemingly condensing time and shrinking space, deterritorializing work and life, and creating the mobile work lives described by the authors in this volume.

As editors, we observe four salient themes that form the basis for conceptualizing the defining aspects of mobile work and lives. The themes are grounded in the patterned

NAPA BULLETIN 30, pp. 148–155. ISSN: 1556-4789.
DOI:10.1111/j.1556-4797.2008.00025.x

behaviors and strategies (cognitive, relational, and physical) mobile workers use to manage their daily lives and relationships in the context of uncertainties brought about by the social and economic flows of the changing global landscape. We review the four themes here to highlight what we believe are this volume's contributions to our understanding of the intersection of self, work, place, and technology by framing new concepts or by expanding existing concepts in the context of mobile work and mobile lives. We conclude with some summary remarks and suggestions for future research.

PERFORMANCE, PRESENTATION, AND MEANING OF WORK

The ongoing popular and scholarly discussion about work-life balance and the blurring of work, personal, and family activities is expanded by the articles in this volume to address the impact of mobile or remote work on the patterning of daily life. The authors do not dwell on balancing work and life but, instead, discuss their difficulty in maintaining any sense of definition or meaning for what is productive work and what is not work. This meaning is invariably connected to how they choose to present what they are doing to others, whether these "others" are collocated or remote. Activities are interwoven and routines are broken, reestablished and broken again as the authors struggle to establish agreements with others about how time should be spent and what the rules of engagement should be in social and work activities. Standard practices, such as arriving and leaving a physical desk at the traditional office at the end of the day, which signify when work begins and ends, as well as what activities constitute work, no longer apply. Entry and exit from the workplace is sometimes invisible in virtual spaces and creates challenges in communicating when one is or is not at work. Instead, we see the interwoven lives in which activities form an overlapping pattern, not always harmonious, of multiple threads that make up daily living with implications for the meaning of work and the work process and how to communicate the accomplishment of work as a remote or mobile worker.

For example, Lange introduces us to the concept of "intertasking" in her engagement and exploration of virtual work spaces. Intertasking refers to personal and work tasks that are interleaved in short intervals to satisfy multiple and often-conflicting work demands. It is an attempt to understand and frame different meanings for work and the work process, and for work interruptions, especially when the work is invisible or unclear to collocated or remote interactants. The behaviors associated with work and what it "looks like" are often distinguished by where work takes place, its visibility, and, therefore, its influence in the different and often conflicting ways these behaviors are defined as "working." Youngblood talks about the meaning of work as it relates to the difficulty of displaying professional selfhood, of determining who is in the work community, and of performing work in a remote or mobile landscape so it will be seen by others as efficient or productive.

To communicate work status, some mobile workers explicitly define boundaries between work and nonwork activities. Others attempt to blend activities, thus giving up the struggle for clarity. Still others try to keep family, friends, and coworkers updated continuously about what they are doing, when they are working, and when they are not. With these updates, mobile workers are seeking to have work "recognized" as such when it is invisible to others. Youngblood observes mobile work performance as constructing "presentness" by signaling that work is taking place through periodic instant messaging and e-mail updates. In Strawn's case, feeling as though she has "fooled" people into believing that she is actually physically present in the office causes her to feel defensive about her remote status. She has a strong need to prove that she is spending sufficient time in the office. Similarly, Meerwarth has difficulty reconciling the discomfort surrounding the perception others may have of her desks that remain unoccupied while she travels between Michigan and New Jersey. All of these examples from the authors' lived experiences indicate that the meaning of work and the work process is in flux for mobile workers, as their work performance in compressed time-space is continually juxtaposed with more traditional workplaces bounded by time and place.

In the realm of mobile work, the meaning of work is being negotiated and is unfolding. For example, work could be transitioning to emphasize results (e.g., deliverables) more than activities. Results, usually in the form of completed and shared documents, are more visible in virtual spaces and are, therefore, more likely to be perceived as efficient or productive work than are the individual tasks that make up the work process itself. The meaning of work, the value of work activities, and the measurement of work performance are all central to the relationship of both mobile workers to organizations and to their colleagues in more traditional workspaces. As organizations become less spatially or time bound, and as the "where" or "when" of work matters less, the negotiations that take place to provide definition and agreement about all aspects of work and work processes will be increasingly important to negotiate. This is important if we are to enable mobile lives that are not only functional from the point of view of employers and coworkers but also from the perspectives of mobile workers themselves and the people closest to them. For anthropologists, it would be helpful to learn more about the ongoing negotiation and reconstitution of work through the lens of mobile workers. Anthropological perspectives and ethnographic research can make important contributions in articulating how work is being redefined in the global economy.

MULTIPLICITY OF IDENTITIES

Because mobile workers are engaged in ongoing interaction with people in different cultural, social, and physical contexts, they must personally assume multiple situational and social identities simultaneously. This enactment of different identities is true for workers in traditional workplaces as well, especially those in multinational corporations. However, for mobile workers the simultaneity and mediated nature of the negotiation and performance of a multiplicity of identities is nearly constant. The ability of the mobile worker to activate multiple identities almost "on cue" to interact appropriately in multiple contexts and in a variety of relationships is a skill that must be acquired and managed in mobile work. For example, simultaneously, the casual coffee drinker in the corner café is also the corporate project team leader, as well as the spouse of the other person seated at the table. This multiplicity creates uncertainty and ambiguity, thus increasing stress and anxiety for mobile workers. The articles in this volume provide evidence of the concurrent presentation of the "expected" self to friends, family, and colleagues, with consequences for personal, social, and organizational identity. Identity is in fluid motion, almost from moment to moment.

Community and belonging are roughly interconnected with identity in mobile work. How does the mobile worker maintain a sense of community identity or belonging if he or she is a member of a formal organization but functions primarily as a remote or mobile worker? How does organizational socialization take place, and how is culture created or maintained in mobile work? As a temporary, independent, or nomadic worker, is it possible to be part of a community and feel a sense of contribution to a shared effort? The authors reveal their own answers to these questions in their narratives of mobile work and provide some insight about emerging trends.

As a corporate executive who chooses to work remotely, Strawn negotiates an operational strategy for maintaining her association with the home office by traveling frequently to be physically present and by managing interaction with colleagues in her hotel when she is in a remote location. Youngblood talks about the importance of using virtual technologies that enhance vocal inflection and visual imagery to help reduce the isolation remote workers might feel as well as to communicate a "deeper" sense of connection and identity among remote coworkers. On-line communities also can help forge a collective sense of identity and a common culture outside the boundaries of the traditional permanent corporate workforce, or with disenfranchised teleworkers, according to Gossett. In addition, Gluesing points out how bonds formed among remote workers outside traditional organizational boundaries can generate feelings of inclusion and a more permanent sense of identity.

However, there is a consistent emphasis in these narratives on the sense of loss, of missing out on the spontaneous interaction that occurs in physical co-location and the camaraderie it can generate. Gossett stresses the importance of websites created by temporary workers to make up for this loss. These websites act as virtual meeting places to share humor and meaningful strategies for teleworkers. Meerwarth talks about the sense of liminality, displacement, and in-betweenness that comes from living a nomadic life and the feeling of fractured identity she feels as a result. Strawn also discusses the sense of fragmentation that results from constant relocations because of travel among work, home, and other locations. This concept of nomadicism is one that should be explored in future research, as it is a lens through which to view both the activity and the consequences of mobile life. Similarly, Goldmacher draws on and expands on the concept of "located mobility," capturing the meaning of obligation and belonging to more than one place at the same time, attempting to demonstrate presence in both. To maintain connections with family and friends, Gluesing and Lange both discuss their strategies for "training" the important people in their lives about what it means to be mobile or how to communicate with virtual technologies, negotiating expectations, "manners," and protocol.

Although insights from the narratives in this volume add to our knowledge about identity, community, and mobile work, there is still much work to be done on this topic. We need to know more about how mobile workers perceive and are managing their multiple identities. What personal characteristics are required to operate in multiple contexts simultaneously is important, as is determining how socialization takes place outside physical contexts. Questions about power and status, in-group and out-group behavior, and the perceived value of the work mobile workers do, are all tied to the personal and professional identity and ability of the mobile worker to perform successfully in work and in life. How effectively organizations transmit their identities via their mobile workers is also a rich area of future investigation that can be explored in tandem with studies focusing on mobile workers.

CONTEXT, DECONTEXTUALIZATION, AND RECONTEXTUALIZATION

Deterritorialization is a consequence of mobile work. Mobile work by definition spans multiple work contexts, and mobile workers cross multiple geographic, organizational, and cultural boundaries in their personal and professional lives. In so doing they move themselves, their ideas, and their artifacts across contexts. Because much of meaning is based in context (e.g., social, organizational, historical meaning) or is situationally bounded, this movement implies that the meanings for ideas, artifacts and relationships are thereby in continual flux, requiring cognitive, emotional, and behavioral flexibility. In this volume, we learn how the authors decontextualize and recontextualize elements of their lives to perpetuate meaning across contexts as well as create new meaning.

Goldmacher and Meerwarth use boundary elements to help them create a sense of a more stable work and home space, moving meaningful artifacts from one context to another in an attempt to duplicate especially their own personal meanings for home in temporary physical locations. This is not new behavior, as travelers have engaged in this type of symbolic behavior for centuries. For mobile workers, however, the behavior may be intensified in frequency and importance.

What is also intriguing about the deterritorialization and decontextualization of work is its recontextualization in "third spaces," "transitional spaces," "meditational spaces," and "voluntary spaces" that attend to the need for some sort of physical connection of mobile workers to space or place, or for a way to move more easily from one physical location to another with less cognitive, emotional, and relational disruption. Youngblood tells us about the habitués in the local café and the creation of routine, and we hear from Meerwarth and Jordan about the airport spaces and other makeshift offices that they claim and rearrange as their own temporary "third spaces," "colonizing," or recontextualizing a workspace by giving their own new meaning to these locations. For Meerwarth, this recontextualization means abandoning long ago socialized connections between physical space and the integration of family, friends, and community. Lange also talks about the need for a "room of one's own" to think and to write. She mentions the frequency with which people in on-line communities use spatial terms, wondering what this "room" might look like for people in on-line communities. All the narratives in this volume raise questions about the importance of physical space and the alteration of meaning for their work and their lives as they move from one space to another. The nature of physical space and how meaning is derived from it in the context of mobile work and lives is worthy of further investigation.

The processes of decontextualizing and recontextualizing meaning across local contexts can provide a starting point for examining the implications of the deterritorialization of work in the global arena as well. The fluid movement between local work processes and the global flow of work via virtual technologies results in a hybrid workspace in which the global and local are copresent. To succeed, mobile workers find they must sometimes consider both the global and local implications of their actions. Mobile work, because it brings an influx of the different and the new from remote locations into the local arena, requires adaptation and adjustment in daily activity. Youngblood, in his descriptions of the cultural misunderstanding that arose over the frequency of e-mail one of his informants, Rajiv, sent, illustrates the different cultural interpretations that are prevalent in global workflows and must be negotiated. Mobile work is fertile ground for investigating the consequences of distributed work that crosses geographic and cultural boundaries, but that is not tied to stable physical locations that provide the context for interpretation. Further study of mobile work can help us better understand how local practices can also become global practices when mobile workers create new work processes that establish global protocols for interaction, as Lange demonstrates in her reflections about her engagement in virtual workspaces.

TECHNOLOGICAL CHANGE AND DEXTERITY

The integration of communication technologies into everyday activity is a requirement for mobile work, as these technologies are central to the integration of work and life and the structuring or interweaving of activities across multiple work, social, and personal arenas. These technologies, of course, are also part of the work life of people in more traditional office spaces. In this volume, there are multiple viewpoints about the prevalence of technology and its role in the movement or colonization of work into non-traditional workspaces. Technology is alternately seen as creating work interference (Lange) or as facilitating mobile work and the integration of home life and work life (Jordan).

Mobile work requires technological dexterity. The exponential developments in new technologies that facilitate mobile work require continual awareness and retraining to keep up. They take lots of time and, particularly in the case of independent mobile workers who are not part of formal organizations, require purchasing power to buy the technologies. This is a real issue because the technologies change so rapidly. Just staying abreast of the technologies is a challenge, let alone incorporating them into work patterns or adjusting work patterns to accommodate them.

The relationship of technology to control also is raised. In the context of the independent mobile worker, control can come from owning one's own business (Gluesing) or being a teleworker (Gossett). For these individuals, engagement in mobile work takes place on a more or less voluntary basis. Technology can be more easily molded to suit the life of the independent mobile worker. However, when control is less and involvement is mandatory, mobile technologies can be perceived as more intrusive, creating uncertainty and ambiguity in work and life routines (Goldmacher). In considering control, an interesting question about the importance of routine or rhythm in alleviating stress is raised. Establishing rhythm and routine in mobile work (Jordan) can be an important strategy in alleviating feelings of fragmentation and removing the uncertainty of this type of work. Rhythm, routine, and their role in managing mobile work and life, as well as how mobile workers' strategies for incorporating technology differ from the strategies employed by workers in more traditional office spaces, could be fertile ground for further inquiry and add to our knowledge of technological change and society.

The mobile technologies that are condensing time and space and allowing collaboration to take place quickly, almost spontaneously, are also establishing new forms of organization, outside any kind of localized traditional work, or even virtual work in traditional organizations. People are increasingly becoming actors in multiple networks that form quickly to accomplish tasks, and that dissolve just as quickly, leading to more temporary associations. Such was the case in the production of the current volume. It is not yet clear what are the cultural implications of this new form of mobile life enabled by technology. By observing what is happening "on-the-ground" and engaging in mobile work as participants as well as researchers, the authors in this volume have provided us a glimpse into work and life at the intersections of identities, of organizational boundaries, of places and spaces, local and global.

SUMMARY REMARKS

The performance and presentation of mobile work, both locally and globally, the multiplicity of identities mobile workers enact, and the contextual and technological challenges they face are redefining the meaning of work and work processes. Mobility not only provides the opportunity for more flexibility, control and freedom to choose how, when, and where we work, but also brings with it uncertainty, ambiguity and challenges as boundaries blur and space–time compresses. The opportunity brought about by technological advances to organize quickly, to accomplish work both locally and globally, is countered by our struggles to relate to each other and to determine our own places in an economic environment that is in continual flux and promises to be so for the foreseeable future. It is clear that by studying mobility in the workplace, we can tap into a variety of emerging social processes that are redefining not only the meaning of work but also how work is situated in our lives and in the global economy as a whole. As researchers and mobile workers engaged in our own personal and professional investigation of mobile work, we are inquisitive about the unfolding of the future workplace. We hope we inspire you as well to explore the mobile workplace for yourselves and to contribute to the ongoing conversation and the emerging, important anthropological research about mobile work and its meaning for all of us.

Biosketches of Authors

Michael D. Youngblood received his Ph.D. in anthropology from the University of Wisconsin–Madison and is currently an independent consultant working at the intersection of ethnography and design. His work on social organizing and popular culture in India has received numerous awards, including the Joseph Elder Prize in the Indian Social Sciences, the Sardar Patel Award for Best American Dissertation on Modern India, the University of Wisconsin's Robert Miller Prize for Innovation in Anthropology, and fellowships from Fulbright-Hays and the American Institute of Indian Studies. Youngblood launched his own New York–based consulting practice in 2002. In his consulting work, he studies human interaction with environments, interfaces, products, services, and messages to solve usability breakdowns and identifies new opportunities for his clients and their customers. His clients include for-profit and not-for-profit enterprises representing a broad span of specializations, ranging from health, nutrition, food, and beverage to telecommunications, automotives, and public transportation. (mikedyoungblood@earthlink.net)

Brigitte Jordan trained as a medical anthropologist (Ph.D., University of California, Irvine). Jordan has carried out ethnographic research for more than 30 years in academic and corporate settings, most recently as a principal scientist at Xerox PARC (now the Palo Alto Research Center). A freelance consultant, Jordan's research and consulting interests revolve around new "lifescapes" she sees emerging in a globalizing world under the impact of new communication and information technologies. Her special interests and expertise lie in the adaptation of ethnographic methods to physical, virtual, and hybrid ecologies. She is particularly concerned with the evolution and design of learning and knowledge ecologies that support productive work settings in the society of the future. (www.lifescapes.org; gitti.jordan@gmail.com)

Loril M. Gossett received her Ph.D. in organizational communication in 2001 from the University of Colorado at Boulder. She is an associate professor at the University of North Carolina at Charlotte in the department of communication studies and organizational science. Gossett draws on a variety of qualitative methods to study nonstandard labor arrangement such as temporary workers, independent contractors, telecommuters, and volunteers. She examines how these alternative work relationships impact what it means to be or communicate as an organizational member, specifically with respect to issues of identification, power, and control. She is on the editorial board of Management Communication Quarterly, Communication Research and Reports, and Women's Studies in Communication. She is also a member of the National Communication

NAPA BULLETIN 30, pp. 156–158. ISSN: 1556-4789.
DOI:10.1111/j.1556-4797.2008.00026.x

Association, the International Communication Association, the Society for Applied Anthropology (SfAA), and the Academy of Management. (lgosset1@uncc.edu)

Julia Gluesing is a business and organizational anthropologist and research professor in industrial and manufacturing engineering at Wayne State University, specializing in global teaming and global product development. She is currently principal investigator of an NSF grant to study the diffusion of innovation across the global enterprise by tapping into an organization's information technology infrastructure. With more than 25 years of industry experience, Gluesing also frequently serves as a consultant and trainer to help business teams develop strategies and skills for working globally. She conducts research in global work practices and in cross-cultural and organizational communication for companies such as Ford Motor Company, Nissan Motor Corporation, Aegon, EDS Corporation, and Sun Microsystems. She has published professionally, most recently as a contributing author in *Virtual Teams that Work: Creating Conditions for Virtual Team Effectiveness, Handbook of Managing Global Complexity*, and *Crossing Cultures: Lessons from Master Teachers*. Gluesing received her M.A. (1985) from Michigan State University in organizational communication and her Ph.D. (1995) in cultural anthropology from Wayne State University. (j.gluesing@wayne.edu)

Perri Strawn is a senior manager with a professional services firm in Washington, D.C. She holds a B.S. in journalism from Northwestern University, a master's degree in East Asian studies, and a Ph.D. in anthropology from Yale University. Her dissertation explored national identity among high school students in Taiwan following the end of Taiwan's martial law. Currently, she works with leaders in healthcare and education on strategic management challenges. (strawn@aya.yale.edu).

Tracy L. Meerwarth has worked as an anthropologist and contract researcher at General Motors Research and Development (GM R and D) since 2001. She graduated with an M.A. in applied anthropology from Northern Arizona University with an emphasis in organizational anthropology. She and her team at GM R and D have published articles in scholarly journals such as *Human Organization, Journal of Manufacturing Management,* and *Space and Culture.* Meerwarth has presented at numerous annual conferences including the American Anthropological Association, Society for Applied Anthropology (SfAA), and the Ethnographic Praxis in Industry Conference (EPIC). She has applied her interest in cultural modeling, cognitive, and symbolic anthropology to various projects at GM, including collaboration, space, and architecture. In 2007, she and her team at GM R and D filed a patent entitled "System and Model for Performance Value Based Collaborative Relationships," and received a U.S. Copyright Registration entitled "Collaboration Tools for Designing and Implementing an Ideal Manufacturing Culture in the U.S." Meerwarth is also a competitive golfer, yogi, and triathlete. (tlm@consbrgs.com)

Amy Goldmacher is a Ph.D. candidate in the department of anthropology at Wayne State University in Detroit, Michigan. She received her M.A. in anthropology from Wayne State and her B.A. in anthropology with honors from Grinnell College in Iowa. Prior to graduate school, Goldmacher spent six years in the publishing industry working in the editorial, marketing, and sales divisions of a college textbook publisher. Currently, she is a teaching and research assistant in the department of industrial and manufacturing engineering at Wayne State University. Some recent automotive industry projects in which she has been involved include an assessment of cost reduction processes and an implementation strategy for a new engineering process. In addition to conducting research on the relationship of technology and culture and diffusion of innovations, Goldmacher is also improving the ways in which anthropology students receive training that will enable them to find jobs in industry following graduation. (a.goldmacher@wayne.edu)

Patricia G. Lange is a postdoctoral fellow in the school of cinematic arts at the University of Southern California. She is researching video production, exchange, and reception on YouTube for a MacArthur Foundation–funded project on digital youth and their use of new media. Lange's prior work on how participants negotiate identity information and technical knowledge in online groups has appeared in journals such as *Journal of Computer-Mediated Communication; Anthropology of Work Review; International Journal of Technology, Knowledge, and Society; First Monday;* and the *Proceedings of the Thirteenth Annual Symposium about Language and Society-Austin.* Lange is a cultural and linguistic anthropologist who received her Ph.D. from the University of Michigan in 2003. She has been researching cultural and linguistic aspects of Internet communication since 1998. (plange@cinema.usc.edu)

Geoarchaeology
An International Journal
Volume 23
Number 3
May/June 2008
Editors: Gary Huckleberry, Arizona, USA
Jamie Woodward, Manchester, UK
WILEY-BLACKWELL